WILL DONALD J. TRUMP (OR A CLONE OF HIS) - BLOW UP THE PLANET WHILE IN OFFICE OR INDEED, ONE OF HIS CHILDREN - IF IN THE SAME POSITION?

BY: BRIAN V. PECK

Copyright © 2023 Brian V. Peck

All rights reserved

ISBN 9798852396297

DEDICATION AND ACKNOWLEDGMENTS

To the whole medical profession in the UK (Private & NHS) and everyone on Planet Earth who devotes their life to this noblest of causes…. As without their amazing skills this author would not be here.

Again, I just want to thank all the teachers at the Darwin Boarding School (near Goose Green, Falkland Islands) who taught me the importance of the acquisition of knowledge between 1956 - 1962 and all the knowledge and skills I learnt with the Open University in 1983/1984. Also, the many academics and intellectuals I met during my subsequent studies at Wolverhampton Polytechnic/University, Cardiff University, and the University of the West of England.

Contents

INTRODUCTION 13
CHAPTER ONE 77
CHAPTER TWO.. 174
CHAPTER THREE 214

INTRODUCTION……

In this book I have attempted to explain and analyse themes relevant to the power structure invoked when someone like Donald J Trump gets elected to the White House. Drawing a close parallel between the personality traits of Caligula the 3rd Roman Emperor (37 - 41AD) and the 45th president of the United States

CHAPTER ONE

Is not about the tens of millions of altruistic and caring Americans but about American Foreign Policy carried out mostly by the very small elite egged on by the ARMS INDUSTRY and the MILITARY INDUSTRAIL COMPLEX who have committed outrageous atrocities (often by proxy) all over the world, for most of their history, which could end with the destruction of mankind for good?

CHAPTER TWO

The idea behind this chapter was to explain some aspects of China's amazing history over the last 10,000 years or more and to understand why China is now such a threat to USA Hegemony?

CHAPTER THREE

On 'The Road to Armageddon for the World' or 'How I Learned to Stop Worrying and Love the Bomb'…..after Dr Strangelove, could or will become a reality if Trump or a clone of his gets elected on the 5th November 2024

OTHER TITLES BY BRIAN V. PECK

WALKING ON THE MOON

THE MYTHICAL WORLD OF 'MIDDLE ENGLAND' DOES IT REALLY EXIST?

NOTES FROM A SMALL PLANET (VOL ONE) - TRAVELS IN INDIA – THAILAND – VIETNAM –
CAMBODIA – AUSTRALIA (BIG OZ) & NEW ZEALAND

THE MYTH OF REAL DEMOCRACAY AND OTHER MYTHS OF MODERNITY

MARGARET HILDA THATCHER: THE LIFE AND TIMES OF A TYRANT

PREFACE

This book was started at the beginning of 2019 and by the time I completed it in 2023, recent events in Ukraine may have rendered the basic premise of the book completely wrong. It might be said that long term China is the biggest threat to USA hegemony and still is. Russia has nuclear weapons like China but the economy is not that large, which may have been the real reason that Vladimir Putin has marched his troops into Ukraine which has valuable commodities like cereal grains, Lithium reserves etc. Albeit the impression given by RT TV (now thrown out of Europe, for being a threat to liberal democracies) was that Putin was only going to protect the Donbass region of Ukraine, where mostly Russian speakers live, which turned out to be not completely true, and to me was somewhat counterproductive! Jeffery Sachs (BBC Radio4 4th March 2022) however has been one of the very few (apart from Jeremy Bowen on the same radio station) that I have heard on the mainstream media who tried to tell the truth about how after the fall of the Berlin Wall in 1989 and the old Soviet Union in 1991, NATO would not go East. They lied about this process through and through, like the weapons of mass destruction in Iraq and went East anyway. Russia suffering massive humiliation by a few Oligarchs taking control of most of the economy with the help of the USA and the Western world and in many cases taking their stolen loot to London, with tens of millions ordinary people in Russia starving. Probably the biggest theft in history, albeit people like Mikhail Khodorkovsky fell out with Putin and was locked up for over ten years and at least part of ill forgotten gains taken back by the Russian federation. NATO going east was very chilling for the Russian Federation especially under President Putin because of past history covering over 200 years of invasions, which included Napoleon and Hitler and the coup in Ukraine in 2014, the reason he went into Crimea to save the deep-sea port in the Bay of Sevastopol where the Black Sea Fleet is stationed. This threat from NATO and the major theme of this project about USA hegemony is real and very dangerous all over the world. Lloyd Austin (April 2022) Secretary of Defence for Jo Biden has said that the West must weaken the Russian Federation so that they cannot invade another country and are provoking them by supplying arms to the Ukrainian forces, which they also did under Trump (Chomsky 2021 ironically according to Fiona Hill et al Putin was trying to weaken USA hegemony?). Pope Francis also said that NATO was 'barking at Russian's door'. This whole insanity is very serious because according as Donald Trump said, (Piers Morgan interview for Talk TV 25/26 April 2022) that when he was president Putin kept mentioning the 'N' word (nuclear) in meetings with Trump and threated Putin that he should never think of using it because the USA was the most powerful country in the world and America would win the fight? Apparently, this was also said to president Xi Jinping of China? Hence, my basic premise of this book is as true when I started it in 2019 as it is now…. And Trump hinted to Morgan that he will probably run for the presidency in 2024 (is now…so he says) and if he had been president in 2022 that 'war would not have happened under me'…meaning the Ukraine conflict? However, if Ian Sinclair et al are correct, when Boris Johnson flew into the capital of Ukraine on the 9th April 2022, more or less unannounced, he brought two simple messages. 'The first is that Putin is a war criminal; he should be pressured, not negotiated with. And the second is that even if Ukraine is ready to sign some (peace) agreements on guarantees with Putin, they (the Western powers) are not'.

The following quotes might well be said to illumine and provide a framework for the portrayal of the model of leadership I am both constructing and deconstructing within the body of this project.

'Cultivation to the mind is as necessary as food to the body'...Cicero born 3rd January 106 BC assassinated 7 December 43 BC.

'I'm the most honest person I know'? Donald Trump interviewed by Piers Morgan for Talk TV 2022

'Let them hate me, so long as they fear me' Gaius Caligula but probably first used by the Roman playwright Accius (170-c.86 BC)

'The Evil that men do lives after them' says Mark Anthony in William Shakespeare's Julius Caesar….and very relevant to this project.

'In the past decade 33 million people have been purged from voter rolls - predominantly in districts with large percentages of non - whites voters' reported in the… The Sunday Observer UK 11th August 2019, about the state of USA democracy, or not?

Trump isn't really a politician, of course. He's a strong-man act, a ridiculous parody of Nietzschean superman…quoted in Matt Taibbi - Insane Clown President p, 42.

Michael Moore described Trump as a 'wretched, ignorant, dangerous part-time clown and full-time sociopath'….and very far from compos mentis, like Caligula?

'Politics' said Albert Einstein, and with good reason, 'is much harder than physics'…. quoted by Frank Ninkovich.

John Oliver: TONIGHT HOST… Noted in 2016……'incredibly, we may be on the brink of electing such a damaged, sociopathic narcissist that the simple presidential duty of comporting the families of fallen soldiers may actually be beyond his capabilities'…. quoted in…. Donald Trump in 100 facts by Ruth Ann Monti 2018

'Make America Great Again '. This was a direct lift from Ronald Reagan's 1980 'Let's Make America Great again', but Trump brandished it with an unambitious nativist bite. Mark Singer - Trump & Me 2016 p, 100.

Challenged by Chris Mathews to assure the whole world, after giving a foreign policy address on the campaign trail in 2016 at the Mayflower Hotel: 'that he would never consider using nuclear weapons in Europe, Trump replied, 'I - I'm not going to take it off the table' Mark Singer - Trump & Me 2016 p, 101.

'What we have to understand about Ed Koch is that he's a bully, pure and simple. Bullies may act tough, but they're really closet cowards. The only people bullies push around are the ones they know they can beat. Confront a strong, competent person, and he'll fight back harder than ever. Confront a bully, and in most cases, he'll fold like a deck of cards'…. p, 306 Trump - The Art of The Deal - 2016 edition.

'On November 8, the most powerful country in world history, which will set its stamp on what comes next, had an election. The outcome placed total control of the government - executive, Congress, the Supreme Court - in the hands of the Republican Party, which has become the most dangerous organization in world history'. P, 120 Optimism Over Despair - Noam Chomsky… (Meaning 2016)

Snowden said to Ewen MacAskill: 'GCHQ is worse than the NSA. It's even more intrusive'…. about its spying operations around the Globe….*The Snowden Files* by Luke Harding p112.

'Even though the historical use of asbestos still kills 40,000 Americans annually, Trump believes asbestos is '100 percent safe, once applied', and has blamed the collapse of the World Trade Centre towers on the absence of asbestos'. P26 Trade Secrets…Nick Dearden.

WILL DONALD J. TRUMP (OR A CLONE OF HIS) - BLOW UP THE PLANET WHILE IN OFFICE OR INDEED, ONE OF HIS CHILDREN - IF IN THE SAME POSITION?

BY: BRIAN V. PECK

INTRODUCTION

AN INTRODUCTION AND BACKDROP TO A MODERN DAY CALIGULA (GAIUS – AD 37 – 41…….3 years and 10months)

In essence this book is about the future, but also about the past, because without some sort of ontological knowledge of history we could not compare a tyrant for example like Trump to that of Caligula who seemed to have a lot in common, (who don't appear to be compos mentis). Without this sort of knowledge, it is very unlikely we have any idea whatsoever how we got to where we are now. Meaning for example, that if you have not read the Jean-Jacques Rousseau (1712 - 1778) book on the origins of inequality (1), which Voltaire hated, you may not understand how static society originated, (possible hypothesis for which depends on how we define 'the true state of nature'). Similarly, you may not have been aware of the great Henry Wallace, who was the vice president of the USA under Roosevelt and was deselected from this position in 1944 by very dubious means and was replaced by Harry Truman, who with Winston Churchill et al started the cold war. So, if Henry Wallace had become the new president after Roosevelt's death in 1945 the cold war probably would not have happened at all (2). All the available hard scientific empirical evidence seems to suggest that for most of human history we were Hunter-gatherers, and any form of static civilization is probably no more than 10,000 - 12,000 years old, a very short span of time in the whole evolutionary process of the last 3 billion years, in which, according to Professor Steve Jones, there was no male species, just single cell creatures for about a billion years of this time (but if this is so who would have taken Mrs Theresa May's bins out - sic)? Henry Ford once said 'history is bunkum' but as Steve Edwards has recently informed us in the Sunday Observer on the 18th of November 2018 and as Noam Chomsky and others have written, the founding fathers of the USA were nothing more than a 'group of rich, white, slave-owning tax dodgers. The USA was then built on slavery and discrimination and the slaughter of two million natives'. This group of very rich people built the American system for themselves against the rest. 'The result is a nation in thrall to a constitution still stuck largely in the 18th century and an election game where entrenched elites hold all the high cards and make all the rules. The "shining city on a hill"? No. A democratic swamp, allowing the perfect place for monsters such as Trump to evolve' (3). This I should add is very similar to the English system in the UK, where the very wealthy aristocrats, worth tens of billions and still owning between one third and half of all the land, and still living a life that has hardly changed in centuries. The English system also has an unelected Head of State, who has hundreds of servants mostly paid for by the millions of hard working 'wage slaves'. This could be costing as much as a million pounds a day and millions are now living in abject and relative poverty with millions going hungry, every week, as they do in the USA (Chomsky et al ...45,000 homeless in Los Angeles 2019 according to Simon Reeve, but maybe in excess of 100,000). Marx & Engels writing in the 19th century called this process a 'class struggle', between the rich and the rest of us, which it is, (see also Owen Jones in modern times). Strange as it may seem, from what I have just written above - the Queens second son, Prince Andrew, according to Private Eye (No 1487) spent £14 million over ten years on flights, hotels and security, in the name of 'promoting business' then describing this as 'cheap at the price'... and all from State funds?

I should also note, that the British system of Royal wealth, especially after the death of the Queen Elizabeth 11 (September 2022) seems to me a bit opaque as the 'Crown Estate' is now worth probably £17, billion and with the other estates added the Royal family own etc...altogether maybe worth a staggering £20, billion, according to the Sunday Times on the 18th September 2022. The new King Charles 111 seems now to own at-least 6 homes, worth millions. According to the Guardian 13th December 2022 a left-leaning think tank (NEF) predicts that '30million to fall short of decent standard of living by 2024'...a shocking indictment of another 13 years of a Tory Government in the UK?

Also, according to the book *'Wikileaks Inside Julian Assange's War on Secrecy'* Prince Andrew was very dismissive about the press like the Guardian, who poked their noses into other people's business, which made it harder for the British to do business, abroad, so he concluded. He also emerged as rude, blustering and guffawing about local bribery, for example, in countries like Kyrgyzstan. Ironically, in the USA, the educated class perceived Britain's Royal family with amused disdain, as a Ruritanian throwback, which it is. The brilliant Scottish comedian Frankie Boyle noted in April 2023 on Channel 4 show called *Farewell to the Monarchy* that the British Royal family were nothing more than a 'boring crime syndicate' which they are? While writing this book, Prince Andrew is also in big trouble over his relationship with the billionaire Jeffery Epstein who committed suicide in prison (or may have been killed by the Ruling Elite in the USA) who may have known too much about the rich, powerful and famous and their misdeeds over decades. In theory Prince Andrew slept with at-least one of Epstein's sex slaves, called Virginia Giuffre, at least 3 times, (while she was under-aged in the USA) which Andrew denies in an interview by Emily Maitlis on the BBC News-night programme last November (2019), which turned out to be a disaster for the Royal Family. Andrew has been virtually disowned by the 'Firm' (sic) from carrying out any so-called Royal duties…. not too sure what the definition of a 'working royal' is? Andrew finally paid Giuffre millions in compensation in 2022, for not sleeping with her?

The Americans are also very cynical about the so-called 'special relations' between the USA and Little Britain which it seems to them is a bit of a joke, nothing more than the 51st state of the USA. As such, they will do what Big Brother wants them to do, in arms sales, "buy mine you bastards" and sanctions and so on. They even told the foreign secretary David Miliband, (at the time…now living and working in the USA for a charity on a salary of 1 million dollars+), to get in line when it suited them, over places like Diego Garcia. We should never forget it was mostly the British Aristocrats and the new emerging merchant class who gained the most out of the brutal slave trade practised in the UK - along with a few other European powers, where 'approximately 20 million healthy young Africans were forcefully transported as slaves to the "new world" between the sixteenth and mid-nineteenth centuries, and this had a critical effect on Africa's own development' (4). The hold on power of the British Aristocracy is beyond belief in the 21st century and how they can keep-up the legitimacy of it all, which is a 'bulwark against progressive change', beats me. Here is some evidence of how they do it now - en-camped in the USA Harry and Meghan have done a deal with Netflix to the sum of about £75 million for future events on film and this supersedes the cost of the Invictus bash according to the Sunday Times (6th September 2020). The Net Flex deal is now apparently worth £112 million and Harry & Megan are still receiving millions from Prince Charles, I presume? Albeit Harry & Megan have given a huge interview to Oprah Winfrey in early March 2021 in the USA, in which Harry said that his father had cut him off from receiving funds a year ago. They also drove a coach and horses through some of the more ridiculous anachronisms of Monarchy, like the close symbiotic relationship between the press and the palace, which has been a state secret, up until now. It was even revealed that the colour of Megan's future child was questioned by a member of the family and so on. Most of the time in the UK especially in the down-market tabloids, the Royal Family are always wonderful and do no harm to anyone, so the billionaire press owners are controlling the narrative and the minds of the uneducated. However, if Irving Krauss is correct, 'stratification could have started with the myth of God', which in Britain is on the wane but still seems very strong with the traditional 'upper class', which believes in the 'natural order from God to serf'. This means that 'keeping up with the Joneses is a never-ending affair in the UK and elsewhere. According to the Sunday Times Rich List (2019) the Queen of the UK was only worth £370 million, in 2020 her wealth was down £20 million to £350 million, whereas in 1989 (the first time the rich list was published) it was suggested she was worth £6 billion, the richest person in Britain, or was before her death in September 2022. She was probably one of the richest women in the world, and probably still was with land and property worth billions at the time of her death. I presume, she was downgraded from the 1989 stats because of the embarrassment of being so rich in comparison with her down-trodden wage slaves/subjects and non-citizens and afraid of the guillotine, sometime in the future? In fact, George Monbiot (Guardian 21st June 2019) reminds us that just before the French revolution, according to Charles Dickens, the majority had to jump out of the way of carriages driven by the very rich, especially in places like Paris. Over two hundred years later in London (same source different story) an old lady of 83 was run over causing broken limbs by a police bike escorting William *and* Kate (Duke and Duchess of Cambridge) and family to Windsor castle, so showing that in the UK nothing has changed whatsoever in how society is structured over centuries and the sooner we have a revolution the better?

I was thinking that if we do not send the British aristocracy to Mars or the guillotine, we could set up special 'world beating' aristocratic Zoos, run by Richard Branson and Alan Sugar type characters (sic) who could charge the proletariat to visit them and perhaps even feed them with some scraps, so they would not need hundreds of servants…. this maybe high satire, or the script for a future reality TV show? Last night on Yesterday (British TV - 10th June 2020) there was an excellent series about *True Evil: The Making of a Nazi*. This specific one was about Heinrich Himmler, who was obsessed about the norms and values of the British Aristocracy and built the 'SS' and their derivatives on this model. He and his lieutenants were mostly responsible for the killing of the leader of the Brown shirts in 1934 and setting up the infrastructure for the holocaust. In fact, many British 'upper class' people like Lord Halifax, admired Hitler as a bulwark against communism. We still have these ghastly people, but much richer than they were in the 1930s and still doing what they have been doing for centuries, looking down on the whole population as 'oiks'. The Duke of Westminster at 29 is worth over £10 billion in the 2020 Rich List, (up £195 million from 2019), and now down £240 million in 2021. The family fortune was founded on 300 acres of prime London property. From the 1720s they developed bogs, pastures and orchards into a new district called Mayfair.

Another very good example of this phenomenon is the life and times of Lord Mountbatten of Burma, nick-named Dickie (who according to Andrew Lownie was bi-sexual), his wife Edwina, who was born 'a rich little girl lost' who had numerous affairs and did lots of travel with servants in tow. Dickie was the last British Governor-General of India, living in New Delhi where they had 5000 servants.

According to the great Kitty Kelly in the book she wrote about the British Royals and published in 1997, one of Prince Philip's sisters (all brought up in Germany) was married to a Nazi who worked for Himmler, not too sure if he survived the war? The Duke of Windsor, who was only King for most of 1936, but not crowned because he wanted to marry Wallis Simpson, a USA divorcee (twice), stood down from being King for that reason and met Hitler. In 1940 until 1945 Edward was the Governor of the Bahamas, and if 'Yesterday' is to be believed (TV digital channel - 23rd June 2020) he may have been involved in the cover up of a murder in 1943, of Sir Harry Oakes. Oakes was an American who made a fortune from gold mines in Canada and gained British Citizenship with a Baronet title and ended up in the Bahamas for tax reasons, and while there probably was the richest man in the whole British Empire, worth perhaps £200 million. The night he was murdered one of his best friends stayed in his home called Harold Christie, who apparently heard nothing when Harry was brutally killed. His son-in-law Count Alfred de Marigny was married to Oakes' daughter, when she was just 18, against her father's wishes; Count Alfred was 14 years her senior and became the prime suspect. He was put on trial but got off because of a dispute over fingerprint evidence which was probably planted. The duke at the time of the trial was away from the Island, for good reasons as he may have been caught up in all-sorts of economic crimes with his rich friends and a cover up of the murder by the British Establishment. The FBI had kept files on him and Mrs Simpson because of their pro-Hitler beliefs. I should also add a postscript to this paragraph about Henry Ford who according to Oliver Stone and Peter Kuznick in *The Untold History of the United States* 'did more than supply trucks for the German military; he also helped the Nazis hone their hateful ideology. In 1921, he published a collection of anti-Semitic articles titled *The International Jew*, which was widely read by future Nazi leaders' (p, 79) Hitler also hung a portrait of Ford in his Munich office and also told the Detroit News 'I regard Henry Ford as my inspiration'.

When history is written about the 21st century, more than likely Boris Johnson and Donald J. Trump will go down in history as a new form of nationalistic fascist – whose raison d' etre is to lie and cheat 24/7 so that he and friends can get very rich, at the expense of everyone else and it seems that God is on Trump's side feeding his notions of grandeur and like Caligula wanting to be worshiped like a God? With the power of God in the Oval office, according to a BBC documentary shown on 29th October 2020 his rationale is that he is never wrong and all foes must be opposed and destroyed. It is obvious to me and many others that the UK and the USA are not democracies anymore but plutocracies, where the extremes of wealth and poverty are now beyond belief in both countries and a disgrace and the reason, I am utilising intellectual property from both sides of the Atlantic in this book. Trump claims to be a billionaire and Johnson is very wealthy with several homes and probably seven children, compared with millions of poor UK 'wage slaves'. In fact, Boris Johnson had told friends he needed a million pounds a year to live on according to an edition of the Sunday Times in March 2021……and come September 2022 Boris Johnson will no longer be prime minister of the UK. Kicked out of office by his own party because his Tory MPs thought they would lose the next general election, in 2024.
Mary L. Trump's book about her uncle called *'Too Much and Never Enough…..How my family created the world's most dangerous man'* helps us to understand the phenomenon Donald, who had a very disturbed childhood, whose mother was often ill and not there and whose father Fred was a sociopath which includes 'a lack of empathy, facility for lying, an indifference to right and wrong, abusive behaviour, and lack of interest in

the rights of others'...something I first noticed in the West Midlands about uneducated small businessmen, when I first went there in 1975. Mary L. Trump a trained clinical psychologist with a PhD says that in such circumstances as Trump's, with a mother being away a lot and their father, not interested in bringing up his children, (he had five of them) but just in being a successful businessman, it may not be surprising that Trump's character was affected. Fred senior became successful with some important input from other family members such as Mary's great granny. Basically, without love from someone, in the family or elsewhere, your growth as a human or probably any animal, is restricted. The extreme individualism in the USA/UK and its wider culture does not help this whole process along, where for example in most cultures in Africa everyone in the extended family helps with bringing up the children. 'Child abuse is, in some sense, the experience of "too much" or "not enough". Donald directly experienced the "not enough" in the loss of connection to his mother at a crucial developmental stage, which was deeply traumatic. Without warning, his needs were not being met, and his fears and longings went un-soothed. Having been abandoned by his mother for at least a year, and having his father fail not only to meet his needs but to make him feel safe or loved, valued or mirrored, Donald suffered deprivations that would scar him for life'. Mary says that the resulting personality traits - displays of narcissism, bullying, grandiosity etc - finally made Trump's father take notice but not in a way that ameliorated any of the horror that had come before... (p, 26). Donald's personality traits are it seems very similar to those of his father, who saw first-hand how his older brother Freddy (Mary's dad) was being treated and humiliated, most of the time. Albeit that the oldest son was being groomed to take over the business into perpetuity. Making money was everything to Fred, as it is to Donald and bragging about it is his raison d'etre with very little help from his father - or so he likes to boast, which is not true according to Mary L. Trump. But what is true is that 'he has no principles', calls all men who are savvier and more accomplished than he 'losers', all women he considers ugly 'fat slobs' meaning the dehumanization of people was common parlance at the dinner table, which is very similar to how the Bullingdon boys behaved at Oxford University - Boris Johnson being a member of that specific club when studying there. When Trump's family learned that he was running for the president they were mostly amazed, like his sister Maryanne who told Mary, his niece, that Donald was 'a clown' and 'this will never happen' because he had not accomplished anything on his own, apart from 'five bankruptcies'. This is also what Tiberius soothsayer Thrasyllus of Mendes said about Caligula becoming an emperor. Unfortunately, Trump did become the president in January 2017, beating Hilary Clinton against all odds, maybe with a little help from the Russian State? Caligula also made it to become an emperor after the death of Tiberius, the suspected murder of whom may have 'shortened the odds'. Only Melania, Trump's third wife, thought he would win which she was not too keen on. Ironically, while travelling back from A to B with a billionaire friend on his aircraft, who was with his girlfriend, a foreign model, who Trump was trying to impress, suggesting they could drop into Atlantic City to tour his casino there. The billionaire friend was not impressed and said it's full of 'white trash', what is the point? The foreign girlfriend had not heard of this term before and asked what 'white trash' was, to which Trump replied, 'they are like me but poor' (5). Trying to impress women seems to have been Trump's second aim in life and 'made life worth living' and sleeping with them, especially with his rivals' wives often by tricking their husbands in his office to brag about their adventures with other women outside of their marriages with their wives listening in on their conversation in another room. Again, this seemed to have been a trait of Caligula's who liked sleeping with other men's wives and after the event bragged about it. Out of the thousands of books I have read (not bragging) I do not think I have ever read of such immoral and unethical behaviour, about a modern-day politician (6). The hype he created around himself in the 1970s and 1980, as a self-made man, was of course a total myth, albeit many Americans may have believed it when he ran the *Apprentice TV show*. This portrayed Donald as the self-made dealmaker, to pass on to his recruits. However, if Mary L. Trump is correct in her amazing book about her uncle, I would have thought that in the last 224 years of American history, since 1776 there has never been a president who was less was qualified to be the president. His knowledge 'about history, constitutional principles, geopolitics, diplomacy' etc was/is nil. Everything is about the glorification of Donald J. Trump at the expense of everyone else; hence the lying about the huge crowds in Washington in January 2017 (alternative facts) has been presented as the truth from day one and ever since. If a lie is repeated often enough it can become the truth, in many people's perception of social reality, a new form of gaslighting. For me when the 'Right' tries to blame everything that is wrong with society on the Left, it is nearly beyond belief as it is the 'Right' who lie 24/7 to legitimize the role of the Rich and Powerful in society and apparently in the USA, Trump is 'the chosen ONE' by God? The power of positive thinking is also Trump's mantra which does not seem to add up when like Boris Johnson, in the UK, he is determined to set groups of people against one another. 'Black Lives Matter' the brilliant opposition group against racism, now a worldwide phenomenon, is apparently a terrible 'socialist' idea according to Trump in the BBC documentary shown on the 29th of October 2020.

The total wealth of the top 1000 people in the UK is now worth £771.3 Billion, according to the Sunday Times Rich List (2019), up £50 billion from 2018, so very hard for most of us to keep up with the 'Joneses'. 50% of all the land in Britain is owned by many of these same people, some say just 1% of the total population. Ironically according to the Sunday Times 12th

May 2019, the 'Rich prepares to flee Corbyn's Britain', because of the fear that a future Labour Government may raid private wealth. How shocking? As I write the labour party was badly beaten in the general election of the 12th of December 2019 - through the insanity of the Brexit idea, thought up by the Tories to stop factions in their own party killing each other and the outrageous behaviour of the extreme right-wing press spewing out lies and propaganda about Corbyn and the labour party, the press being mostly owned by billionaires. In fact, as I noted in my last book about Thatcher, (and others) we are drifting into a cruel and brutal 'One Party State', which may last for the rest of the century, unless the majority stand up for themselves and overthrow the whole rotten British Establishment. Amazingly, because of the covid-19 crisis, according to the Sunday Times Rich List 2020 - the top 1000 richest people are now worth £743 billion, down £29 billion from last year……only the second time since the first edition in 1989.

It's perhaps very ironic that Trump calls himself 'a nationalist', without understanding the true nature of this concept. Having read Hannah Arendt's famous book on *the Origins of Totalitarianism*, I conclude that what Nationalism has done is to hide the real class conflict built into modern day society by the invention of this idea.

As Arendt notes: 'The relationship between the state and society was determined by the fact of class struggle, which had supplanted the former feudal order. Society was pervaded by liberal individualism which wrongly believed that the state ruled over mere individuals, when it ruled over classes, and which saw in the state a kind of supreme individual before which all others had to bow. It seemed to be the will of the nation that the state protects it from the consequences of its social atomization and, at the same time, guarantees its possibility of remaining in a state of atomization.

To be equal to this task the state had to enforce all earlier tendencies toward centralization; only a strongly centralized administration which monopolized all instruments of violence and power-possibilities could counterbalance the centrifugal forces constantly produced in a class-ridden society'. (7)

I would also suggest that very few would understand the above quote, and most have not got a clue how the capitalistic epoch/society works just for the small elite and no one else, in fact a constant theme of Polly Toynbee's writing in the Guardian for decades. Lucky for Polly she does not write for the Murdoch Empire as well, but according to Matt Taibbi, Murdoch (who Trump looks up to like a God...or did?) 'has succeeded in accruing enormous power across the globe. In the United States, its impact on political affairs has been incalculable. It's led us into war, paralyzed Democratic presidencies, helped launch movements like the Tea Party and effectively spread so much disinformation that huge majorities of Republicans still doubt things like the birthplace of Barack Obama'. (8) Trump apparently told the UN General Assembly last year to 'reject the ideology of globalism, and embrace the doctrine of blue-collar patriotism' something that I have never heard of, or to my knowledge, have never read in a textbook, unless I am behind the times, or living in a parallel universe to Trump? This may mean that the CEO of McDonald's could earn '2100 times' more money than the workers are doing on the shop floor, flipping hamburgers and still claim to be one of them? Amazingly by the end of June 2020 Trump may be in real trouble with his followers, mostly middle class/working class groups, because of the covid-19 crisis causing real harm to the economy when tens of thousands are dying. The evidence for my proposition seems overwhelming. 'Fifty years ago, a US CEO earned on average about 20 times as much as the typical worker. Today, the CEO earns 354 times as much' (source the Guardian 6th June 2019) see also above. In the UK, the same thing has happened between the rich and powerful and poor wage slaves.

What has emerged about Trump is that he is a pathological liar on a grand scale and a con man of the highest order; as the Washington Post suggested he may have told 30,000 lies by the time he left office. In fact there is very little evidence that what he has said over the last few years has had a grain of truth in it - as it was with David Cameron (who thought he was born to rule & was part of the Patrician guard going to Eton a & Oxford) and then Theresa May in the UK, who resigned, kicked out of office by her own party on the 7th June 2019, and leaving office completely on the 26th July 2019, a departure akin to Mrs Thatcher's! Theresa May had the gall to peddle a story, (which was not true) about the Human Rights Act article 8, namely that an illegal immigrant had used his cat as an excuse to stay in the UK, and won the case, as part of the family life tradition. Now we have Boris Johnson, a lying, cheating, conman as prime minister, (now thrown out of No 10) who if not very careful may end up in prison. In 2019 he earned £700,000 on top of his salary as an MP and after Mrs May stood down as the PM, she has earned about £2 million or there about on top of her salary as an MP (source Sunday Times)? We are living in a 'post-truth' world whether you know it or not! Alan Townsend, a former deputy mayor of New York, a sage of the place so it seems, said: 'I wouldn't believe Donald Trump if his tongue were notarized' (9). While visiting the UK on a State visit in June 2019, Trump even had the gall at a press conference with Theresa May, to claim that he heard cheers of approval, while in fact, there were 75,000 protesters out on the streets of London protesting about his visit. This he called "fake news". At the same protest Jeremy Corbyn (who he refused to meet) addressed the protesters accusing 'Donald Trump of spreading hatred and division as he addressed tens of thousands of protesters within shouting distance of Downing Street, demonstrating against the US president's visit'. Others who addressed the protest were: Emily Thornbury, Caroline Lucas, Francis O'Grady, the head of the TUC who Trump suggested was a 'nasty woman' - like 'Megan Markle' – (who Trump accused of being another one), I presume because she is telling the truth about his outrageous remarks about women and refugees (10). My own view on this State Visit is that it is very suspect, because albeit the British Head of State has invited some nasty pieces of work to the UK over decades, mainly to encourage trade between other Nation States and Britain, in this case she did not need to invite Trump in his first term in office, based on the assumption he will get two terms, so what was the reason? So, was it because it looked as though Britain was going to leave the EEC trading block and needed as many friends as it could get? Or was it because of the 75th anniversary of D-Day on the 6th of June? Or was it simply that the British 'ruling class' are in cahoots with the USA ruling class who want to maintain the status quo at all costs, in both countries, and help Trump get elected in 2020, which he probably will, (thank God he didn't) because most Americans think the Royal family are wonderful?

Prince Charles may have accumulated as much as over £300 million for himself and his family according to Private Eye…. albeit the Royal family are now worth billions as a family! Michael House from London NW6 notes that after the death of Elizabeth 11 in Private Eye (1583) we got 'a fortnight of Ruritanian rubbish, with the parasite family to the fore, sporting uniforms and bedecked with medals they mostly did nothing to earn, not to mention the fawning sycophancy of the whole media'…well done Michael, my feelings completely.

Johnathan Alred reminds us in the Guardian on the 6th of June 2019 that even Warren Buffett, a billionaire, seems to think that in the USA there has been a nasty form of class warfare going on for the last 20 years which the rich have won, mainly due to the economic and social policies carried out by Reagan and Thatcher in the 1980s, especially by cutting what the rich pay in taxes, and then having to create a narrative that if you are unemployed and on welfare you are lazy, which has always been a very powerful weapon to legitimatize the power of the rich and the rewards they give themselves. Paradoxically it was Karl Marx in the 19th century who noted that the ruling class writes the rules of the big game and asserted that the class who owns the economic base of society writes those rules and ideas within the parameters of the superstructure. So, nothing has changed in essence and certainly not in the UK and the USA. Liberal Democracy for a long time has been a cruel joke played on the majority. Johnathan Alred nicely sums this up in this quote: 'Much of the inequality we see today in richer countries is more down to decisions made by governments than to irreversible market forces. These decisions can be changed. However, we have to want to control inequality: we must make inequality reduction a central aim of government policy and wider society. The most entrenched, self-deluding and self-perpetuating justifications for inequality are about morality, not economy. The great economist John Galbraith nicely summarized the problem "One of man's oldest exercises in moral philosophy...is the search for a superior moral justification for selfishness. It is an exercise which always involves a certain number of internal contradictions and even a few absurdities. The conspicuously wealthy turn up urging the character-building value of privation for the poor"'. (11) It is very unlikely, I would have thought that: Trump, Thatcher, Reagan, George W. Bush et al, has ever read a book written by a moral philosopher. Thatcher claimed she had read Friedrich A. von Hayek, who was no moral philosopher but to me an extreme neo-brute and nothing else, who helped to legitimize massive inequality, as was Karl Popper who died on the 17th of September 1994. Hayek died on the 23rd of March 1992. I should have also said in my fourth book that Milton Friedman (died 16th November 2006) should have come under my mantra of a neo-Brute as well as Hayek (after Aristotle) because of his insane ideas about monetarism, which caused economic chaos all over the world. This started in Chile after the overthrow of President Salvador Allende, engineered by Nixon and Kissinger, both very dangerous men at the heart of power in the western world, in the 1970s…see below. As the great Naomi Klein (a true freedom fighter) wrote about this process many years later in *'The Shock Doctrine'*…. 'What Chile pioneered under Pinochet was an evolution of corporatism, a mutually supporting alliance between a police state and larger corporations, joining forces to wage all-out war on the third power sector - the workers - thereby drastically increasing the alliance's share of the national wealth. That war - which many Chileans understandably see as a war of the rich against the poor and middle class is the real story of Chile's economic "miracle". By 1988, when the economy had stabilized and was growing rapidly, 45% of the population had fallen below the poverty line. The richest 10% of Chileans, however, had seen their income increase by 83%. Even in 2007, Chile remained one of the most unequal societies in the world - out of 123 countries in which the United Nations track inequality, Chile ranked 116th, making it the 8th most unequal country on the list' (12). In this amazing book, Klein also documents other countries in South America that copied this crazy idea of Friedman, and the UK under the tyrant Thatcher, which I wrote about in my 5th book, called *Margret Hilda Thatcher: The Life and Times of a Tyrant.* In that book I tried to copy my hero Socrates, in some ways whose rationale is still with us to this day, in questing to get to the truth of any problem. For example, questioning whether people are actually educated to a level that they pretend they are - he apparently said, according to Plato, 'that the un-examined life is not worth living'. The great Frederick Douglass, born in 1818, did something very similar escaping as a slave to become an abolitionist, orator, writer and statesman...dying in 1895, truly one of the most amazing men of USA history and living at the same time as Karl Marx.

Ironically according to Michael Wolff, if he is correct, it was Donald J. Trump himself who fed the press half-truths and lies for decades, especially to the National Enquirer (which they printed before he came up with the idea of 'fake news'), and any news organization that would not go along with his ideas of truth, (meaning 'alternative facts') like CNN et al. Even at the beginning of October 2019 he was charging CNN with doing 'fake news' at a press conference with the President of Finland, see also below. Never forgetting that it was a man as great as Professor Noam Chomsky who has been critiquing the mass media for decades for not being honest with Jo public (especially about foreign adventures) and at-least since 1916 when public opinion had to be swayed, that it was a good idea to come into the First World War, the first mass slaughter of the innocents in History. Albeit that Julius Caesar was also pretty good at it over two thousand years ago, even writing his own history in the process, with a scribe doing all the hard work, (the great Cicero did the same thing it would seem?) which even one of his lovers Cleopatra, who also bore Caesar a son, may have read... 'that the Alexandrians called Caesarion'? I was also not aware until researching this project, that Cleopatra, who was fascinated by the current fashions of the time, was probably one of the first women in history to fall in love with silk from China, which had reached Rome by 50bc. According to Joe Studwell Cleopatra 'was among the first to promote a fashion for transparent dresses in the exotic fabric' which was silk and she must have used it to its full potential in history (14)? 'By the end of the fourth century silk was a universal accoutrement in civilized society throughout the empire' (15).

According to Plutarch in *Fall of the Roman Republic* over a ten-year period in Gaul, Caesar 'took by storm more than 800 cities, subdued 300 nations, and fought pitched battles at various times with three million men, of whom he destroyed one million in the actual fighting and took another million prisoners' (13). The National Enquirer was not around at the time of Julius Caesar, having been founded 1926. It is the US publication of legend, known for its high level of sensationalism and dubious veracity, at one time selling millions, now just a few hundred thousand. If it had been around at the time of Caesar, he would have loved it as from what I can see of the 22 June 2020 edition, it is mostly about Hollywood stars doing this and that. This paper was even mentioned by the one of Hollywood's greatest actors, Orson Wells in Citizen Kane. The reason that I have bought this specific magazine was because last night, on June 24th 2020, it featured on BBC 4 TV in the UK, as part of the Storyville series. It was titled *'How the National Enquirer became the most infamous tabloid in America'*. It was probably bought outright by Generoso Pope Jr with the help of Frank Costello, a mafia boss, in the 1960s when Pope ran on fear, like a mafia boss and the circulation soared. This was mostly due to gore, road accidents and the whole nonsense about celebrity culture, at the time of Elvis Presley's death even paying for picture of the King in his coffin. Money at this time was no object so on Elvis's death 6 journalists set off from Florida on a private jet with 50,000 dollars in a suitcase to buy what they could get on the King of Rock and Roll, who in the 1950s was also called 'white trash'. The theme of the paper was to expose all the scandal they could get their hands on, from Elvis to O. J. Simpson, from many different sources and pictures of Hilary Clinton looking under the weather in the 2016 election. The impression given on the TV story/exposure was that once David Pecker, who was a friend of Trump, bought the paper, he helped to hide the truth about Trump's infidelity with other women by buying up the stories called 'catch and kill' and basically helped Trump to win the 2016 election. Ironically at the time of the O. J Simpson trial/saga, the National Enquirer was taken seriously by other news agencies, due to fact-checking the fine details such as the shoes he wore etc. Michael Cohen a lawyer who worked for Trump as a fixer between 2006 and 2018 got convicted and sent to jail for lying to Congress and for facilitating hush money payments to two women, Stormy Daniels and Karen McDougal, who allegedly had affairs with Trump. Cohen got 3 years in prison and a 50, 000 dollar fine and was sent to prison in May 2019, but got out of prison early on the 21st of May 2020, due to concerns over the covid-19 crises.

I should just add a VIP bit of information which I was not aware of until I was watching BBC Four on British TV last night (7th October 2019) called Ian Hislop's Fake News: *'A True Story'*. This explored the history of dishonest news reporting over the last two hundred years, so predating Noam Chomsky's ideas about state propaganda. Starting in the early 19th century in the USA, with stories about life forms on the Moon, etc.... nothing was beyond the pale, so it seems in the down market and very cheap newspapers of the time. Very similar to the tabloids in the UK in the 21st century that are read by the 'working class' and are often believed to be reporting the truth? This of course they are not, especially as about 80% of them are produced by extreme right-wing press Barons spewing out half-truths and lies 24/7. My old Mother who is 91 reads the Sun in the UK and believes it.... a form of gas lighting, on a huge scale. For example, Jeremy Corbyn is the devil and if elected the Labour government would ruin the economy and the UK would become as poor as Venezuela, albeit millions are starving already under a brutal Tory Government, in power since 2010

(Coalition with the Lib Dems for 5 years, who put student fees up to £9000 a term) …. Isn't the truth wonderful in the 21st century?

The premise of this book may not be obvious to most, but it is to me, as we have already been warned by an academic as famous as Joseph Stiglitz, Trump has 'fascist tendencies'… and is perhaps a modern-day Caligula in the making as I show throughout this chapter and project. 'The eccentric Roman appointed his horse to the office of consul and made it a priest. He also liked to say of his subjects "oderint dum metuant" (let them hate me so long as they fear me)', which I could also say about Trump summoned up in three Latin words, (with thanks to Geoffrey Bindman for this bit of information) and Suetonius (born 70 AD) in *The Twelve Caesars.*

It has also been suggested by UK TV Channel 5 on the 16 March 2020, that Henry V111 and Trump had a lot in common which I tend to agree with. The programme was called *'History repeating itself'* informing us that both of these neo-brutes were 2nd sons and both did not like be upstaged by their wives. In Henry's case, Cromwell made up stories that were not true about Ann, which resulted in her having her head cut off. When Henry was getting bad press in Scotland, he called it fake news (or whatever was the term at the time) and used other agencies of social control against his tormentors as does Trump in the 21st century. Steve Bannan Trump's right-hand henchman, now retired, played a similar role to Cromwell, who got the chop in 1547. Cromwell and Bannan used power and fear, on their terms. This was also a trait that both men used to frighten their opponents. Ironically, Barack Obama told Malcolm Turnbull (ex-prime minster of Australia) in 2016, that the Americans would never 'elect a lunatic' like Trump. How wrong can you be? A lesson Turnbull learned from other bullying billionaires is that you must stand up to them (16). I presume that this quote got back to Trump, and was probably the reason that he seems to hate Obama and why he is turning everything he achieved on its head? Luckily for USA citizens, Obama is informing graduates all over the States (May 2020) that Trump has made a complete mess of the coronavirus pandemic, in a very similar way to Boris Johnson in the UK. Before this project is completed 700,000+ Americans will have died of this terrible virus and in the UK at-least 150,000+ will have died.

In fact, like Rome 2000 years ago, in the USA, since its inception in the 18th century, American foreign policy has always been expansionist, while denying it outright, and pretending that they are always the good guys, which was just aping the British Empire, and all other power-hungry brutes and tyrants in history, before them, like Caligula. The idea behind it is to rob and exploit other peoples' resources, and is what Noam Chomsky calls the 'fifth freedom'….an axiom that could never be repeated by most academics and journalists, in the Western world! Hence, what is so worrying, if Stiglitz is correct, is that the 'President of the United States as commander-in-chief of the armed forces' (17) could press the nuclear button in a heated situation and kill us all? Even Sadiq Khan, the mayor of London, is virtually repeated the Joseph Stiglitz warning when critiquing Trump's State visit in the Sunday Observer on the 2 June 2019 by pointing out that Trump was to be given the full pomp and red-carpet treatment on the 3rd of June. Khan asserted that Trump was now the major political figure head at the front of the far-right movement on the global stage and we should not be welcoming him as his values are not compatible any more with ours. As he said: 'in years to come, I suspect this state visit will be one we look back on with profound regret and acknowledge that we were on the wrong side of history'. Simon Tisdall, writing in the same paper on the same day noted: 'Trump is no friend to Britain: it's time to end this knee-jerk subservience to Washington. We are in essence acting like a timid mouse afraid of the big cat, roaming the world ripping up agreements, left right and centre. The US has taken a number of high-profile unilateral foreign policy decisions that are contrary to the interests of the UK the committee said in a report, (UK Foreign Policy in a Shifting World Order), debated in the Lords (the second Chamber of the UK system) last month'. Agreements like the Paris accord on climate change, the Iran nuclear deal, the United Nations human rights council and the impositions of trade tariffs on USA allies, are 'undermining efforts to tackle pressing global challenges of critical importance to the UK'. Even the International Criminal Court, which the UK helped to create, has been effectively outlawed by Washington, as have many other factors that help to cement the international order in a rational way, between nations, according to Tisdall. He also suggests that at this crucial time in history we need Europe more than ever, just when the Tory party is tearing itself apart, deciding to have a referendum that went the wrong way for David Cameron. This in the short term could make us a lot poorer and long term could drive us into having a third world country status. As it turned out Trump wanted everything on the **tabl**e once we left the EU, including the NHS, in any future trade deal with the UK. The NHS is already being salami sliced by this brutal Tory government, which has always hated this socialist idea since its inception in 1948. Now the Tories are pretending they love the NHS and are going to put billions more into it and other public services, because just around the corner there is going to be a general election, which the Tories are hoping to win? They did win in 2019 albeit 15 million did not vote at all and 71% who could vote did not vote for the Tories, a story of outright chicanery and fraud played on the British public repeatedly.

Throughout history whenever an emerging power, is a threat to the dominant one, the dominant one will try and destroy that threat, by whatever means it can, at its disposal, so when Sparta saw Troy as a threat, they combined with other City States to destroy it, according to Homer. When Rome saw Carthage or at least perceived it as a threat, they destroyed it after several attempts with the swords and skills they had learned over hundreds of years. At its height Carthage had a population equal to Rome. In a similar way Julius Caesar, perceived the threats from Gaul and killed hundreds of thousands in response and in the bloodbath that followed enlarged the Roman Empire, even invading Britannia in 55bc and 54bc. By the time, the First World War in Europe broke out in 1914, mostly caused by the ancestors of Queen Victoria fighting over land and commodities and each one of them wanting to be top dog, fighting had become industrialized, on a massive scale, with huge shells and weapons that could travel miles before they killed their opponents. This also happened in the Second World War which was a direct cause and effect from the First World War, in other words if the First World War had never happened, Hitler would never have come to power, and about 100+ million people would not have died in the 20th century? Ironically, we should also never forget that if Hitler who was quite good at being an artist/painter (source: Yesterday TV Channel UK and the excellent min-series…. Starring the amazing Robert Carlyle as Hitler, from 2003) and had not been turned down by a college of Art, the Second World War may never have happened, well certainly not under him? This is something that the brutal Tories seemed to have forgotten, concerning Brexit? As one of the main reasons the EEC was set up in the first place in the 1950s was to stop this madness that had happened in the 20th century in the whole of Europe, albeit it was only a trading arrangement originally. In fact, Brexit is turning out to be such a disastrous economic shamble that if it had been a Labour government who had started the whole insanity, I believe the Labour government would have been overthrown by the British State, led by the Army? David Cameron, who will probably go down as one of the worse prime ministers in history, (an old Eton & Oxford graduate & Bullingdon boys club member), and may have been paid 10 million dollars by Greensill before its demise, only started this madness because of infighting in the Tory party between different factions in the first place and the rise of UKIP under the right-wing nationalist Nigel Farage (pretend friend of Trump)? So, to pretend it was all in the 'national interest' is beyond belief, and that life will be better for all is a down right lie. Most Tories are millionaires like Cameron who owns at-least 3 homes, as do most of Boris Johnson's cabinet. Rishi Sunak the Chancellor of the exchequer has 4 homes worth £10 million (and is worth with his wife £730 million…Sunday Times Rich List 2022 and now the new prime minister but lost £201 million in the last year ST Rich List 2023) and his father-in-law is a billionaire, so do not have a lot in common with the poor working class, mostly paid a pittance for selling their labour power in the labour market, and very hard to escape from, if at all. Therefore, their wealth insulates them from the economic ill effects of leaving the EU.

And as I have just written above this process was also behind the so-called Cold War, which some say was just an 'American fiction', through the pen of the great late Gore Vidal. Reagan and Thatcher, who were simply two 'lower middle class' representatives of the people, really believed they were fighting Lucifer, when they were in power and nothing else, all over the world in the 1980's, during this zeitgeist. The crimes carried out in Latin America, killing hundreds of thousands often by proxy, when Reagan was in power, was a war crime, which it seems that even Mrs Thatcher ministers, went along with at the time. According to Matt Taibbi 'Reagan's attention span was so short, the CIA had to make mini-movies to brief him on foreign leaders. George W. Bush not only did not read the news, but he also was not interested in it. "What's in the newspapers worth worrying about"? He once asked, without irony (18). This was a constant theme of all the Republican presidents in the USA after Richard Nixon, the president from

1969 until he resigned in disgrace in 1974. He was the 37th US president and basically brought down by Bob Woodward and Carl Bernstein of the Washington Post – who were persistent at getting to the truth of the break in of the Democratic headquarters in Washington D C. Nixon received a full scholarship to Duke University Law school in Durham North Caroline and could have gone to Harvard, but his family could not afford the travel and living expenses. He also served in the Second World War, without seeing action, in the Navy Reserve and became a member of Congress in 1946 in the House of Representatives and in 1950 was elected to the Senate. Nixon was born poor in Southern California and even worked in Washington on New Deal projects, but later became an enemy of anyone on the Left of the political spectrum. This is a phenomenon I find very hard to understand, when you are born poor and basically working class why do you want to switch to support the boss class, and in Nixon's case to become part of them, although he seemed to hate mankind in any form according to Stone & Kuznick. In Britain, the famous actor Michael Caine has gone the same way as Nixon; where the great Scottish actor Brian Cox is a socialist, like me. Albeit I have become educated but have never had a middle-class job, so was often despised by the workers when they discovered I have had six years of Higher Education and am probably hated by the established 'middle class' who may not be as well read as I am?

In fact, the 20th century was probably the first time in history on a large scale that businesses understood the true nature of warfare which is not only killing the so-called enemy and stealing resources, but making huge profits, especially in the USA. On a much smaller scale it would have been known for centuries. For the real evidence see for example: Hannah Arendt - The Origins of Totalitarianism and Will Hutton's 2007 book, in which he notes: 'The great medieval Italian banking families grew fat by financing war; the same demand would spur banking families to become the first commercial banks' (19). According to Warren Beatty's take on *Ten Days that Shook the World* turned into a movie called Reds in 1981, when the great crusading journalist John Silas 'Jack' Reed (1887 - 1920) was asked at a meeting what the mass slaughter was all about when carving up the rewards from the First World War, he just said 'profits'. Joseph Choonara adds an extra layer of truth to what I have just said above: 'Imperialism is not simply the domination of colonies by the great powers themselves as they seek to redivide the globe at the expense of their rivals. Hence, the rapid development of Germany late in the 19th century brought it into conflict with existing powers such as France and Britain, leading to the First and Second World Wars' (20).

It was mostly the events of 1939-45 that helped the USA to come out of the economic depression of the 1930's with businessmen making vast fortunes on making armaments with factories running 24/7. The 'Military Industrial Complex' in the USA - now sometimes called the 'deep state' - which even President Eisenhower warned about, albeit while he was President the increase in nuclear weapons went through the roof - we could say is behind most conflict in the world today (according to: William Blum + Joseph Choonara + Seumas Milne). Certainly, since the Second World War, albeit the UK, France, Russia, China et al, also make money out of arms, but not on such a large scale as the USA, who now sell '36%' of the global total arms. According to the Stockholm International Peace Research Institute, a very high per cent of total sales go to the Middle East, especially Saudi Arabia. It has been reported on RT TV several times (2018) that to pretend that Russia spends anywhere near as much on defence, compared to the USA and NATO, is just a joke beyond belief. Under these circumstances we are not going to have peace for a very long time, and as I'm hoping to elucidate, maybe never, before the end of the World, particular in light of the current situation in Ukraine. We should always remember that '11 million' including 6 million Jews and others were murdered under the Nazi regime between 1941 -1945. However, like the arms companies in the UK and the USA that made vast fortunes out of two World Wars and the slaughter of 100 million people, we very rarely hear about the German companies who also made a killing out of killing? Peter Frost in the Morning Star (25th January 2019) helps to expose a small part of this missing knowledge. Basically, it was the capitalist class in Germany that helped to build the concentration camps, and weapons of killing, often using slave labour. 'German industrialists from many of Germany's biggest businesses met Heinrich Himmler once a month to discuss how they could best work with those running the camps. Large companies like IG Farben helped to build the camps as did Siemens. Farben also developed and sold the poison Zyklon B used in the gas chambers. 'Today German chemical and pharmaceutical giants like Bayer and Hoechst can still trace their origins back to IG Farben'. Krupp also used slave labour from Auschwitz to build armaments, tanks and super-guns for the Nazis. Other companies also helped Hitler with the war effort like: Daimler-Benz, Volkswagen Hugo Boss et al, often using slave labour, as did some American companies: but ironically none of this will ever be mentioned on January 27th each year which is now called the Holocaust Memorial Day? Amazingly on BBC Radio4 on the 27th of January 2019 between 8am to 9am from St Martin-in-the-Fields, celebrating this day, it was admitted perhaps for the first time ever on BBC Radio4 that slave labour from the death camps were used by the German War machine? According to the great Kitty Kelly, an American author, in her book on the 'Royals' (First Published in 1997 and banned originally in the UK) all of Prince Philip's sisters were married to German Officers and one of them worked for Himmler, another secret kept hidden by the whole rotten British Establishment, until Kitty Kelly exposed it.

A constant theme of John Pilger's work and Noam Chomsky and several others for that matter is the sheer brutality of USA and the British foreign policy over decades and with the British, over centuries. This applies especially to the bombing of civilians by the USA and the British near the end of the Second World War, as Victor Grieg who is now 100 years of age informed BBC Radio4 Today programme's listeners on the 11th of February 2019. Mr Grieg so it seems was a prisoner in Germany, who escaped twice from captivity and was sent to Dresden to be killed, lucky for him but not for tens of thousands of German civilians who were burnt to death in the bombing of Dresden, as he noted, adults and children were literally 'roasted to death'. This whole process, as he went on to inform us, was a 'worse evil then the enemy we were fighting'….as the 'war had already been won' so there was no need to bomb innocent civilians? I should note that this interview was one of the most unusual and honest that I have ever heard on BBC Radio4 - while listening to this station for over 46 years and a backdrop to my life while living and working in the UK, since 1964.

I was not aware that the great John Pilger had made a documentary/film called *The Coming War on China* until I read about it in the Morning Star at the end of June 2020. After reading about it I bought it on Amazon and a few days later was able to view it. Filmed over two years it is an excellent film and his 60th about the crimes of American foreign policy over decades. The film came out at the time that Trump was running for the presidency. The blurb on the back of the DVD says 'The United States may well be on the road to war - and with a noose of bases now encircling the world's newest superpower, nuclear war is not only imaginable but a nightmarish prospect. *The coming War on China* is both a warning and an inspiring story of people's resistance to war and the occupation of their countries'. This sums up nicely what it is all about, America flexing its muscles again surrounding the whole of China like it did with the old Soviet

Union, with hundreds of bases. This process started with the blowing up of Bikini Atoll in the Marshall Islands with nuclear tests over years and without caring a hoot about the indigenous population of those Islands, who suffered terribly because of the tests. One of the Islands not blown up is now called the Ronald Reagan missile site - testing Mace missiles aimed at China. Rather ironic don't you think as is the idea that women's swimsuits are now mostly called bikinis and blowing most men's minds up while on the beach? The film also gives us an overview of previous atrocities carried out against China like the opiate wars and the boxer rebellion. A Chinese social scientist also informs Pilger that 'China does not want to run the world', unlike the USA who have at-least 3000 bases in America and 1000 around the globe, while saying they do not want to be like the British Empire. Really? What of course is a real threat to USA hegemony is the new economic strength of China, China being the new capitalist kid on the block. I have not been to China, but I have visited Vietnam and the same can be said of that country in a smaller form. The 'Yellow peril' still exists, but in a new form. The rise of the new middle class in China is an amazing event in the history of the world and no doubt will be discussed for centuries to come. China is now a market economy, based on capitalist principles albeit the Communist party is at the centre of this new power structure, whereas the USA and the UK are both nothing more than 'One Party States', while claiming not to be, and might be said to be a mirror image of China. Most journalists certainly in the UK are so brainwashed and uneducated by agencies like the BBC and the extreme Right-Wing press that they cannot see it, although many were educated at Oxford University, as was Boris Johnson who for most of his life has been a journalist for a right-wing magazine and the Daily Telegraph, (sometimes called the Daily Boris by Private Eye). He is also a hard right-wing nationalistic lunatic and a very dangerous man indeed, like Trump. As Pilger so rightly suggests 'China is now a class society' the same as most of the world but more like the USA and the UK in becoming very unequal, with lots of protests about the theft of land and so on by the more powerful, which in modern times started with the Tiananmen square (gate of heavenly peace) riots/protests over several months in 1989, based on ideas coming out from the old Soviet Union at the end of the 1980s. Pilger is also correct in his brilliant analysis, that Mao's 1949 revolution caused a paranoid rage in the West which I have noted throughout this discourse, from many sources. Mao also 'wanted to be a friend' of the USA according to Pilger. This particular film was made at the time Barack Obama was the president, who upgraded the military establishment like many before him, and now Trump after him, 'preparing for mass murder'. The difference about Trump is that 'he has a thing about China' which makes him so dangerous and is the reason I am writing this book. According to Pilger the USA has now got bases in 147 countries in the world which are often pushing against China's development programs in many regions and 'confrontation is growing by the day'. This confrontation often breaks out in the Far East, for example over women, and how they are treated by American troops and the building of new bases. According to Google/ internet (27th June 2020) the Philippines officially told the US that they were scrapping a security pact that allowed US forces to train and take part in joint exercises, which must have been a real shock for Trump as President Rodrigo Duterte had long threatened to move away from his country's long-time ally and pivot towards China and Russia. Duterte is a nationalist like Trump and may have had 1400 citizens killed by death squads for drug dealings between 1998 and 2016. Ironically, under Biden, the USA seems to be moving ever closer to conflict with China over the question Taiwanese autonomy?

Following the fall of the Berlin wall and the end of the old Soviet Union, where State assets were stolen on a gigantic scale (see below) by the very few oligarchs helped by the Western powers, millions were left in destitution. The big idea of the day was that there would be an economic dividend from the end of the Cold War, for the Western world. Francis Fukuyama even wrote one of the most stupid books ever written by an academic, called *The End of History and the Last Man... (1992)* suggesting that Liberal democracy and the American model/form of Capitalism was here to stay forever...total tosh of the highest order? I should note here that the same could be said of Marx writing in the 19th century, albeit as I understand it, Marx's assumptions were based in the belief that once all contradictions had been overcome in society and we all moved into a communist epoch, we would all be free to do what the hell we wanted to do, like farming, writing or whatever; similar so it seems to what Jeremy Clarkson's life is all about in the UK now - although he appears to be a right-wing lunatic (ex-Top Gear presenter, on TV worldwide), when writing articles for Rupert Murdoch's empire, on a weekly basis and other stuff? In Britain, to my mind one of the most stupid countries in the world, considering we still do have Pharaohs, the aristocracy, living a lifestyle that those 5000 years ago also lived, in Egypt.

An agreement was given by the Western powers to Mikhail Gorbachev at the end of the Cold War that NATO would not move east (Oliver Stone & Peter Kuznick et al). This agreement was broken, the main reason being that there was no economic dividend, or very little from the end of the Cold War, to justify its existence. NATO carried on in the same belligerent manner. The legendary crusading journalist and documentary film maker John Pilger, on the RT channel's excellent programme called *Going Underground*, in late 2018, was very critical of this move and of how NATO had done exactly what Hitler had done in 1941 and gone right up to the

Russian border, thus threatening Russia, while at the same time playing the same old games that the Western World played during the Cold War, suggesting that they are the enemy again, or I should say one of several states threatening NATO? Ironically, at about the same time, Trump was complaining that European countries were not contributing enough economically to NATO for USA protection, meaning not buying enough arms from the USA? The Western powers have used sanctions in recent times against Russia, for so-called misdemeanours, in Crimea and the Ukraine and other incidents - including the Salisbury affair in 2018 (sic) in the UK, where in theory two GRU men tried to kill a double agent, called Sergei Skripal and his daughter with a poisonous substance. Months later, when a local woman called Dawn Sturges died after her boyfriend picked up a perfume bottle that had a deadly cocktail of poison in it, the Tory Government tried to link the two events. I would suggest that no one knows for sure, the true conclusions of this incident, but I was always very suspicious of the immediate outcry from Theresa May, the prime minister at the time, blaming the Russians, before any investigations had taken place. The latest truth or pack of lies about the Skripal saga seems to be that the two GRU men may have had a 'backup team' in the UK, according to the Guardian on the 20th of May 2019. Detectives now think the two GRU men 'applied the lethal nerve agent novachok to the door handle of Skripal's home and caught the train back to London', receiving a phone call from the backup team after returning to the capital, albeit there is no real hard scientific empirical evidence that they, did it? This article also now seems to contradict what the Tories were saying after these events, in that detectives are not too sure where the bottle of novachok came from that caused the death of Dawn Sturges, in the first place. Therefore, I presume not from Porton Down, just down the road from Salisbury, a science park which is off limits to the public, being a site of the Ministry of Defence. Porton Down (Defence Science and Technology Laboratory - Dstl) - known for over 100 years as one of the UK's most secretive and controversial military research facilities, which occupies 7,000 acres and is a site of Public Health England. Interestingly top-secret papers from Porton Down were recently found in a bin in London carelessly dumped…. could the perfume bottle of novachok also have been carelessly dumped? The BBC made a documentary cum movie on this subject with actors playing real people shown over several nights (2020) and basically parroted what the Tory government had said happened about the Salisbury incident, even suggesting that Sergei Skripal had told his best friend in the UK that Putin was after him? Apart from joining in with USA's Russian phobia, including trying to silence RT (which they have now done), Mrs May oversaw the continuing brutal and corrupt Tory government driving millions into poverty through low paid crap jobs and pressured by the introduction of universal credit all in the name of 'austerity' for the masses, while the 1% grow richer. Her legacy from the home office has been shown to be a wave of broken lives, especially those of the Windrush generation conned by the illusion of being British citizens, only to be told that they do not belong here. According to Private Eye No 1487 she knighted 16 people in two and half years of being PM thus taking full advantage of her position. The new home secretary under Boris Johnson's regime (and probably the most corrupt government in the history of the UK) called Priti Patel, wanted to be more ruthless than Theresa May, so it seems, cutting immigration and making it even harder for anyone who wants to come here to work and play. Ben Jennings in the guardian (15th November 2019) made jokes in a brilliant cartoon that even Father Christmas was not welcome under this ghastly woman. The latest Tory legislation (2021) wants to make anyone who comes here illegally a criminal who can be locked up for four years. Strangely the same government now wants immigrants to join the workforce to increase productivity. (October 2022)

I would also suggest that what terrifies me more than anything about Brexit, is that once we leave the EU, there will be no counter-lever whatsoever to another brutal Tory government sometime in the future, probably this century, starving millions to death through more economic and social policies that only benefit the 1%, at the top. If you think this is over the top, you have never read history or understood that the British ruling class for centuries have been one of the most brutal and cruel in the whole world. The evidence for my premise here is quite simple; in modern times a recent UN report on Britain by Philip Alston stated that 14 million people are living in poverty. The massive inequality with many scenes taken from the 19th century, written about by Marx and Engels and others, like Charles Dickens - is becoming as stark as in the USA, which we seem to copy as a wonderful model for capitalism. The upside-down world of Tory rhetoric by the party, denying everything, does not mean anything according to this report. Philip Alston noted that this terrible poverty, will in two years' time, mean that 40% of children will be living in poverty with unheard levels of loneliness and isolation and that without a reversal of all these social and economic polices things will only get worse, according to this brilliant report.

Another UN expert we should look up to is Nils Melzer, the special rapporteur on torture, who has suggested that 'Julian Assange is showing all the symptoms associated with prolonged exposure to psychological torture and should not be extradited to the US'. Having lived in the Ecuador Embassy for nearly seven years, virtually living in a prison type situation and after being dragged out by the British police by force and given 50 weeks in Belmarsh prison in London, for skipping bail, so would most people in the same situation, also be displaying the same symptoms? As Ben Quinn who wrote this in the Guardian on the 31st of May 2019 asserts 'Assange is accused of violating the America espionage act by publishing secret documents containing the names of confidential US military and diplomatic sources. After meeting Assange this month in the company of medical experts who examined him, Melzer will condemn what he describes as the deliberate and concerted abuse inflicted for years on Assange'. Melzer was also concerned about how quickly Assange was convicted after being dragged out of the Embassy and how the whole rotten British Establishment seem to be ganging up on one individual who did nothing wrong apart from exposing some of the seedier sides of war, carried out by the USA et al in Afghanistan and Iraq, kept from the public until WikiLeaks exposed them. In fact, the book called *Wikileaks -Inside Julian Assange's War on Secrecy* by David Leigh and Luke Harding, should be on all University reading lists, as Julian Assange is a real freedom fighter of the 21st century and should go down in history as ONE. Ironically because of the corona-virus crisis he cannot be extradited to the USA, so should in theory be out of prison, which he is not, to my knowledge (still in prison in March 2023) probably against all rules of fair justice, that the British ruling class pretend to abide by. When this sort of behaviour happens elsewhere, it is the end of the world and hits the news with a vengeance.

Continuing in this vein, with Theresa May having to resign on the 7th of June, pushed out by her party like Margret Thatcher in 1990, we get Boris Johnson. Brian Reade in the Daily Mirror informs us on the 25th of May 2019 that Johnson 'is a shallow, friendless disloyal, deceitful...a womanising, mad-haired, narcissistic liar' which is not far from the truth and means that things can only get worse for most of the population, in the future. For further evidence of his behaviour everyone should read Private Eye. In fact, for anyone who understands what has been going on in the UK in recent times and in the past, (see for example my book about Mrs Thatcher) and many other authors, Theresa May does not seem to have had any analytical skills whatsoever, or intellect and was promoted above her pay grade when she became prime minister. All the rhetoric about 'burning injustices' and so on did not mean anything. The Tory government has been carrying on with their austere social policies, increasing poverty and stress in society especially through their hostile immigration ideas. Paul Mason on BBC Radio4 Any Questions (24th May 2019) even asserted that she was 'serving the rich and not the poor' and trying to save her party from disintegration, which has very little to-do with the 'national interest'. This has been true about the Tory Party for getting on for nearly 200 years and will not stop until the whole rotten British Establishment are overthrown, hopefully this century? I am only repeating this axiom from the great Hugh Thomas, editor in chief of *The Establishment* published in 1959/60 containing another 7 essays, by other authors. He noted: 'To those who desire to see the resources and talents of Britain fully developed and extended there is no doubt that the fusty Establishment, with its Victorian views and standards of judgement, must be destroyed; the authors of the following essays make their own suggestion as to how (as well as why) this should be done; the editor, however, cannot refrain from pointing out that it is in childhood that the men who make the present Establishment are trained; and that therefore we shall not be free of the Establishment frame of mind, permeating all aspects of life and society, and constantly re-appearing even when apparently uprooted, until the public schools are completely swept away, at whatever cost to the temporary peace of the country'(21). A year into Boris Johnson's reign as prime minster (August 2020) an all-mighty row broke out in the UK over education, something that happens every now and then, as in the UK only 7% of parents can afford to send their children to private schools, but millions want to be middle class with A levels and degrees. In its most simplistic form, because of covid-19 most children have not had a full-time education for months, so they have not sat the end of term exams but had sat mocks and had been assessed earlier on in the year by their teachers. However, it seems that Ofqual who oversee the whole exam system in the UK, decided to use an algorithm that was weighted in favour of smaller class sizes that are only found in the private sector, whereas the state sector, especially the comprehensive schools, have atleast 30 pupils in each class. So, what happened was that many privately educated children were given higher grades and the children from larger size classes in the state sector were downgraded. Ironically even the Sunday Times (16th August 2020) is getting upset about 'this debacle', because Boris Johnson and the Tories have tried to pretend, they were on the side of the working class, especially in the so-called 'red wall' (sic) constituencies, won from labour at the general election in December 2019 with an 80-seat majority. They called it a 'levelling up' exercise when this whole debacle is about levelling down, which is the norm for this brutal and cruel ruling class. Most educated people like me have no idea whatsoever what levelling up means, because as I just noted and as reinforced by people like F. A. Hayek, (Mrs Thatcher's favoured guru) noted, that there is no greater danger to society then an educated proletariat, with nothing to do. Hence, the reason that for most of the 20th century and into the 21st, all Tory governments have tried to attack the education system, when any progressive forces had tried to alter in favour of the majority and have always made sure it favours the 'upper classes and no one else. Albeit that Mrs Thatcher, as education Secretary in the 1970s, closed more grammar schools than anyone else, because that was what many sociologists had, in the 1960s, said needed to be done to make the system fairer. We could say that while writing this we have been going through an epoch of madmen and women, running America and the UK, which seems not far from the truth.

As from Monday the 18th of August 2020 all changed from what I have just written above and there has been a massive U turn, (something Mrs Thatcher said she would never do, when in power), on education and exam results. So, I will let the Morning Star of the same date, report to you what happened in England, called A-levels U-turn….'As the Morning Star went to press the government was in panic mode as the full implications of the A-level fiasco became apparent to Tory MPs. The government could have tolerated a chorus of complaints from Labour about admissions if it solely affected the daughters and sons of the labouring classes who aspire to a university education. But the perverse effects of applying a defective algorithm across such a wide spectrum of secondary school pupils has inevitably produced a storm of personal disaster stories in which the reasonable expectations of many thousands of brighter students were dashed. The normal functioning of the school system conceals any number of factors which compound the discrimination faced by working-class children, but this is obscured by the fact that in the examination hall the human factor moderates, to some extent, the systemic class bias. Now the arbitrary operation of the mechanism adopted by the government to "moderate" teacher assessment resulted in a myriad of injustices, forcing a chaotic U-turn at the last moment due to mounting public pressure, including by demonstrations on the streets. This was a full spectrum cock up by the idiot in charge, though Labour felt unable even to echo the Liberal Democrats in demanding that Education Secretary Gavin Williamson resign. This U-turn must not be allowed to detract from the struggle against an education system whose injustices have been made obvious by an algorithm imposing the prejudices of the Tory Party on working-class kids'.

Returning to the situation in the USA, sanctions have been used against North Korea, Iran and several other countries including Venezuela. Iran was threatened with annihilation by Trump through his twitter feed 19th May 2019, because of so-called misdemeanours. When it comes to Venezuela it would seem to me and many others - not only do they want to ruin the country economically through sanctions and currency speculation but also their long term aim probably is to steal the oil reserves, which are the biggest in South America, so just repeating history from 1928 (Chomsky 2003) as they did in Iraq in 2003.

Until Trump fell in love with Kim Jong-Un, he called him the 'little Rocket man' and other derogatory terms. He said such things as: 'North Korea best not make any more threats to the United States. They will be met with the fire and fury like the world has never seen'. He has been very threatening beyond a normal state, and as I said they will be met with fire and fury and frankly power, likes of which this world has never seen before, Thank you.' (22). The reason for this over-the-top rhetoric was that North Korea had got hold of nuclear secrets and were in the process of making nuclear weapons, probably to protect themselves from American aggression? After the second meeting between Trump and Kim Jong-Un in Hanoi at the end of February 2019, which it seems, may have not gone so well as the first; the North Korean leader wanted all sanctions to be lifted, which Trump would not do. It would seem however that this may have been a million miles from the truth, according to the foreign minister, Ri Yong Ho of North Korea, who asserted that Pyongyang 'had only demanded partial sanctions relief'....'those that hamper the civilian economy and the livelihood of our people'. He said that in return they would permanently and completely dismantle all the nuclear production facilities in the Yongbyon area, in the presence of US experts (23). If this were true about Trump, we may see more bullying tactics being employed in the future, by the USA Rogue State (William Blum - see below). Again, according to Cohen this process of bullying is part of Trump's psychological makeup, similar in essence to Thatcher whose whole life was based on conflict, where in Trump's case he has threatened at-least '500 people'. Or as Matt Taibbi wrote in 2017: 'The problem, of course is that Trump is crazy. He is like every other corporate tyrant in that his solution to most things follows the logic of Stalin: no person, no problem. You're fired. Except as president he would have other people-removing options, all of which he likes: torture, mass deportations, the banning of 23% of the Earth's population from entering the United States, etc' (24). In fact, his ego is getting so big it seems to resemble an Egyptian Pharaoh or another Caligula. If Taibbi is correct again, Trump wanted the wall to be called, when it's built, between Mexico and the USA, the 'Great Wall of Trump'...so he told Maria Bartiromo? The wall received funding from the so-called emergency funds from the Pentagon budget of about 1 billion dollars, as of the end of March 2019. According to the authors of a new book (October 2019) called *'Border Wars: Inside Trump's Assault on Immigration'* by Michael D. Shear and Julie Hirschfeld, two New York journalists (from inside sources) suggest that at one meeting in March, Trump wanted to shoot illegal immigrants in the legs to slow them down, electrify his border wall and surround it with a moat full of snakes or alligators. Apparently, Trump 'exploded with rage when advisers told him his suggestions were unworkable, illegal or would cost a fortune'.... (Several sources in British newspapers, 3rd October 2019). Now we hear in another new book called *'A Warning'* - that Trump wanted to call all migrants entering the US without permission as 'enemy combatants' so they could be sent to Guantanamo Bay in the east part of Cuba. 'Enemy combatants were the legal definition the Bush administration seized upon as a way of skirting international law to justify indefinitely held al-Qaida and Taliban suspects picked up in the so-called "war on terror" after the September 11 attacks. Its use was to bypass federal courts and hold terror suspects in the extrajudicial military setting of the US naval base at Guantanamo Bay, which was condemned around the world'....as stated in the Guardian on the 15th of November 2019. The war on terror was an idea that became so ludicrous that it was going to go on for ever, something very similar to the enemies at Rome's door 2000 years ago, but as Oliver Stone and others have noted, war, or we should say killing and bombing people is very good for business, albeit mostly immoral.

This sort of rhetoric and barbaric behaviour has been on-going in America virtually since breaking away from Great Britain in 1776 (Chomsky, Pilger, Klein Oliver Stone & Kuznick et al). While in office George W. Bush in 2002 called North Korea, Iran and Iraq the 'Axis of Evil'. This was a year before the USA and the UK invaded Iraq against all the norms of UN convention etc and was a mountain of lies and propaganda, to legitimize the invasion. According to Greg Palast in *'The Best Democracy Money Can Buy'* George W. Bush only won the 2000 election from Al Gore because of: 'Florida's Ethnic Cleansing of the Voter Rolls' and other scams? Oliver Stone (DVD) also noted that this whole process was nearly so surreal you could hardly make it up in a so-called modern first world country, pretending that it is a liberal democracy when it is a plutocracy, like the UK, and both are 'rogue states' according to Noam Chomsky. Paradoxically according to most well-informed sources, for example Channel4 news in the UK and others, if it were not for the invasion of Iraq, we would not have had ISIS fighting Assad in Syria who were mostly from the minority Sunni ethnic group, which Saddam Hussein belonged to and not the majority who were Shia? For ten years before the invasion of Iraq the Western Powers had put sanctions on that country, enforced by fly overs with fighter jets for having so-called weapons of mass destruction, which may have killed half a million children through starvation, and lack of medicines and during and after the war another million may have died according to George Galloway and others, like Seumas Milne? A similar process is now happening in the Yemen by proxy, with arms mostly bought from the USA and the UK and sold to Saudi Arabia who are bombing and killing thousands and starving millions. Maybe as many as 14 million are in dire need and while writing this, Yemen is the biggest humanitarian crisis in the world. According to the Morning Star on the 24th [of] January 2019 'last night there was an arm's dealing shindig' in a very posh hotel in London where it cost non-members £425 for dinner and one of the speakers was Alan Johnson - an ex-labour

MP and one of Tony Blair's ministers between 1997 and 2010, who like many of Blair's ex MPs are now millionaires, as is Blair who may be worth £60 million or more, with at-least 10 homes? Saudi Arabia was the first country that Trump visited after gaining the presidency, and he is always bragging about his friendship with MBS (sic). When Mrs May came back from a visit to the same country probably selling more arms, she said 'we shared the same values' ...as Saudi Arabia; you madam maybe - but not mine or most educated people in the UK, I would have thought? It is also worth noting the outcry from this brutal Right-wing Tory government over the Salisbury incident, with added further sanctions against Russia, and the near silence about the death of Khashoggi. If Russia is now a 'mafia state' which according to the Wikileaks book mentioned above they are, with Vladimir Putin et al getting very rich and up to all sorts of misbehaviour in other countries according to the Western powers, surely, he is only copying the Americans & British elites doing the same thing...the pot calling the kettle black, comes to mind here!

You would think by what I have written so far that Russia is the number one enemy along with North Korea and Iran. In fact, to pretend that North Korea is an enemy of the West, is nearly beyond belief, or Iran for that matter, described as 'not a threat to anyone' according RT on the 21st February 2019. The USA and their friends in the Middle East have been itching for years to destroy the place? In fact, less than ten countries in the world have nuclear weapons, and the biggest danger to the world is the USA, as noted by William Blum in *Rogue State* and a few others like Noam Chomsky and John Pilger et al. In the past we have had warmongers like Dwight Eisenhower and Jack Kennedy who nearly helped to blow up the world in 1962, the year I started work at the age of 14 in Port Stanley. Others of the same ilk have included Richard Nixon, Jimmy Carter, Ronald Reagan, Bill Clinton and George W. Bush and now Donald J. Trump in the

White House and Tony Blair the ex-Prime Minster of the UK. George W. Bush even had the gall in 2001 to unilaterally scrap the anti-ballistic missile treaty, the agreement that the USA had signed with the old Soviet Union in 1972 based on the assumption that 'the world had changed'. Trump also did away with the Intermediate-Range Nuclear Forces (INF) agreement on the 2nd of August 2019, which was made in 1987 between Mikhail Gorbachev and Ronald Reagan, suggesting that Russia broke the agreement in the first place by developing a land-based nuclear-capable cruise missile, which the US and its NATO allies said violated the above agreement. Jack Kennedy was the first President to sign a Partial Nuclear Test Ban agreement on the 24th of September 1963, and ratified on 7th October, which was something Kennedy was very proud of, and only a few weeks before he was killed probably by the whole USA establishment and others, and not a lone killer, if the great Oliver Stone is correct in his movie about these events in JFK and his book written with Peter Kuznick?

Robert De Niro the double Oscar winner and one of American greatest actors of all time called Trump a 'racist' and bordering on a 'fascist', noting how Hitler and 'Mussolini looked funny and other dictators and despots look funny' as well. The danger being that over time others may imitate Trump and be more dangerous than him. As De Niro notes, about the current President: 'He's a con artist. He's a huckster. He's a scam artist. And what bothers me is that people don't see that. I think that *The Apprentice* had a lot to do with that, which I never saw but once, maybe. It's all smoke and mirrors, it's all bullshit'. When at the Tony awards last June (2018) De Niro had a rant against Trump and said, 'fuck Trump' he got a standing ovation. Trump replied on Twitter the next day by saying De Niro had a low IQ and had taken 'too many shots to the head'. Robert De Niro is also a critic of Trump's 'anti-immigration ideology' along with Fox news owned by Rupert Murdoch which is just nothing more than 'a mouthpiece for the government'. The low IQ jibe about De Niro is rather cruel, considering that Trump has maybe read only a few books in his life, or perhaps ONE or TWO *'All Quiet on the Western Front'*, according to Ruth Ann Monti and *Fountainhead* by Ayn Rand published in 1943) albeit he wrote a few; all written by ghost writers. Several people have called him a 'moron', who wanted to build a wall across the USA to stop terrible people like illegal immigrants coming over from Mexico, and get their government to pay for it? Albeit he said on the 10th of January 2019 that he never said this, while shutting part of the Federal State down and trying to blackmail Congress into finding 5 billion dollars to build the bloody thing, which if CNN was correct would cost billions more? How Trump ever got hooked on the whole idea of anti-immigration is questioned by Matt Taibbi in his excellent savage critique of the President Trump called *'Insane Clown President'*, where he considers that the USA economy has been built on immigration virtually from year dot, when the Europeans first invaded the place? He also makes another very important political point about a rigged system, as he asserts: 'Republicans won middle American voters for years by taking advantage of the fact that voters didn't know the difference between an elitist and the actual elite, between a snob and an oligarch. They made sure their voters' idea of an elitist was Sean Penn hanging out with Hugo Chavez, instead of a Wall Street bank financing the construction of Chinese factories' (25).

Michael Cohen, Trump's lawyer, fixer and an ex-friend of Trump for ten years - virtually repeated what the great De Niro had said sometime before (see above), calling Trump: a 'racist, liar and conman' in an extraordinary appearance before Congress at the end of February 2019. Trump's family in 2016 also knew in advance of the dirt Wikileaks were going to leak from Russian sources on Hilary Clinton. He also lied about his business interests in Russia, hoping to build more Trump Towers during/after the 2016 election jamboree.

Fusion GPS was a commercial research and strategic intelligence firm based in Washington whose owners may have been trying to do a Woodward and Bernstein on Trump in 2016 (my hypotheses). They hired Christopher Steele a former British spy MI6 operative (like James Bond) to investigate Trump's repeated brags about his relationship with Vladimir Putin and the Kremlin. Steele did what was asked of him and produced an explosive 'dossier' on Trump with the help from insider sources (maybe) which suggested that Trump was being blackmailed by the Kremlin for misdemeanours with prostitutes in hotels in Russia. Steele briefed reporters from several newspapers with this story in September 2016, but the day before CNN broke the outlines of the dossier on TV and Buzzfeed published the whole story. According to Michael Wolff's account of this story in *Fire and Fury,* Trump completely denied this accusation many months later including what Cohen had said in Congress. Albeit he had been in Moscow with the Ms. Universe competition bragging that he could be the president running the USA as well as his business interests around the world. It was at this news conference that he attacked CNN directly calling them a 'fake news' organisation and refusing to answer any questions from their journalists. He then noted: 'that report first of all should never have been printed because it is not worth the paper it's printed on. I will tell you that should never happen. Twenty-two million accounts were hacked by China. That's because we have no defence, because we're run by people who don't know what they are doing. Russia will have far greater respect for our country when I'm leading it. And not just Russia, China, which has taken total advantage of us. Russia, China, Japan, Mexico, all countries will respect us far more, far more than they do under past administrations'. (26) To my mind there do seem to be some contradictions here, especially with his views on Russia, where in theory

Steele's 'dossier' came from, and the idea that they had no defence against hacking from China is so bizarre its straight out of a John le Carre novel.

Stormy Daniels a porn star who was paid thousands of dollars to shut her up - claimed she had an affair with Trump and has now written a barn storming book about the whole process, even discussing the size and shape of his penis. But to me one of the biggest blunders he made if Cohen is correct is on 'racism'? And this is what Trump said to Cohen: 'if I could name a country run by a black person that wasn't a "shithole"'. (This was when Barack Obama was president). 'While we were once driving through a struggling neighbourhood in Chicago, he also commented that only black people could live that way, and that black people would never vote for him because they were too stupid' (27). To me as a very well-read social scientist, from an impoverished background this may show us all how uneducated the man might be said to be. He seems to have no clue about the structural nature of the epoch. The same could be said about many extreme right-wing journalists and radio hosts in the USA and in the UK, for that matter, some working for Rupert Murdoch? I would also agree with Matt Taibbi in *'Insane Clown President'* that 'the Republican Party under Trump has become the laughing stock of the world, and it happened in front of an invading force of thousands of mocking reporters who made sure that not one single excruciating moment was left uncovered' (28). Ironically, Trump pretended he is not a racist, but during July 2019 he has tweeted several nasty remarks about members of congress of colour, that they should go back to their own crime ridden shitholes. In at-least 3 cases these members of congress who were born in the USA. Then afterwards he is trying to blame the victims of his tweets for saying terrible things about the USA that they should apologize for, just as the USA informed Vietnam that they should apologize for the deaths of millions, caused by the foreign policies at the time of several USA presidents, in essence turning social reality on its head, a form of societal inversion. A day later when at a Trump rally in North Carolina (Wednesday 17th July 2019) Ilhan Omar was picked on by Trump (as were three other women of colour in Congress), and got the crowd so riled up they were shouting 'send her home' but by the next day in the White house he said he was not happy with the chants? From what I could see on my TV in the UK this whole process was straight out of the Hitler's playbook, and why I believe that Ilham Omar was correct in calling him a 'fascist', and one of the most dangerous persons ever to come to power in the world and the reason I am writing this book before I die and perhaps the whole human race may die with me, if he goes mad. In the Guardian on the 18th October 2019, Gary Younge backed up what I have just said - when he noted 'don't question Trump's sanity: ask how he got into office'. In fact, 'following a 2017 conference, 27 psychiatrists, psychologists and other mental health experts wrote a book called: *The Dangerous Case of Donald Trump,* arguing it was their moral and civic duty to warn America that for psychological reasons, Trump was more dangerous than any president in history….as did Noam Chomsky. They diagnosed him with everything from severe character pathology to delusional disorder which can be added to the more common verdicts of narcissistic personality disorder and antisocial personality disorder which are regularly offered'. The theme of this article is that he may be deteriorating psychologically because of his erratic behaviour in virtually everything he says and does with foreign policy initiatives and meetings, with all sorts of people and groups. Constant lying is another theme of this article, about Trump, as it is with Boris Johnson in the UK, which is one of the main themes of this chapter. An excellent British TV documentary about Trump shown on the 15th of October 2020 called *The Trump Show* was mainly a scathing attack on a human who had no idea what he was taking on as president of the USA. He was just thinking that it was all about making deals like he had been doing for 45 years as a businessman. Of course, it is not, but is mostly about diplomacy and getting to grips with the complexity of world affairs. Rex Tillerson who had been appointed Secretary of State at the start of Trump's presidency and lasted just over a year, an oilman all his life from Texas, decided after one of his first briefings about world affairs with Trump, that his boss was a 'fucking moron'. The reason seems to be that as far as Trump is concerned being a politician is just another branch of show business, and nothing else. For example: when meeting Kim Jong-un, the Supreme leader of North Korea, he wanted to direct the whole show especially where the cameras were going to be, at the event, etc - as for him it was 'gold dust'…. John Bolton thought the whole thing was a mistake. From day one when Trump questioned how many people were at his inauguration, as there were many empty spaces (where there was not with Obama) there has been dynamic tension between most of the media and the Trump administration, with some it was a declaration of war. If we need any more evidence than I have already written from many sources about Donald J. Trump, they should watch now *Unfit: The Psychology of Donald J. Trump, directed by Dan Partland* and why he should never have been elected president in the first place in 2016! This is one of the most powerful documentaries I have ever seen in my life, albeit I have seen dozens and dozens, especially about the Second World War. Apparently to work for the USA military, especially in a serious capacity of responsibility, you must be 'compos mentis'. Everyone interviewed in this documentary stated categorically that Trump was not 'compos mentis' and was a threat to the world. The list including being: a 'malignant narcissist'…. 'sadist'…. 'Enjoying degrading other people' …'constantly lying' and even cheating at golf, 'gaslighting and abusing' people and a very dangerous sociopath, who could blow up the planet with nuclear weapons. He only got away with this because like Mussolini and especially Hitler in Germany, millions were desperate for a better life. The major tool that Hitler used was to have perceived enemies like the Jews;

Trumps perceived enemies are the Left, fake news organisations and immigrants. And very similar to Hitler he keeps repeating lies until many believe him, or the more intelligent of us would say 'gaslighting' is the weapon of choice that he uses: so, millions are so confused about what is going on that they believe him. Noam Chomsky being interviewed by Piers Morgan on Talk TV (UK version - 9th June 2023) said Trump was a 'megalomanic and a psychopath' and a 'disaster for the world'.

Not only is Donald Trump a very 'dangerous' person when it comes to using his power, including economically against his foes as he sees fit, but he is also a climate change denier and is doing everything in his power to get rid of scientists or down grade them in the government bureaucracies. The British Guardian did an excellent article on the 18th September 2019 called 'Science became irrelevant'. This was about 6 scientists who became 'whistle-blowers who revealed how the experts were silenced in Trump's climate whitewash'. The 6 were all searching for the truth about how different aspects of society effects the environment, which Trump and his team of cronies do not want to hear, especially from big business-like oil and gas exploration. As Chis Fry noted about this whole process under Trump, 'political appointees are picking candidates sympathetic to the administration, even if they have fringe views, like climate change isn't happening'. A week later Trump gave a 36-minute speech to the UN general assembly which Ben Rhodes, Barack Obama's foreign adviser and speech writer, called a 'warmed-over nationalist garbage delivered like a late-night talk radio host trying to put you to sleep'. I watched it live on TV in the UK and the tone did seem down beat in a muted monotone format, reading off an auto-cue, very slowly. Trump's speech asserted stuff like 'the free world must embrace its national foundations' and 'it must not attempt to erase them or replace them. The true good of the nation can only be pursued by those who love it, by citizens who are rooted in its history, who are nourished by its culture, committed to its values, attached to its people'.... patriotism being the main theme of his speech, in other words 'the future belongs to patriots not globalists'. Trump did not mention climate change or arms control - but was bragging about what he has done for the military spending trillions according to him. He later tweeted a video link of the amazing and wonderful Greta Thunberg saying 'she seems like a very happy young girl looking forward to a bright and wonderful future. So nice to see' which was maybe a side swipe at her as she got quite upset when giving her dynamic short speech about climate change and was one of the stars of the whole event (29).

However, for all the rhetoric against China, Iran, Venezuela and so on in this speech, (but not Russia), I believe that to return to Rome and Carthage, former colony of the Phoenician's (destroyed between 149 – 146BC), the analogy that represents this most closely is the USA verses China now. Trump has been complaining about China for several years, and they will probably over-take the USA economically by halfway through this century, or before, so representing a real threat to USA hegemony. Ironically, it has been China who has been the most successful at becoming a Capitalist country by doing it in their own unique way, while in Russia it was forced on them in the most brutal way, forcing millions into poverty over two financial crises in the 1990s. These were mostly caused by agencies of the Western Powers according to Joseph Stiglitz (30) and the Oligarchs got away with murder. For example: Russian industrial production fell by almost 60% - even greater than the fall in GDP of 54% between 1990-99 which was bigger than the period between 1940 - 46 in the old Soviet Union where industrial production fell by 24%. Hence, 'The result of giving away its rich natural resources before it had in place a system to collect natural resource taxes, was that a few friends and associates of Yeltsin became billionaires, but the country was unable to pay pensioners their 15 dollars a month pension'. (31) As Seumas Milne has described about these times in *"The Revenge of History"*, 'far from opening the way to emancipation, these changes led to beggary for most citizens ushering in the most cataclysmic peacetime economic collapse of an industrial country in history. Under the banner of reform and the guidance of American-prescribed shock therapy, perestroika became catastroika. Capitalist restoration brought in its wake mass pauperisation and unemployment; wild extremes of inequality; rampant crime; virulent anti-Semitism and ethnic violence. All combined with legalized gangsterism on a heroic scale and the ruthless looting of public assets' (32). Also, as Naomi Klein wrote in *'The Shock Doctrine'*......'In Russia in 1993, it was Boris Yeltsin's decision to send in tanks to set fire to the parliament building and lock up the opposition leaders that cleared the way for the fire-sale privatization that created the country's notorious oligarchs' (33). Further evidence again comes from Seumas Milne about this whole rotten process. As he noted 'The case is made throughout the years of market idolatry. When western prescribed market shock therapy was used to restore capitalism in Russia and Eastern Europe, Western elites hailed it as a dawn of freedom and prosperity. But opponents of the new order predicated it would lead to economic and social disaster. Sure enough, Eastern Europe's 1990's slump was deeper than the Great Depression of the 1930's. And the neoliberal medicine of deregulation and mass privatisation that Russia was forced to swallow ushered in the greatest peacetime collapse of an industrial economy in history, driving 130 million into poverty and millions to premature deaths' (34). What this says about the crimes of Stalin as portrayed by western academics and others, must be left to historians, 'to expose the lies and tell the truth'. Of both events? Oliver Stone & Peter Kuznick also repeat what I have just written above, in *The Untold History of the United States* which according to these two authors; even Alexander

Solzhenitsyn was not impressed. He noted in 2000 'As a result of the Yeltsin era, all the fundamental sectors of state, economic, cultural, and moral life have been destroyed or looted. We live literally amid ruins, but we pretend to have a normal life…. great reforms…. being carried out in our country…were false reforms because they left more than half of our people in poverty…. Will we continue looting and destroying Russia until nothing is left? God forbid these reforms should continue' 35). It may take several centuries for these crimes to come out completely, I would have thought.

What Donald J Trump will never admit to is that the whole economic system, especially after the Second World War, was designed for the benefit of the USA and in theory the other winners of the war, who gained the most out of mass slaughter of at-least 60 million people, with the old Soviet Union losing maybe between 20 to 27 million of its population depending on which source one finds credible, and a lot of the basic infrastructure destroyed by the retreating armies.

This also applied to the creation of NAFTA in the 1990s which helped to close factories in the USA relocating them to cheap labour in Mexico, which also helped to force down pay rates in low paid jobs in the USA. The idea was to raise living standards in Mexico, but 'instead both have plummeted harming the economic prospects for workers on both sides of the border' (36). I presume that when Trump quoted this specific case, on the campaign trail, it was not the poor wage slaves in Mexico he was concerned about, but some of his core supporters who suffered under this agreement, enforced during the Clinton period in office? In fact, one of the most important films ever made, in 2007 about the NAFTA agreement is called *Bordertown,* written and directed by Gregory Nave. Starring Jennifer Lopez, who was also one of the producers, and based on real facts about the brutal exploitation of Mexican workers in Maquiladora factories and the murder of perhaps thousands of poor women. One excellent line in the movie says this is nothing to do with free trade, but 'slave trade'!

Again, when China opened its economy to the West it was often big business and Plutocrats around the Globe who gained the most out of it, people like the Walton family in the USA: also, between 1990 and 1999 there was inward investment into the USA of 8 billion dollars (1990) as against 41 billion dollars being invested in China in 1999, something never mentioned by Trump, to my knowledge? (37). Neither were the terrible working conditions that pertained in China and vice-versa in the USA, often using serving prisoners according to Noam Chomsky, writing in 1994 about Human Rights contradictions of U.S Foreign policy. Simon Reeve also explained this process in his excellent TV programme for the BBC while exploring America, which suggested there were 3 million locked up prisoners in the USA which cost the State 80 billion dollars a year. The downside for the USA of these policies was that cheap goods did flood into the USA and to everywhere else from the Far East, often causing a balance of payments problem, between imports and exports. Trump is trying to blame China for this which I find very ironic indeed, considering that Communism was the big Satan that the Western Powers had to destroy! I did notice that when I was visiting Vietnam in 2007, as part of writing a travel book on the Far East - that it was virtually a Capitalist country but calling itself a Socialist one. However, I enjoyed it just as much as the old BBC Top Gear team (Clarkson et al) did when they visited the place, several years after me.

And now a very short lesson on the works of Keynes, who Trump may have heard of through his advisers? Well Trump does want to build a wall and improve the infrastructure, so he said when campaigning in 2016. What John Maynard Keynes understood more than most in the 1930s was that free-market Capitalism left to its own devices will create unemployment through 'suppressing wages and cutting costs by replacing labour with technology' (38). This whole process creates a chain of events where if the workers cannot buy the goods made in factories, (Henry Ford understood this phenomenon and was a hero to Hitler) and demand drops, including abroad through similar processes - so aggregate demand falls further, factories close and a recession is in inevitable. Therefore, at Bretton Woods Keynes was the leading light, as he was in the eyes of Roosevelt in the USA with the 'new deal'. If businessmen will not invest in these situations the Government must step in to create a demand in the whole economy, by 'priming the economic pump', investing in infrastructure, dams, etc, in the case of Britain in the NHS, training and so on. Even if the Government goes into debt, it does not matter as when the economy picks up, they will gain through the taxation system, and stable employment saves government money overall. This major idea was taken up by most Western States for at least 30 years. However, Keynes did not get his own way at Bretton Woods when it came to the creation of a 'reserve currency'. He wanted to create a world 'reserve currency' administered by a global central bank. This would create a more stable and fairer world economy 'by automatically recycling trade surpluses to finance trade deficits' (39). This did not suit the USA 'Power Elite', so they chose the dollar, which in theory was set at 35 dollars to an ounce of gold, so becoming the major currency for trading throughout the world, with fixed exchange rates. According to the brilliant professor Steve Keen speaking on RT ((July 2021), who calls himself a post-Keynesian sage, this whole process has helped China to become a powerhouse in the world, today - which would not have been the modus operandi originally, I would have thought? Wayne Ellwood notes that Britain was the first country in modern times (1816) to adopt this idea that a specific currency had to have a direct relationship to gold, a very simple idea, which may have been around thousands of years ago, in a different form? In other words, 'if a country's imports exceeded its exports, then gold had to be shipped to those countries who were owed in order to balance the books' (40). To keep an equilibrium (or at least in theory), you could only print money if you had the gold reserves to allow it, so less money in circulation would tend to lower prices and vice-versa. With the depression in the 1930s this whole idea was dropped so that countries could devalue their currencies; so, gaining an advantage over the competition by making their exports cheaper. In 1971 -1973 Richard Nixon again suspended the exchange of American gold for foreign-held dollars at fixed rates, mostly because of the expense of the Vietnam War (and probably the space race to the Moon, which cost a fortune) and made the dollar just another commodity to be traded in the marketplace with restraints, so as not to make it worthless. To control the processes designed at Bretton Woods the: IMF the World Bank and the General Agreement on Tariffs and Trade (GATT)/(WTO) was set up, with in theory, different controlling mechanisms. For example: the IMF was to oversee a system of fixed exchange rates and to facilitate the expansion and balanced growth of international trade and maintain a high level of employment and incomes. The idea of keeping an eye on fixed exchange rates was so that countries would not return to the 1930s chaos. The IMF also had control of a system of quotas called Special Drawing Rights (SDRs) linked to certain criteria, set out by the most powerful Nation, the USA. The World Bank's primary objective was to rebuild the economies that had been devastated by the Second World War (International Bank for Reconstruction and Development), especially in Europe, mostly was destroyed after 6 years of total war and to supply loans for infrastructure, like: dams, power plants, roads and airports around the world that were badly needed (Ellwood 2001). Gatt, now named WTO standing for World Trade Organization from 1994 - was to establish a set of rules to govern global trade, with a clear objective to reduce national trade barriers and to stop countries from gaining competitive advantage over their neighbours.

Over the years there have been numerous meetings all over the world to try and achieve these objectives, sometimes with success and other times without gaining much. In 1986 while Mrs Thatcher was Prime Minister of the UK the WTO meeting was held in Uruguay. The reason for these impasses was that it has always been a rich man's club with the powerful Western nations setting the agendas - like the big idea of free trade. Disputes arise for example, over something as simple as the export and import of bananas, where the USA did complain to the EEC that ex-colonies were having an advantage over the USA owned companies in Central America. In this case it seems the Americans won, by threatening the livelihood of small farmers in the Caribbean, who often just rely on one commodity, and could be put out of business if they cannot export their product/products to the EU or wherever. There is real danger of side effects with power imbalances, which in essence affect most people most of the time. For example, when Canada wanted to export asbestos to the EEC (the larger block) it had to be proven scientifically that it will not harm anyone. You would think this was self-evident truth, but apparently not? Again, when the EEC said we do not want cattle fed on hormones from America, the WTO panel decided in favour of the USA, (the larger block) albeit you were not allowed to feed home grown cattle in the EEC on hormones. For not agreeing to these commodities being imported into Europe the EEC had to pay compensation to the USA and Canada for lost export earnings and in retaliation the USA imposed 100% tariffs on a range of European goods (41). A constant theme of this project will be these effects on trade, especially between the USA and China, which is always a contentious issue, in a capitalist epoch.

'US trade deficit hits highest level in 10 years despite Trump's tariff campaign' - so says the Guardian of the 7th of March 2019, despite Trump's efforts to restrict imports. 'The gap between the goods US companies sell to China and Chinese imports to the US ballooned to a record 419 billion dollars (£318bn), while the total deficit in goods with all countries jumped to 891 billion dollars'. The reason so it seems is obvious because USA consumers like the goods made in China, such as: phones, laptops and computer accessories and the dollar are overpriced to the yuan making exports more expensive. Trump's answer to this thorny contradiction was to impose more tariffs - says Philip Inman who wrote this article. Tariffs, not only on China, but on other countries he feels are ripping the USA off, like India who gets preferential trade treatment and now, duties on steel and aluminium made in the EU, etc. The Morning Star on the 14th August 2020 describes the 'US tariffs economic as vandalism costing thousands of jobs'. For example, the USA, through the WTO, thought that Airbus was receiving state subsidies, disadvantaging the commercial position of Boeing. This was not true as Boeing has been subsidized by the State in America for at-least 80 years (Chomsky et al). The USA put £6 billion of tariffs on 100 items in the EEC, which including 25% on some commodities like whiskey, in Scotland. The sale of Scotch exports dropped by a third to the USA, therefore some of us understood the insanity of leaving the EU, one of the largest trading blocks in the world without tariffs.

During the research and writing of this book very dramatic change of events occurred, which is that Donald J. Trump may end up being impeached (summer/autumn/winter 2019)? Albeit there probably are not enough votes in the Republican controlled senate for this to happen; only two other presidents, Bill Clinton and Andrew Johnson, have been impeached before and Richard Nixon resigned in disgrace before it happened to him.

It all started with a telephone call to the new president Volodymyr Zelenskiy of Ukraine on the 25th of July 2019 when it seems Trump tried to blackmail the new president 'by withholding military aid unless it helped to investigate a political opponent'. Joe Biden who ran against Trump in the 2020 election and who Trump maybe seemed afraid of. Hence Trump was trying to find dirt on Biden and his son Hunter, who worked as vice president for a gas company called Burisma and was paid 50,000 dollars a month. The company was investigated for corruption. Hunter was part of a successful international effort to have Ukraine's chief prosecutor dismissed and Joe Biden was vice-president of the USA at the time. You would think that a phone call between two heads of state would be secure, but apparently not because a whistle-blower, who worked in US intelligence, blew the whistle and filed a complaint in August about multiple acts involving Donald J. Trump. He of course is denying that he did anything wrong and is accusing the Biden's of being corrupt; well 30,000+ lies can't be wrong, can they? Nancy Pelosi, the speaker of the House of Representatives moved full speed ahead with their investigations despite the White House declaring it illegitimate, pushing the US towards a full constitutional crisis (42). The reason for this accusation is that Pat Cipollone, counsel for the White House, wrote a letter to Nancy Pelosi et al in the Democratic Party saying 'that the House did not formally vote to begin the impeachment inquiry' (the same source) in the first place. The trial itself turned out to be bit of a damp squib and a forgone conclusion because the Republicans would not allow any evidence from the Trump administration itself to be heard and on January 31st a Senate majority of 51 Republican senators voted against allowing subpoenas to call witness or documents. So, on February the 5^{th,} the Senate acquitted Trump on both impeachment articles, as neither article obtained the support of two-thirds majority of the 100 senators. If John Bolton had been allowed to give evidence, perhaps the conclusion may have been a little different? Trump was only the third person ever in USA history to be impeached, so will go down in history. He is now the only president in history to be impeached twice, as of January 2021. As further evidence of what I believe is a close correlation between a 'lunatic' like Trump and a tyrant like Caligula who was killed in a similar manner to Julius Caesar in 41AD, is that they both fell ill in their rule and recovered; also, they both seemed obsessed by construction projects - albeit in Caligula's time at-least some projects were for the improvement of society. In Caligula's day, some say he was disturbed, self-absorbed, and short tempered, indulged in too much spending and sex, a list of qualities maybe not too far removed from the former President. And instead of a Trump tower Caligula stole an Obelisk from Egypt and erected it in Rome, weighing 326 tonnes and now in Vatican City. There was also a famine in Rome at the time of Caligula which may have been caused by a shortage of transport; just as In the USA and the UK many people are going hungry in the 21st century.

A final act of madness was when on the on the 6$^{th\ of}$ January 2021 a semi - uprising was instigated on Congress, some attributing the instigation to Trump himself. Caligula's height of insanity was when he had boats built, (two biggest ever built at the time) and formed a pontoon for two miles from the resort of Baiae to the neighbouring port of Puteoli and rode his favourite horse 'Incitatus' across the pontoon, wearing Alexander the Great's breastplate, or may have done? This whole charade was only done because Tiberius the soothsayer (see above) said he had less chance of becoming emperor than of riding a horse across the bay of Baiae. In a very similar way to Trump's family thoughts and Obama's thoughts, about him ever becoming president of the USA.

According to Oliver Stone and Peter Kuznick in *The Untold History of the United States* Barack Obama, who most of us on the left perceive as a good guy, was not so great according to these two, especially when it comes to secretive behaviour. They note, 'In many respects, Obama has been more secretive than the pathologically secretive Bush-Cheney administration. His government has classified more information and responded more slowly to

Freedom of Information Act requests than his predecessor. It has prosecuted more government whistle-blowers than all previous administrations. Employing the 1917 Espionage Act in six separate cases, compared to a total of three in the ninety-two years before he took office' (43). So, it seems there are good whistle blowers and bad ones like Bradley Manning, Julian Assange and very recently, under Trump, Jeffery Sterling who was locked up for whistleblowing as was Daniel Hale, both for 'exposing lies and telling the truth' ...about USA foreign policy. Edward Snowden was in my eyes, and in the eyes of many intelligent people on the Left, also a good guy, but not according to the Ruling class in the USA and the UK. Snowden exposed the level of spying all over the world especially by the USA spy agencies and GCHQ in the UK and elsewhere around the world? Luke Harding's book on this case should be a must read before you die, published in 2014, called: *The Snowden Files...The Inside Story of the world's Most Wanted Man.* Explaining how Snowden escaped the clutches of the USA power Elite with the help of Laura Poitras, Glen Greenwald and Ewen MacAskill and a few others. Harding's book reads like an Ian Fleming and John Le Carrie novels combined, in fact most of it is so outrageous we are now all living in StasiLand. How ironic!

SOURCES

(1) Jean-Jacques Rousseau - Discourse on the Origins of Inequality f/p 1755.
(2) Oliver Stone & Peter Kuznick – The Untold History of the United States – paper edition 2013.
(3) The Sunday Times Rich List - several editions.
(4) Tony Bilton et al - Introductory Sociology – 1987 edition p, 40.
(5) Michael Wolff - Fire And Fury 2018 hardback edition p, 23.
(6) IBID p, 23

(7) Hannah Arendt – The Origins of Totalitarianism f/p 1951 paperback edition Penguin Classics p, 301.
(8) Matt Taibbi – Insane Clown President – 2017 p,228.
(9) Mark Singer - Trump & Me - 2016 p,89.
(10) The Guardian -5th June 2019.
(11) The Guardian 6th June 2019.
(12) Naomi Klein - The Shock Doctrine – 2007 - p, 86.
(13) Plutarch – The Fall of the Roman Republic – Penguin Classics – p, 230 f/p 1958…..(in this version).
(14) Joe Studwell – The China Dream – p,3 2002.
(15) IBID
(16) The Guardian 20th April 2020.
(17) Joseph Stiglitz - Globalization and its discounts – 2002
(18) Matti Taibbi – Insane Clown President – 2017 p, 280.
(19) Will Hutton – The Writing on the Wall China and the West in the 21st Century
(20) Joseph Choonara – unravelling capitalism, p, 107
(21) British Establishment – editor by Hugh Thomas f/b 1959/60 p, 18
(22) Michael Wolf - Fire & Fury - 2018 p, 291
(23) The Guardian 1st March 2019
(24) Matt Taibbi – Insane Clown President – p,15
(25) IBID p, 51.
(26) Michael Wolf - Fire And Fury -2018 Hardback edition, 39
(27) The Guardian…UK edition.
(28) Matt Taibbi – Insane Clown President – 2017 - p, 209
(29) The Guardian – 25th September 2019
(30) Joseph Stiglitz – Globalization and its discounts – 2002
(31) IBID – p, 159
(32) Seumas Milne – The Revenge of History – p, 17
(33) Naomi Klein – The Shock Doctrine – 2007 – p,10

(34) Seumas Milne – The Revenge of History – p, x1v & xv
(35) Olive Stone & Peter Kuznick – The Untold History of the United States – 2013 – p, 485/486
(36) Wayne Ellwood – No Nonsense guide to Globalization -2001 p,65
(37) Bill Quinn – How Wall-Mart is destroying America (and the world) And what you Can Do About it – 2005 3rd edition + Joseph Stiglitz 2002 p, 26.
(38) Wayne Ellwood – as above – p, 26
(39) IBID – p, 28
(40) IBID p, 34
(41) IBID p, 34 to 37
(42) The Guardian – 10th October 2019
(43) Olive Stone & Peter Kuznick – as above p, 563

OTHER SOURCES

Internet
Professor Steve Jones - The Descent of Men - 2002
Greg Palast - The Best Democracy Money Can Buy - 2002
Donald Trump in 100 Facts 2018
Francis Fukuyama - The End of History and the Last Man - 1992
Private Eye: One of the most important satirical magazines in the world.
Morning Star - 24 January 2019.
Ibid - 25th January 2019
Frank Ninkovich - The Wilsonian Century US Foreign Policy since 1900
Bilton et al - Introductory Sociology - 1987 edition.
Irving Krauss - Stratification, Class and conflict – 1976
Michael D. Shear & Julie Hirschfeld Davis – Boarder Wars – Inside Trump's on Immigration

John Pilger - The Coming War on China (DVD)
Sunday Times Rich List: several editions
Kitty Kelly: The Royals – 1997
Andrew Lownie: The Mountbatten's - Their Lives and Loves: Hardback edition 2019.
BBC4 TV channel in the UK.
Citizen Kane starring the legendary Orson Wells.
National Enquirer: 22nd June 2020.
Yesterday - digital TV channel in the UK.
Simon Reeve a brilliant young journalist/travel maker on BBC 2….UK
BBC TV Top Gear, with Jeremy Clarkson, James May and Richard Hammond.
C. Wright Mills: The Power Elite….
RT TV: Going Underground - various editions.
F A Hayek: The Constitution of Liberty - f/p 1960
Owen Jones: The Establishment 2014
Marx & Engels: The Communist Manifesto f/p 1848
David Leigh & Luke Harding: Wikileaks – Inside Julian Assange's War on Secrecy – 2011
Unfit: The Psychology of Donald J. Trump - directed by Dan Partland – 2020
Luke Harding: The Snowden Files – The Inside of The World's Most Wanted Man 2014
Suetonius: The Twelve Caesars…. Penguin Classics.
Nick Dearden: Trade Secrets: The truth about the US trade deal and how we can stop it 2020.
Talk TV Piers Morgan interview with Noam Chomsky….9th June 2023.
David McClure: The Queen's true Worth - 2020.

CHAPTER ONE

SOME ASPECTS OF AMERICAN FOREIGN POLICY, SINCE ITS INDEPENDENCE IN 1776, AND ITS MANY CONTRADICTIONS WHICH HAVE LED TO IT STILL BEING THE BIGGEST BULLY IN THE PLAYGROUND.

Before I start my critique of USA foreign policy, I should state categorically that the USA 'ruling class's' rational/logic seems to be based on an idealism and set of beliefs that they are setting people free, sometimes educating the locals how to be civilized, especially with the idea that western religion was a force for good and so, on which was similar in nature to that of the English Elite and others over centuries. At the same time, they were doing the complete opposite of setting people free in the countries they invaded abroad and likewise at home, to the native population. This had all started in the 17th century, on the east coast of the USA by the British and Dutch settlers often attacking and killing the indigenous population. The British carried on with this course of action all over their empire, especially in places like India and from the days of Adam Smith in the mid-18th century, they knew that the 'division of labour' was very good for the economy but made people completely stupid (and I would suggest still does), if they do boring repetitive jobs all day. As the complexity of this system has progressed over the centuries the division of labour now resembles a military operation with ranks accordingly fixed to their arms with very tight social control over the 'wage slaves' at work. While trade unions must be smashed as they have been in the USA and the UK, for these operations to work, you must have total control of all human agencies. Even in hospitals now you have line managers based on business model. Without this tight social control of the labour force the '1%' would not be able to get very rich indeed with the majority often living in relative poverty and millions going hungry. The third world is now following the first world with this model but this is mostly hidden by the power of the mass media spewing out lies and propaganda 24/7. The structural nature of the epoch is very rarely understood by the journalists who influence the political agenda, as far as I am concerned. In the UK Richard LittleJohn for example who works most of the time for the Daily Mail and earns £20,000 a week from them while living in the USA throughout the winter, probably knows very little of this phenomenon. 2000 billionaires now own as much as 4 billion people - half of the population of the world. However, Simon Reeve is one of the few great travel TV documenters (born in the UK and working mostly for the BBC) who seems to try and understand how this whole process works all over the world and I think would make a great general secretary of the UN? Simon comments not only what he sees but also on the political and historical background to peoples' daily lives.

Woodrow Wilson the USA president between 1913-1921 was just aping the English Elite in that the vast majority had to be controlled if not by force, then the ideology, of the ruling group, saying for example 'an elite of gentlemen with "elevated ideals" must be empowered to preserve "stability and righteousness"' (1). At the same time according to Noam Chomsky, Woodrow Wilson 'celebrated his doctrine of self-determination by invading Mexico, Haiti and the Dominican Republic' (2). I should also state that I have nothing against most Americans, which means over 328 million people plus, who probably have not got a clue of the crimes that the USA and its proxies have carried out around the globe, especially in the 20th century? I have also set foot on USA soil at Los Angeles Airport for two hours on my way back to the UK from New Zealand at the end of 2006, researching my very amusing and informative travel book. This was the last item on the bucket list undertaken by me, to set foot on every continent on the Planet apart from Antarctica, before I was 60. And like most people of my age, I still like many aspects of the USA culture; for example, most American movies (see above), pop stars like Elvis Presley et al and many of the great groups from the 1960s like the Mamas & Papas and so on. However, my innocent pursuits, like millions of tourists roaming the globe, as I write and research this book, are not the reason the Ruling Elite roam the globe. Their motive is normally to steal land and commodities, for the greater good of the Empire, be it Rome, Greece, under Alexander the Great, Britain, Germany in the Second World War and before that in Africa. This is nothing new as anyone who has studied history and the Social Sciences like me (see above) will know! According to Hannah Arendt, the Belgian ruling class in the Congo decimated the population from about 40 to 8 million peaceful people. Spain in modern times (last 500 years) has been one of the most brutal nation states, since first discovering the new world in 1492, apart from Hitler's Germany, which the USA might be said to be catching up fast? Ironically, according to John Pilger, the term 'imperialism' has been dropped from American textbooks and 'declared a European affair' (3). With the birth of the USA in 1776, and the subsequent killing of Native Americans (probably in excess of two million) there is always a cross over between who was responsible for all the deaths, the English or the new American elite and I cannot remember reading a recent source that has ever tried to define this dilemma. Therefore, throughout this chapter I have inserted some aspects of the UK experience which overlap with the USA, historical facts in many ways, as we shall see. In Latin and South America, it was either the Portuguese or the Spanish who were responsible for millions of deaths, either through over work or terrible diseases that the Europeans had given them. In an excellent BBC4 TV programme on the 17th August

2020, Ade Adepitan who was born in Nigeria and disabled but an amazing young man, noted that there were probably a million slaves who died on ships and were thrown overboard for the sharks to eat, during the 400 years of European slavery. By the mid-nineteenth century some Europeans could see the rise of USA power on the world stage, demonstrating the 'Monroe doctrine' of 1823. In other words, 'leave this part of the hemisphere to us to-do whatever we feel is correct in our eyes'. And it was Spain, who had one of the biggest Empires before the British, who first had to give way to indigenous groups, fighting for their freedom all over the world, as Spain's Empire started to fall apart, which subsequently happened to the British in the 20th century. The theft of Texas from Mexico was one of the first adventures into imperialism by the USA Ruling Elite. These adventures were glorified by Hollywood in the 20th century, in several westerns, some of them quite good. Reservations were set up for the indigenous Indians, who are still relatively poor compared with most Americans, as are the indigenous people in Canada and Australia, to this day. The movie 'Hombre' (1967) starring the great late Paul Newman was one of the most significant and empathetic films ever made about the true state in which indigenous Indians had to live their real lives in the USA - for example, often having to eat dogs or starve, partly due according in this movie, to a crooked white business man? Starvation was not seen in the movie but talked about in the abstract by Hombre. In Australia, the aborigines may have been there for over 50,000+ years before the white man invaded and set up a completely new culture and laws to be obeyed, by everyone, albeit that it had nothing to do with aboriginal culture in its many forms and languages whatsoever…. something very few people seem to understand! Again, the Hawaii deep water port at Pearl Harbour was used as a very useful tool in 1898 during the Spanish-American war, so was annexed two years later into a formal US territory and in 1959 Hawaii became the 50th State of the USA. Therefore, intellectuals like Chomsky say categorically that the attack by the Japanese in December 1941 on Pearl Harbour was not an attack on USA soil itself because it had been stolen in the 19th century but not legitimised as a formal state until 1959, which was true. Nicaragua was first attacked by the USA in 1854 to 'avenge an alleged insult to America officials and the millionaire Cornelius Vanderbilt' (4). A year later they supported William Walker's puppet government, and then in 1909 the US Marines landed in support of a US-British inspired revolution. This ushered in 25 years of chaos and military occupation, which lasted until the murder of the nationalist leader Sandino and the establishment of the brutal Somoza dictatorship using the US-trained National Guard to control, rob and torture the captive population.

What of course is as ironic about imperialism as I have noted above, is that these high ideals are often the pretence for an invasion. Even Mrs Thatcher returning the Falkland Islands to its old ruling masters after the conflict - in June 1982, was saying tosh - straight from the UN play book - with reference to 'self-determination and freedom' and returning our people to our islands and so on, albeit it is a vassal country (sic). But when Mrs Thatcher met the locals, after the war she was not impressed, she: 'was disillusioned with the locals, whose lethargy shocked her, and fell asleep in their company '. Something very similar, but worse was said about the Philippine people, by the Americans after the USA kicked the Spanish out of Manila, and paid 20 million dollars for the whole country. It was said that they were 'ignorant, superstitious, and credulous in remarkable degree'. The locals were not too impressed swapping one colonial master for another and fought back over three years. As many as 300,000 locals may have died in the civil war and 6000 Americans who fought under Col, L. W. T. Waller. He stated that 'following higher orders to take no prisoners and to kill every male filipino over age 10', for action he was court martialled, but got off in spite of being a nasty piece of work and also a racist. According to Noam Chomsky the young Winston Churchill told a New York audience 'that concentration camps and execution of prisoners and hostages were necessary because the Filipinos did "know when they are whipped"'. So, in essence Churchill was another nasty piece of work. Well, he was part of the English Ruling class, dating back to the time of Queen Anne (8th March 1702 - 1714) when Sarah Churchill (nee Jennings), married John Churchill who became the Duke of Marlborough. On marriage she became the Duchess of Marlborough and was a direct ancestor of Winston Churchill. When the Duke of Marlborough beat the French at Blenheim (1704), Ramillies (1706), Oudenarde (1708) and Malplaquet (1709) and numerous other conflicts before these, his fame was well established in British history, and Queen Anne had Blenheim palace built for him, in Oxfordshire. Sarah may have nicked all sorts of knick-knacks from the royal residence according to the wonderful and beautiful Lucy Worsley (BBC4 British TV February 2020… who reminds me of my darling daughter who is just a little older) after falling out with Queen Anne, who paid for most of Blenheim palace.

Continuing the same theme as above, a similar number of Philippine people (300,000) or more probably died between 8th December 1941 and 1945 when Japan invaded the Philippines, and the Americans, under General Douglas MacArthur, were ordered out and fled to Australia, before the Axis won the war. In January 1941 'President Roosevelt announced that the Allies were fighting for freedom of speech, freedom of worship, freedom from want and freedom from fear. The terms of the Atlantic Charter, signed by Roosevelt and Churchill the following August, were no less elevated' (5). As I noted just above these were very high ideals with very little truth in them, especially on ventures abroad, like the threat of installing Batista in Cuba when it was feared that US commercial interests might be threatened by the civilian government of Dr Ramon Grau San Martin. However, as Michael Woodiwiss has informed us in *Gangster Capitalism,* Roosevelt did manage to tame the wild beast that was/is industrial Capitalism/monopoly capitalism, at least until Nixon and Reagan reversed virtually everything he had tried to do. President Roosevelt even at the time of the Bretton Woods agreement did seem to have most of the USA population and of the world at heart according to Woodiwiss, with empathetic values. Albeit that 'rhetorical commitments' to human rights and democracy were frequently made, the overriding aim of America foreign policy since the Second World War has been to keep the world safe for capitalism, especially American capitalism' (6). We should never forget also that what politicians are saying to the populace and what other agencies of State are doing are maybe two different ideas/philosophies altogether? In theory, therefore, a free press is so important in this epoch, as is academic freedom - unfortunately, most of the media is owned by very rich people, with their own agendas. In the USA the CIA, State department and the 'Military Industrial Complex' are very powerful and are plotting most of the time against what progressive politicians are saying, a constant theme of the Stone & Kusnick book used as a source throughout this project. For example: in 1948, with the Second Word War only three years over, people like George Kennan, the author of post-war ideas and policies, were saying that when the USA has 50% of the world's wealth and only 6.3% of the world's population, that we cannot be empathetic and idealistic to the other 93.7% population. Therefore, we need to wake up and be realistic about the fact that they are going to want what we have. This could have been a reaction to Henry Wallace's well known progressive ideas (Stone& Kuznick). This notion was repeated by President Lyndon Johnson in similar language in the 1960s at the height of US aggression in Vietnam.

The reason the theory of communism was so dangerous to the Western Elites and why it had to be crushed at all costs was that state collectivism was everything they hated. In the same way the theory of evolution threatened the church hierarchy in the 19th century. Even 2000 years ago the idea of Spartacus that slaves should be free was also a threat to the ruling elite as recorded by Plutarch in his thesis on Crassus, who thought the idea of freeing slaves should be crushed. So, from the time of Eisenhower 'unreal objectives such as human rights, the raising of living standards, and democratization' (7) had to make way for realpolitik, such as the build-up of arms under Eisenhower on a gigantic scale. This was nothing new for USA foreign policy as I have shown above from other sources, but the threat of what most of us on the Left believe in, like: 'social justice', where economic and social polices benefit everyone (which Fredrick Von Hayek, Mrs Thatcher's favourite guru said did not exist), had to be ditched once and for all, and a war against these dangerous ideas had to be waged, once and for all and amazingly is still going on while researching and writing this book, in the 21st century 100+ years after the first Russian revolution, of 1917.

In 1953 an agency of the USA State with the help of British intelligence called 'Operation Ajax' facilitated the removal of Iranian Prime Minister Mohammed Mossadegh, for the crime of nationalization of the Iran's oil reserves and installed Reza Shah Pahlavi back on the throne, who for over two decades waged a war of torture and police terror against anyone who opposed him, propped up by Western powers. The excuse was simple for the coup d'etat to happen. By refusing to buy Mossadedgh's nationalized oil, the USA and the British whose interests he had upset, virtually drove Iran into destitution. Consequently, Iran asked the old Soviet Union for help, giving the excuse that British intelligence and CIA needed to put the Shah back on the throne. According to Stone & Kusnick when the British ruling class were running Anglo-Iranian oil (later BP) it kept 84% of the revenue for itself and paid the local workforce, who runs the oilfields less than 50 cents a day, with no benefits or holidays.

This has been a theme that has been used time and time again by the USA to invade countries and interfere in their elections and economic and social policies throughout the period of the cold war. Now a new narrative has had to be invented for the next invasion, which will probably be Venezuela, or Iran, which often goes like this. Somehow the current Leader/Prime Minster or whosoever was elected by fraud, (according to the USA) even when it has been legitimatized by no other than Jimmy Carter, who was no saint according to Noam Chomsky et al when he was President of the USA for one term only. The USA then tries to install their own 'chosen one' with the support of the mass media and other so-called democracies. The Western World seems obsessed by elections only, as being the only thing that matters in so-called democracies (bourgeois - liberal capitalist democracy) rather than how society is organized and structured, which strikes fear into rich Elites whenever discussed, on very rare occasions. Therefore RT (TV) is such a threat to the West (see above.... as is Al-Jazeera according to Chomsky 2001), as other ideas of how society is organized are openly discussed daily, often with savage critiques of the lies and propaganda of other news outlets, in written form and news channels on TV. In case anyone thinks that I have been taken in completely by RT as well as the BBC news programmes for that matter, I have not, but at least RT allows Noam Chomsky and John Pilger on their channel as well as right-wing views, especially from the USA. Of course, with the Russia/Ukraine conflict, RT has been completely banished from the UK. Over the last few years like many people on the Left of the political spectrum I have become completely disillusioned with the news outputs of the BBC, apart from the BBC World service which at-least in theory is much more objective, attracting some say as high as 100 million listeners?

As I have just noted above about Venezuela, before Hugo Chavez and Nicholas Maduro got elected, this pattern of behaviour actually happened in Chile in 1970, when Allende got elected and was overthrown in 1973 by the Army under Pinochet with the help of the CIA and as Noam Chomsky writes about this whole process, 'Kissinger's aides recalled that he was far more concerned over Allende in Chile than over Castro because "Allende was a living example of democratic social reform in Latin America"' which could be a template for other countries. This even applied to the strong left-wing leanings in Europe at the time, instead of the Castro revolutionary model of change. (9) A good example of the Castro model was when Ernesto Che Guevara, one of the most famous freedom fighters of the 20th century (a modern-day Spartacus, in my eyes and born in Argentina and a qualified doctor) when captured in Bolivia, was shot dead with orders from the USA military/government, for trying to carry out the Castro model to help the downtrodden peasants, of that country. The year that the great freedom fighter Che Guevara was murdered, Evo Morales was only 8 years old. He was born in Orinoca, Oruro, Bolivia, but in 2006 he was elected president of Bolivia and has done wonders for the country that Che would have been proud of according to Oliver Balch writing from La Paz (in the Guardian 8th March 2019). For example, 'the percentage of people living in poverty in Bolivia fell from 59.9% in 2006 when Morales first came to power, to 34.6% in 2017, with extreme poverty more than halving (from 38.28% - 15.2%) over the same period, according to government figures. The reason for this amazing turnaround of events was the boom in commodity prices, with Bolivia having the continent's second largest gas reserves which helped exports revenue grow 'sixfold during his first term, from an average of 1.14 billion dollars a year over the previous two decades, to 7 billion dollars'. The national debt was also reduced to 2.2 billion dollars just as he came into office. 'The same was true of moves to nationalize key hydrocarbon assets. Another success story of most left leaning governments is that they spend money on the infrastructure, which happened in Bolivia under Morales increasing from 629 million dollar's (just before he took office) to 6.5 billion dollars spent on schools, hospitals, power plants, electrification and the like, last year according to their figures'. He won a fourth election last month with a 24-hour delay before declaring the result. Subsequently the OAS (sic) said it was fraudulent, albeit there may have only been a 3% margin of error according to RT TV. Riots broke out probably organized by the CIA, which meant the army generals told him to resign and now he has fled to Mexico with a price on his head. What we should never forget about this specific narrative is that Evo Morales was one of the very few indigenous persons in the whole of South America to be elected President in 500 years, in fact since the plunder by the Spanish and Portuguese imperial powers. The election of Morales was a terrible crime in the eyes of the new ruling Elite. Amazingly Bolivia now has a new interim president called Jeanine Anez aged 52 who is a conservative Christian who likes to display the bible and the cross at the old official residence, without any sign of the indigenous Wiphala (the multi-coloured flag of the native people of the Andes) whatsoever; this in a country where 20% of the population belongs to one of 36 indigenous groups, according to the Guardian (15th November 2019). The new/old political class is now going on the war path and killing indigenous people in the city of El alto, if the Guardian is correct (22 November 2019) during confrontations between Morale's supporters and the Army. 'What happened was a massacre…. They used weapons like you use in war'. The army is denying that they have fired one bullet and calling Morales's supporters terrorists. The Sunday Observer (24th November 2019) noted that a person called Martin Cornejo, who is a local organizer, asserted 'our plurinational state has suffered a coup d'etat led by racist and fascist people'. I would have thought that was not far wrong in summing up the current situation in Bolivia, using the Roman Catholic Church and their bible to legitimize their action? This narrative has changed again since this was first written, for the good of the majority.

The narrative above, about Bolivia's state expenditure under Morales is the opposite of extreme Right-Wing governments like the one we have now in the UK, where, while researching and writing this book, state expenditure is now heading towards 38% of GDP, and dropping, and millions are going hungry, perhaps as many as '8 million', according to the Morning Star. The legal system and local government are being destroyed, millions working in the Gig economy; at-least a million and half people are so poor they must go to food banks; very little is spent on infrastructure and the very small Elite are getting very rich at the expense of the wellbeing of the UK. Lord Heseltine who at the time of the overthrow of Mrs Thatcher in 1990 was worth £50 million is now worth over £280 million, according to the Sunday Times Rich List, with many servants at his beck and call, I presume? The new movie which came out November 2019 called *'Sorry we missed You'* directed by the great Ken Loach (making great movies for 50 years and who I met at the Hay-on-wye book festival several years ago) gives us all a wonderful insight into the structure and behaviour of workers in the 'gig economy' and how most people in this surreal world really live their lives, struggling just to exist and keep out of debt, for most of the time. The gig economy is now getting on for 5 million people. The figures above about the level of GDP expenditure in the UK are now out of date as this project progresses through the terrible covid-19 pandemic…. but was correct at the time of writing.

In the financial sector however, the complete opposite is happening - for example in the UK, thousands of UK bankers are paid 1million euros plus a year according to a recent report published by the European Banking Authority (11th March 2019). The report notes 'that 3,567 UK-based bankers collected more than 1m euros in 2017. Their average pay, skewed by huge pay-outs at the top, was 2m euros and together they scooped nearly 10bn euros. At the top of the scale, 30 bankers were paid more than 10m euros each. One asset manager received 40.9m euros (£35m), of which the bonus alone was 38.3m euros' (The Guardian 12th March 2019). The ironic fact from this report is that 73% of all millionaire bankers across Europe came from the UK and 'much of the revenue used to pay these rather vulgar sums of money comes from leeching wealth off the real economy, rather than creating it'. Aditya Chakrabortty (13th March 2019) confirmed what I have just written above when he asserts, in the Guardian: 'The fact that austerity has never worked matters not. The government did a reverse Robin Hood: taking from the poor and giving to the rich'. Having gone off on a slight tangent, let's return to the main task in hand. Out of the blue, like a bolt of lightning, something happened that is nearly beyond belief. A corona virus previously only known in bats (?) made the jump into humans killing some within a few weeks/days of being infected. This probably started in China at the end of 2019 and is now alive and kicking all over the world, affecting millions. Several countries that could afford it, like the UK, have put into operation a furlough (extraordinary for a Tory government) paying employees 80% of their wages, if the employers keep them on. In addition, society has been locked down apart from key workers, like my daughter who was working as an intensive care nurse in London. This has sent the national debt into the stratosphere, and public spending is up to at least 50% of GDP. Public spending on this scale by a

Tory government appears to be a socialist policy very similar to that proposed by Jeremy Corbyn before the 2019 election in the UK.

Critiquing American foreign policy and their poodles - like the UK under the Tony Blair government (Tory lite as I called 'new Labour' or as we should perhaps say, virtually the 51st State of America) Noam Chomsky calls the USA and the UK a 'rogue states'. In fact, a lot of the underlying problems in the world stem from European powers carving up the whole world over centuries, which the USA just copied from their older siblings. According to Seumas Milne 'The US will in future brook no rival in power or military prowess, will spread still further its network of garrison bases in every continent, and will use its armed might to promote a "single sustainable model for national success" (its own), through unilateral pre-emptive attacks if necessary'. (10) This is markedly visible currently as the USA continues to shore up countries bordering Russia against the negotiated agreement with Gorbachev after 1991.

In the 20th century, many of the disputes in the world stem from countries fighting for their independence from empire builders, often the UK and France being the prime movers especially in the Middle East. Balfour, (former British Prime Minster - died 19th march 1930) in the 1917 Balfour Declaration gave concessions to the Jewish people, so that they would have a homeland, (I presume after the Ottoman Empire had been destroyed, and the Middle East carved up, for their own ends)? Apparently, the British Government never clearly defined the concept of a Jewish National Homeland; neither did they propose a concrete policy plan to implement the notorious Gallipoli campaign orchestrated by Churchill which took place between 19th Feb 1915 - 9th Jan 1916, just one example of a ridiculous mistake made in the region, with huge consequences. The Gallipoli campaign was a costly failure for the Allies, with estimated 27,000 French, and 115,000 British and dominion troops (Great Britain and Ireland, Australia, New Zealand, India, and Newfoundland) killed or wounded. Over half these casualties (73,485) were British and Irish troops. It is worth noting and somewhat ironic that only a few months after this battle/fiasco in which so many Irish troops died, James Connolly was sentenced to death by firing squad for his part in the uprising in Dublin, where amazingly a very few Irish nationals held the British army at bay for at least a week. The Gallipoli fiasco in Turkey (fiasco meaning: 'something planned that goes wrong and is a complete failure'), was one of the main reasons that in 1940 many in the ruthless British Establishment did not want Churchill as Prime Minster. In addition, many in the whole rotten British establishment supported Hitler as a bulwark against communism, from Edward V111 to newspapers like the Daily Mail; even Chamberlain hoped for an alliance with Nazi Germany. Incidentally my brother reads the Daily Mail every day and has done for years. He seems to believe in every word of it and now has caught the 'Affluenza' (sic) virus so bad that I am very concerned for his sanity as of October/November 2020, mainly due to his complete obsession with house prices in the UK that are basically bonkers, (because of the shortage of stock and other illogical reasons...i.e., David Cameron and most Tory MPs having 3 or 4 homes) and with making money, with no intellectual hobbies whatsoever?

Rome saw enemies around every corner; so, does the USA two thousand years later. However, they do not have men as famous as Julius Caesar - but they do have one of the most ruthless 'ruling classes' in the world, very similar to that the UK. The USA is determined to control the energy supplies of the world directly or indirectly or any other commodity that they require, which includes crushing all resistance, in its many forms, now mostly with sanctions (very similar to a siege in the Middle Ages) in theory to make 'America Great Again'? Therefore, after the Second World War 'the United States literally crushed left-wing resistance in Europe and Japan and imposed traditional structures, including fascist collaborators. In Germany, they did not have that much influence, but still imposed their values. In fact, it is not well-known, but it was the American Historian/diplomat George Kennan who in 1946 called for "walling (West Germany) off against Eastern penetration". U.S policymakers were afraid of the German labour movement, and they were afraid of the resistance. The resistance had plenty of prestige after the Second World War. And it was radical democratic, socialist, and communist and so on, so the United States had to crush it. They did that with great brutality in Italy and Greece (my late stepfather Harry Womack was there) and in various other ways in Germany, France, Belgium, and elsewhere. The United States continued to be involved in large-scale subversion of Italian democracy at least until the 1970s. We don't know after that because the record runs dry, but I presume it is still going on. (11) From the same source in Japan General Douglas MacArthur initially, did allow democratic institutions to flourish until Washington heard about it, then in 1947 they put the whole system into reverse gear so they could crush the labour movement and make the country a 'one-party state'. Around about this time with the help of Truman and his reactionary advisers, the warmonger Winston Churchill made his notorious speech, in Fulton Missouri about Soviet Union policies in Europe, from 'Stettin in the Baltic to Trieste in the Adriatic, an iron curtain has descended across the continent' with all countries of the West of this line being wonderfully free democracies and East of the line a sort of tyranny directed by the USSR. Mostly tosh of the highest order because Stalin did keep his word regarding what had been agreed before the end of the Second World War, in most cases. For example, not countering the British in Greece, where my stepfather was helping to put a King back on the throne and killing partisans who had been fighting the Nazis in the Second

World War (pure hypocrisy of the highest order). We should never forget that Churchill was not only fighting Hitler between 1939 and 1945, but also to maintain the British Empire as an entity away from USA market penetration, who wanted part of the action. Very few seem to understand this axiom of the 20th century, because the education system for the majority is lacking the full story and needs severe changes in the curriculum as well as at least £10 billion pumped into it, or more?

Also, to pretend that the UK and other so-called democracies are not living hell for many, even to the current day, is beyond belief, mostly because wage slavery in its most brutal form is a tyranny?

The theme of this chapter is a constant reminder of USA foreign policy repeating itself time and time again in the 20th century and now in the 21st. The USA is either invading countries or intervening in elections to get their **MAN** and his buddies in power, sometimes by proxy. This meant that the USA corporations could rape the country for profit and not care anything about the indigenous people, often killing so called communists, who were often worse off with their new masters. By the middle of the 20th century the USA and their small elite had, in Guatemala, virtually control of all the commodities especially the United Fruit Company. Guatemala had one of the most corrupt and pliable governments in Latin America. Unfortunately for the elites the locals had read about and may have heard Franklin Roosevelt, amazing speeches about the Four Freedoms: human rights, democracy and the New Deal from the Second World War, so they wanted change that would benefit everyone. 'In 1951 they voted for a nationalist, Jacobo Arbenza, to bring them a New Deal of their own'. (12) This was heresy to the Americans as Arbenza soon threatened United Fruit dominance by attempting to improve the life chances of the majority. (13). The company soon recruited lobbyists and publicists to inform the USA government that something had to be done about this new upstart.

'President Eisenhower's Secretary of State John Foster Dulles, as a former United Fruit legal representative, needed little convincing that the company interests needed protection. His brother Allen Dulles, as head of the CIA was given the task of toppling Arbenz and Operation Success was launched at the beginning of 1954. At an estimated cost of around 20 million dollars, an invasion force of mercenaries, trained by the CIA at a military base in Honduras and Nicaragua, was organized under the leadership of Colonel Carlos Castillo Armas. With American air support, the invasion was successful and Armas became the first of a series of Guatemalan military dictators acceptable to and even trained by the United States. In the decades that followed Arbenza's downfall, the country remained impoverished while tens of thousands of dissidents were murdered by official or semi-official death squads. By 1970 the machinery of murder in Guatemala was concentrated in the hands of the military, and civilian terrorist groups acted only under its orders, according to Nick Cullather, a historian given access to previously secret CIA files. The army in effect became an organized criminal enterprise. Officers received subsidized housing and consumer goods, and soft loans; as they rose through the ranks, the perks and opportunities for graft increased'. (14) This is something that Trump et al never seems to understand, how most of the Third world is impoverished through this process which helps to cause the refugee crises in the first place. Globally, some now say 80+ million people are trying to escape wars and hunger in their own countries. But the rich and powerful as I have noted above, always try to blame the poor and downtrodden as if this were an individual problem instead of a structural crisis of the epoch. The new movie called 'Parasite' from South Korea is (February 2020) one of the most important pictures of recent times showing the clear misunderstanding between the rich 'upper class's' and the downtrodden working class, both of whom have no idea whatsoever how the other half really live their lives, a theme throughout this epoch, in all societies. Albeit that the working class in this movie proves that they are not as stupid as the rich really think. This whole process was also pointed out by Noam Chomsky in *Optimism Over Despair* (from other sources), that often the working class in the UK at the time of industrialization, were a lot better read and had a greater thirst for real knowledge than the 'philistinism of the British aristocracy'. I myself was born below the working class in Port Stanley in the Falkland Islands, with only six years formal education and left school at 14 to work in the Treasury department. This is why I could resemble a 'white Frederick Douglass' et al within the structural nature/dynamic of this epoch or born a Dalit within the Indian caste system. My love of reading and assimilating knowledge, like Frederick, for over 65 years has not left me. This author also went hungry for several years in the early 1990s, living in the UK, because the benefits given for being unemployed is far to low to live on.

If anyone anywhere now tries to improve the lot of the majority it is a crime against the Ruling Elites, especially in the United States and the UK, for that matter. For example, the attack on the Cuban economy for over 60 years, by the USA was because it was deemed a dangerous model that could be copied by other States, especially in Latin America. However, if Professor Noam Chomsky is correct the USA elites had wanted to invade Cuba from the days of John Quincy Adams, many decades before the Bay of Pigs invasion between 17th April - 19th April 1961. 'The need to possess Cuba is the oldest issue in US foreign policy. The US sanctions against Cuba are the harshest in the world, much harsher than the sanctions against Iraq, for example, perhaps depriving Cuba of over 500 billion dollars.'(15) We should also never forget that often the American agencies of social control and power elites got their rational/logic completely upside down, (especially at the height of the Cold War), over countries fighting for their independence from a foreign power, or according to the USA becoming 'communist states', like Indonesia and Vietnam, for example. 'The PKI was pro-Chinese, but by 1965, when it was demolished by mass slaughter, (In Indonesia) Russia and China were hardly allies.' (16) This was one of the worst atrocities (see also below) since the Second World War as probably at-least one million peasants were slaughtered just because they believed in social justice for all, like most of the world.

The history of Vietnam is far more complex than most of us understand. What we know for sure is that the French landed in Danang in 1858 after trying to convert the Vietnamese to Catholicism in the 18th century. I visited Danang in 2007 which now has a population of over 1 million and wrote a very amusing chapter in my travel book on Vietnam. In Nha Trang further on, I actually bought a B52 cocktail, (named after the American Bomber) - true story. The French stayed until 1961 and treated the locals as 'inferior beings', like all European colonists everywhere for that matter. Ho Chi Minh had gone into exile in 1911 and did not return until 30 years later, after visiting the USA, Britain, France and the old Soviet Union, doing all sorts of low paid jobs. Paradoxically according to PSB America and their excellent TV series on the Vietnam War, the OSS (an American intelligent agency) saved Ho Chi Minh's life towards the end of the Second World War. The USA has struggled throughout its history between supporting the concept of independence, while maintaining its power (now) throughout the world.

Hence, in Vietnam Ho Chi Minh was hoping that the USA would help them escape their own exploitation by the French. Charles De Gaulle was also aware of this problem and suggested to the Americans that if they did not get help in Vietnam that even France it's self may fall to the red menace, a constant theme of the 20th century after the 1917 revolution in the Soviet Union. The Americans tried to stay neutral in this affair at the end of the Second World War and even the British, amazingly, were involved in the South of Vietnam for a short while. The French returned after the British left and by 1953 they had been involved again trying to put down rebellions for seven years. This was partly resolved in the 1954 Geneva accord which established a partition between North and South Vietnam known as the 17 parallel. Two years later democratic elections had been promised, but the West intervened fearing the spread of communism, from Chairman Mao's China, via North Vietnam.

One reason that there was so much hysteria around the whole idea that communism was taking over the world, was that Chairman Mao had come to power on the 1st of October 1949, beating the nationalists. When we look back on history it is sometimes beyond belief, for example, when John f Kennedy visited Saigon in 1951, he learned first-hand from a very well-informed journalist that the French were not going to win this war, while the French Generals were telling him the complete opposite…. probably why later, when he became President, he was very wary of the American Armed forces and of what he was being told as hard facts and possible outcomes of future events. The better educated in France were calling this whole involvement in south east Asia a 'dirty war' which it was and were protesting against it, just as the USA citizens did in the 1960's with the wonderful and beautiful Jane Fonda, with Noam Chomsky et al leading the fight, and in Jane's case even visiting North Vietnam. She was then for ever known as 'Hanoi Jane' and is one of America's greatest actors; well, her dad was Henry Fonda. The impression PBS America and some other sources have noted is that when LBJ (President Johnson) extended the war in Vietnam and ran out of working-class recruits to fight his foreign wars, he had to turn to the new middle class who resented this form of action. It was this group in society who started the whole ant-war movement, in the USA and elsewhere. There may have been over half-a-million American troops in Vietnam by the time Johnson stood down. The war was orchestrated at this time by General Westmoreland. President Johnson did not seem aware that he was getting himself into a quagmire in Vietnam but if he did not go along with the 'Military Industrial Complex' he would have been perceived as weak, which seems to be a main theme of most USA presidents now over decades….and the real danger why Trump as the president has been such a threat to the whole world and could come back in 2025.

The Pentagon Papers released evidence decades later but probably not known to most of the world, that the USA deliberately ignored the agreement made in Geneva in 1954, that after the French left with at-least half a million Vietnamese dead, the country would be reunited with a general election taking place two years later. The USA went ballistic at the idea that Vietnam should ever become a whole again and that they would even invade **China** if they had to prevent this happening. In essence this was communism on the march, all over the globe and they felt they must stop it at every point on the map, like the Roman Empire did two thousand years before (albeit they were not fighting Communism, but enlarging their empire and crushing all resistance, on their borders). Even Crassus (who crushed and killed Spartacus, at least in theory - who may have also said 'we must destroy this idea of Spartacus as a man and his rebellion for ever') Crassus was killed in Harran in Turkey in 53BC defending the empire, losing his head and right hand as trophies to the victors, according to Plutarch. As Noam Chomsky reminds us regarding 20th century events and the Pentagon Papers in particular 'The phraseology and plans are interesting. The wording was chosen in order to make it very clear and explicit that the United States was going to purposely violate the major principle of international law, the UN Charter, which states that use of force is always illegitimate except when under armed attack and an instantaneous reaction, before the Security Council reacts. But the statement was: in the event of "local communist subversion (we'll decide what that is) or rebellion not constituting armed attack" we will take military measures, including rearmament of Japan, attacks on China, setting up Thailand as the "focal point" for US subversive activity throughout the region, and so on. This blatant and purposeful violation of the fundamental principles of international law was then repeated year after year, in the same wording. It was in the Pentagon Papers - one of the few interesting revelations in the Pentagon Papers. Most of what appeared was obvious, but this was new. It has yet to enter even most scholarly records. Apparently, it's considered a little "too hot to handle" although it's now been 25 years since it was released, and it is very important. Those are the origins of the expansion of the war after the US undermined the Geneva agreements' (17).

As related previously, before the Second World War Vietnam was fighting for Independence from its colonial masters, the French.

'Thus, when the State Department decided to support French efforts to re-conquer its former colony, US intelligence was instructed to prove that Ho Chi Minh was an agent of the Kremlin or Peking (either would do). When it turned out that no evidence could be found, that was taken as proof that the targeted enemy was a mere slave of his foreign masters, in one of the more comical episodes of the history of intelligence (18). Anyone who has studied the war in Vietnam by the Americans, especially from scholars like Noam Chomsky and Oliver Stone (who was there) should understand that it was one of the most disgraceful acts of aggression of all times, especially since the end of the Second World War. It involved chemical warfare on a massive scale. In fact, there is hardly a book, by Chomsky (that I have read) on USA foreign policy that does not mention the Vietnam War. Ironically, in recent times it was also probably the first time since the days of the famous Greek City States that anyone has rebelled against a war, on such a large scale, to my knowledge. These rebellions are now referred in most text books as a 'counterculture', born of the hippy generation that was rebelling not only against the Vietnam war, but also about how society is structured, which did terrify the Ruling Elites at the time, because without brainwashed wage slaves, forced to sell their labour power in the labour market, the whole rotten system itself would not work. According to the Elites in the USA the reason that this rebellion took place was that most nights on the American news networks, the War was being played out in most peoples' living rooms, a lot of it very gruesome indeed. This is also the reason now that they do not like TV companies on war fronts without some sort of social control. By February 1965, the United States escalated the war against the Viet Cong in South Vietnam radically, and, on the side, began regular bombing of the North at a much lower level' (19).

The USA bombed Vietnam with sheer brutality and with impunity, by setting up a Latin American - style terror state in the south, killing at-least '70,000 South Vietnamese by 1960'. This state was very flimsy and as soon as there was any reaction to it its repression, it immediately began to collapse. Hence, Kennedy had a problem of what to do next, so he escalated the scale of the bombing, which included crop destruction, in violation of the Geneva Convention. William Blum also notes that biological warfare was probably carried out against China and Korea along with Agent Orange and all sorts of deadly weapons in Vietnam which may have created birth defects in at-least 500,000 children up to the present day.
By the time that John F Kennedy had become President of the USA in January 1961 the French were packing up to leave …. 'throwing in the towel' as they say in boxing jargon, after 100 years of colonial rule. According to Stone & Kuznick 'The number of U.S. military personnel in Vietnam jumped from 800 when Kennedy took office to over 16,000 in 1963'. (20) The USA remained in Vietnam until 1975.

One of the main themes of *The Untold History of the United States* by Oliver Stone & Peter Kuznick is the real danger to the world of the USA warmongering over decades, especially with the threat of using nuclear weapons not only in Japan (which they did at the end of the Second World War), but also at the time of the Korean war and ever since, (even threatening to drop them on the Soviet Union and China several times) especially with the advent of Thatcher and Reagan, in the 1980s. The paranoia whipped up about the threat of communism in the USA was beyond belief shortly after the Second World War, for consumption at home and abroad. The Vietnam War was just a continuation of the Korean War. Here are a few quotes from this great book, which helps us all to understand this phenomenon: 'On December 9, 1950, MacArthur requested authorization to use atomic bombs at his discretion. On December 24th, he submitted a list of twenty-six targets. He also requested four bombs to drop on invading forces and four more for "critical concentration of enemy power". He calculated that dropping thirty to fifty atomic bombs "across the neck of Manchuria" could produce "a belt of radioactive cobalt" that would win the war in ten days. But that was just the short-term effect. The belt of radioactive cobalt would spread "from the Sea of Japan to the Yellow River". Therefore, he figured "for at least 60 years there could have been no land invasion of Korea from the North" (21).

With the war in Korea continuing and casualties mounting: 'MacArthur began issuing statements from Tokyo blaming others for the military debacle and pushing for all-out war with China. On March 10, 1951, MacArthur requested a "'D Day atomic capability" in response to the Soviet bolstering of air capabilities in Korea and Manchuria and a build-up of Chinese forces near the Korean border. "Finletter and Lovett alerted on atomic discussions. Believe everything is set", Vandenberg wrote on March 14th. On March 24, 1951, knowing that Truman was pressing for a cease fire, MacArthur broadcast his own ultimatum to China. Truman bristled, "I'll show that son-of-a bitch whose boss," but let the incident slide. But when

Republican Congressman Joe Martin read the entire House a letter that MacArthur had written in which he stated that "if we lose this war to communism in Asia, the fall of Europe is inevitable" the Joint Chiefs unanimously recommended that MacArthur be relieved of his command. On April 11, the White House announced MacArthur's firing. MacArthur's eagerness to use atomic weapons did not factor into this decision. Just the week before, the Chiefs had ordered attacks on Manchurian bases if the Chinese sent in another large contingent of forces. On April 6, Truman approved that order and authorized the transfer of nine atomic weapons from AEC to military custody in Guam and Okinawa' (22).

According to Noam Chomsky even before the USA got involved in the Korean War properly, 'about 100,000 people were killed in the late 1940s (in Korea) by security forces installed and directed by the United States' (23). As he notes from the same book, this was a theme after the Second World War about crushing all resistance to the old conservative order. This was often done with 'fascist collaborators', especially in Europe, but virtually everywhere, including what the CIA took to be the most severe threats at the time "radical nationalism" as in Guatemala and Bolivia. It is perhaps also ironic as I have noted in this book, that Trump is up to the same trick in the USA itself (make America great again) as Boris Johnson also tried in the UK, as others are in a few other nation states in Europe and Narendra Modi in India. In fact, while I was researching and writing this book Trump visited India for a two-day State visit where violence broke out in Delhi (February 2020) caused by an act Modi passed in parliament in December 2019 called the Citizenship Amendment Act. Many believe that this act discriminates against Muslims. This hardly seems rational when Trump at a rally in Ahmedabad, in Gujarat, (in his honour) lavished praise on Modi for his 'democratic' and 'tolerant' leadership of India. According to the English Guardian covering this story on the 27th February 2020, the 'death toll from the worst religious violence in Delhi in decades had risen to 24'. In 1984 3000 Sikhs died in Delhi following the assassination of the Prime Minister, Indira Gandhi. And in 2002 at-least 2000 people died in Gujarat over several months, again caused by inter-communal violence while Modi was in charge, as the Chief Minister. The cloud of the 1930s seems to be the theme hanging over us all; now the plutocrats have won the argument for the time being?

Just as England after 1588 (sic) and the so-called defeat of the Spanish Armada, (which was not so splendid as the English ruling class like to pretend to this day - BBC 4 TV 25th February 2020) the USA, from day one after the landing of Puritans, in the 1620s, for some strange reason believed that God was on their side. In essence this is a very dangerous belief, just as the cold war has proved to be. In addition, the big idea of Nationalism forms a very toxic mix of pure tosh. When the UK was part of the EU it was much harder for the ruling class in the UK to pull this Nationalism out of the ether, but it was put back on the agenda, under the right-wing nationalistic persona of the previous PM Boris Johnson. The build-up of the American arms industry, especially after the Second World War under Eisenhower, was all part of this big game and one of the most dangerous periods in world history, as at the time many hands were on the control buttons of the nuclear system according to Stone & Kuznick.

Chapter 7 of Stone & Kuznick is one of the most important in this amazing book called: *The Untold History of the United States* (see also above) because the Cuban missile crisis nearly led to the extinction of humans, something very similar to what happened to the dinosaurs 65 million years ago, when an asteroid hit the planet that triggered the catastrophe in which 75% of all life on Earth perished. However, even under Eisenhower, the USA knew that the so-called missile gap with the old Soviet

Union was a myth as the USA had spy planes flying over most of the country. John F. Kennedy the young junior senator from Massachusetts rose to power on this myth and exploited it to the full…. from 1957 onwards….and on, seeing Richard Nixon on TV said that this 'guy has no class'. He was egged on by his friend the columnist Joseph Alsop. What brought this whole crisis to a head before Kennedy even got to the White house was the overthrow of the Basista regime on the 1st of January 1959 in Cuba. Led by Fidel Castro and Che Guevara, one of the most audacious revolutions in history began after Castro had served a year in prison for the first failed attempt on the Moncada Barracks in 1953. American corporations had dominated the economy of Cuba since 1898, which Castro partly undermined. This was like showing a red rag to a bull, and inflamed American passion to the height of insanity, with a so-called communist 'One Party State', 90 miles from the USA mainland. This led to the 'bay of pigs' fiasco, first thought up by the Eisenhower regime and the CIA. The Americans were determined to wreck the whole economy of Cuba after the revolution, with a plan called 'operation mongoose', using chemical warfare, etc. As Oliver Stone noted in his DVD's (which go with the book) on these related subjects 'anti-communism was good for business', especially the arms business which made a fortune out of the Second World War, and for the most powerful country in the world, after the war also. This was nothing more than aping the Romans of two thousand years ago, a constant theme of this book.

The hatred whipped up by politicians, especially Joe McCarthy and J Edgar Hoover of the F.B.I and the mass media in the USA, made the Soviet Union very concerned that the USA would invade the Island, for the second time following a military exercise in the Caribbean with thousands of troops, called Operation Ortsac, (Castro spelled backwards). They were also very concerned that the USA was going to attack the Soviet Union with nuclear weapons, in a first strike, which was not far from the truth, considering they had thousands more nuclear weapons than the Soviet Union. This whole insanity was the reason that Khrushchev decided to send small battlefield nuclear weapons to Cuba, on 80 ships. The Americans also had nuclear weapons in Turkey, aimed at the Soviet Union, which Kennedy was not even aware of, until someone told him! Stanley Kubrick's great satirical movie called *Dr Strangelove*, brought out in 1964, was closer to the truth, than most people realized at the time. By the end of the film, we are all blown up, and the world ends. This movie was partly influenced by the ideas in Peter George's book called *Red Alert.* This was the movie for which Peter Sellers should have won an Oscar, for playing 3 roles, but because it was taking the piss (sic) out of the USA, he never got it…. but one of the greatest lines ever spoken in a movie was from this film, directed by Stanley Kubrick. When a fight breaks out between the Soviet Ambassador, (invited into the war room) and Buck Yurgidson (joint Chief of Staff) and the president says: 'Gentlemen you cannot fight in here. This is the war room'…. satire at its highest level of understanding. However, not too sure that Donald J. Trump or Boris Johnson would understand the irony here, are we? The great movie 'Vice' (2018) is another brilliant satire on Dick Cheney and others who rose from nothing to become the power brokers in Washington over decades and basically rigged the system in their favour over George W. Bush. The discussion at a table with Alfred Molina as the waiter serving up the menu to Cheney et al of 'enemy combatants' and so on: is just as brilliant as the war room joke in Dr Strangelove.

Once the USA photographed missile sites on the Island of Cuba, Kennedy was caught in a bind, because it appears that if Stone & Kuznick are correct, he only stood for the top job because he thought Eisenhower was leading the country to a third World War. Kennedy, being a war hero himself and injured in the Second World War, wanted to avoid this at all costs, once saying that 'I would rather my children be red than dead'. He also badly messed up the Bay of Pigs fiasco according to the 'Military Industrial Complex' and the CIA, by not allowing the military to use air power, to overthrow Castro. Kennedy was also involved in 163 covert operations around the globe while in office. General Curtis LeMay who sent in 334 planes to attack Tokyo in March 1945, was a dangerous hawk who thought Kennedy was wrong not to use aircraft at the bay of pig's disaster and may have been the main reason Kubrick made his famous aforementioned movie, about a lunatic, something like LeMay or General Thomas Power. After the Bay of Pigs fiasco Kennedy met Khrushchev in Vienna, hoping to calm down the cold war hysteria, but it seems that Khrushchev gave Kennedy hell about USA imperialism, and probably thought that Kennedy was a young man who could be pushed around. Apparently, the meeting shook Kennedy to the core. As a very young man of 14 in Port Stanley, Falkland Islands starting my first job at the Treasury department, as a junior clerk in September 1962, I can remember the Cuban missile crisis as it was yesterday, 60 years later (2022), because most of us thought the world was going to be blown up. One of my next-door neighbours older than me put me straight and said something like 'don't be silly Brian'. Thinking that Cuba was going to be invaded, Castro wanted Khrushchev to attack the USA with nuclear weapons before the Americans did a first strike on them. Khrushchev being a more rational man than Castro did not think it was a very good idea but did send several letters to Kennedy asking for him not to invade Cuba and to remove the missiles from Turkey. At first Kennedy rejected the missile swap but said he would not invade the island of Cuba. After much thought (for all of us), Khrushchev did not think that killing hundreds of millions was a good idea and withdrew the missiles from Cuba and did a secret deal that the Americans would withdraw the USA weapons from Turkey. It was at this point in history, if Stone and Kusnick are correct, that the world was nearly blown up, once and for all, and I would not be writing this 6th book, of mine. During this debacle the Soviets had sent a B-59 submarine to protect their ships, on the way to Cuba. The Americans started to lay depth charges against the submarine. The crew of USS Randolph dropping the charges were not aware that the submarine was carrying nuclear weapons. The depth charges had a profound effect on the submarine crew with some of them fainting in the extreme heat and suffering carbon dioxide poisoning and trying to escape the onslaught for four hours. The Commander Valentin Savitsky tried unsuccessfully to reach the general staff but in vain, so it was at this moment in history that the commander 'ordered the officer in charge of the nuclear torpedoes to prepare for battle' as he was not too sure what was happening above the water and wondered if the third World War had already broken out, and did not want to go down in history as a disgrace to his country? Luckily for all of us everyone was calmed down by Commander Vasili Arkhipov, one of two other senior officers on board the Sub and the world was saved from extinction. I presume the submarine got back to the Soviet Union without breaking up, after such a hammering. The postscript to this saga is also very chilling on three accounts again if Stone & Kuznick are correct. Firstly, Kennedy thought he may be overthrown by the 'Military Industrial Complex', (now sometimes referred to as the 'deep-state') at this time of true dynamic tension between capitalism and Communism; secondly the Americans did not know that the Soviets had already positioned small nuclear weapons on Cuba before the larger ones were discovered. These would have been used if the Americans had invaded Cuba for the second time, with the possible loss of millions of lives. What I was not aware of however I presume until reading this amazing book ('*The Untold History of the United States*') and why I am writing this one is that: 'It has also recently been discovered that on the island of Okinawa, a large force of Mace missiles with 1.1 megaton nuclear warheads and F-100 fighter bombers armed with Hydrogen bombs was preparing for action. Their likely target was not the Soviet Union but **China** (24). The paradox about this whole sad saga seems beyond belief, because Kennedy was an extremely intelligent man who did not want a Third World War that would destroy the world.

This anti-communist stance led to the Berlin wall fiasco which was caused partly by the settlement at the end of the Second World War, where Germany was split in to four elements, being controlled by: Britain, France, USA and the Soviet Union, with Berlin 100 miles inside East Germany. The West deliberately built-up West Berlin into a show case of consumerism, so the Soviet Union said they built the wall to keep capitalism out. The wall was started in 1961 and stayed in place until 1989. The West said it was built to stop east Germans fleeing to the West, which was partly true as millions did flee, but people like Khrushchev were terrified that Germany would be armed again as ONE nation and attack the Soviet Union, (as told to a USA journalist according to Olive Stone & Peter Kuznick) and who can blame them after 27 million Russian souls were lost in the Second World War? As Kennedy admitted it was the Soviet Union who took the brunt of Hitler's insanity in the Second World War and Churchill held off as long as he could to start a second front in Europe (against USA thinking and wishes on this matter at the time). This was the main objective and reason he persuaded the USA to go into North Africa and from there into Italy. The USA came out twice as rich as she was at the start of this madness, and virtually all the other countries involved in the war came out poorer, especially the UK, with 250% of GDP debt - albeit the Soviet Union did turn into a superpower in spite of the infrastructure in the West part of the country being destroyed by 1945. Germany was destroyed and bombed into the ground as was Japan. The bombing alone killed over a million people in Japan - so the west had to put the Marshall plan (designed for reparations) into operation, not for any altruistic motives but terrified that they may go LEFT politically or Communist completely, if this plan was not put into operation. This enabled new markets to prosper and created demands for the entire extra consumer goods made in the USA, as Marx & Engels had predicated in the 19th century. The third world was too poor to buy trainers, guns or whatever; hence the reason Germany and Japan were built up after the Second World War.

By 1963 Kennedy was talking about peace with the Soviet Union and even sharing the space race with them. He also made a speech that he could understand why Castro did what he did in Cuba, in the 1950s. Castro even noted that Kennedy may go down in history as one of the greatest presidents of all time. Kennedy, like Khrushchev in the Soviet Union, was caught between the hawks and the doves, telling some people he wanted to get out of Vietnam but could not do until after the 1964 election, because more than likely a new McCarthy scare could start all over again in the USA. This made him many enemies within the USA establishment, which included the CIA and 'Military Industrial Complex', the anti-Castro factions in Florida, (which is still a very powerful, force to this day) and so on. This was probably the reason he was killed on the 22nd of November 1963, in Dallas Texas - more than likely by more than one man, as suggested by Oliver Stone & Peter Kuznick and others. This was one of the very few events in history I remember as a boy growing up in the Falkland Islands. Well, it is 8000 miles from the UK, is it not? Oliver Stone also made a brilliant movie about the Jack Kennedy assassination called 'JFK' in 1991. Apparently like his subject matter, Stone has become a controversial figure in American film making, with critics accusing him of promoting unsubstantiated conspiracy theories, and of misrepresenting real-world events and figures in his works'. No doubt many people are very jealous of a very clever man who won 2 purple hearts in Vietnam and several other medals, as well. In the movie about JFK, it is suggested that there was more than one killer, on the 22nd of November 1963 and also why it was so controversial when The Warren Commission, 'concluded that Lee Harvey Oswald was the lone assassin'. Jack Leon Ruby, a small-time night club owner shot Lee Harvey Oswald dead on the 24th of November 1963. In the movie Oswald does say he was set up as a 'patsy', meaning a person who is easily taken advantage of, especially by being cheated or blamed for something. Why this story was so dynamic, complex and such a Cold War drama at the time, was that Oswald (born 24th November 1939) had been a U S marine who after being released from the forces, left the USA for the old Soviet Union in October 1959, (and in theory became a Marxist). He lived in Minsk until June 1962 with his Russian born wife Marina and on his return to the USA ended up in Dallas. The twists and turns in the movie are quite complex, but Stone's conclusions do seem to form a ring of truth. Kevin Costner played the main role, in the movie - Jim Garrison, who is very convincing and brilliant. Garrison was the only District Attorney in the USA who prosecuted Clay Shaw (a possible leading conspirator), with many others involved in Kennedy's death? The key evidence Garrison gave to the jury was the Zapruder Film from Life magazine that did seem to show that more than one person was involved in killing Kennedy. Because the Warren Commission had decided that Lee Harvey Oswald was the sole killer in the report, we can only presume that the jury had to acquit Shaw, after only one hour considering the case.

This is what Stone & Kuznick say about these very important times in their own words, 'in the minds of some leaders in the military and intelligence community, Kennedy was guilty of far more than three betrayals: he was guilty of not following through on the Bay of Pigs, disempowering the CIA and firing its leaders, resisting involvement and opting for a neutralist solution in Laos, concluding the atmospheric test ban treaty, planning to disengage from Vietnam, flirting with ending the Cold War, abandoning the space race, encouraging third-world nationalism, and perhaps most damningly, accepting a negotiated settlement in the Cuban Missile Crisis' (25). There is no doubt about the proposition that if Stone, Kuznick, Castro et al are correct; that if Kennedy had lived, he may have been the greatest President of all time, very much in the mould of Henry Wallace, had Wallace been lucky enough to have been in the same position, **in 1945?**

Lyndon Baines Johnson (LBJ) was born in Stonewall Texas in 1908 and died there in 1973. He won an election to the United States House of Representatives in 1937 and the Senate in 1948 and became the majority whip in 1951. He only became president by accident in 1963 because of Kennedy's assassination and then won a large majority in 1964. When Khrushchev heard about Kennedy's death he broke down and cried; when Castro heard about it, he was very concerned it would be blamed on Cuba. The assumption seems to be that Kennedy and Khrushchev saved the world from being destroyed. This was also the view of Jacqueline Kennedy who thought the same thing and wrote to Khrushchev with these thoughts. Stone & Kusnick note how Averell Harriman believed that if LBJ had not got bogged down in Vietnam, he could have been the greatest president ever. 'Sadly, he never came close' because he was not a deep foreign policy thinker and was a dedicated anti-communist, which clouded his judgement. He was basically crude, egotistical, overbearing and insecure and a bully. 'What's new' we could say while writing a book about Trump. Albeit that LBJ once noted that if you do not stand up to a bully he will be in your house and rape your wife as soon as your back is turned. The most important thing LBJ did (four days after he took office) was to issue National Security Action Memorandum (NSAM) 273, 'signalling that the

United States would be taking a more hands-on approach to Vietnam'. However, he did not like the advice that the CIA Director McCone was giving him about the conflict in Southeast Asia, as it was not going too well for the Americans. He also questioned 'what the hell is Vietnam worth to me', in May 1964 when confronting McGeorge Bundy. Twelve years previously in 1954, he seemed to understand why, influenced by its tin and manganese deposits. Henry Cabot Lodge could also see the potential of the whole region with plenty of rice reserves, rubber, and tin for businessmen to chew over in the future. LBJ, was it seems, like many USA presidents in that he did not want to be perceived as a coward or weakling, and was having nightmares about it. This state of mind is in essence what makes them all so dangerous for decades ahead, like Trump. Time will tell if this applies to Joe Biden, regarding his foreign policy objectives. However, he may still be taking a hard line against China on trading practises. According to the excellent programme on the BBC TV in January/February 2021 about the insanity of the Trump presidency China will never again ever be humiliated like they were in the 19th century.

As I note above, basically, the USA has been trying to expand its sphere of influence since its birth as a Nation State in 1776. There was an expansion process within the USA itself and abroad copying previous empires like the Romans and in more recent times the British and European imperialists. This is the reason the USA is so dangerous now especially under presidents like Trump with the rise of China challenging USA hegemony. While the British and Spanish et al just went in with sheer power to crush all resistance, America often does it by proxy helping to bring down a government or kill its perceived enemies and encourage the new regime to do all the dirty work, often pretending they know little about it. This seems to be what happened in Indonesia in the 1960s, a complex story that goes back centuries. Even Marco Polo visited what is now Indonesia in 1292 and the Portuguese were the first European settlers there in 1512. The Dutch slowly became the most successful colonial power in Indonesia by 1800. Their reason for being there was to exploit the spices that made a fortune back in Europe, which may have yielded profits as high as 400%. The British were often fighting the Dutch for these rewards. Sukarno, (who later became the first president of Indonesia) was fighting the Dutch empire and became the most important person as a nationalist (a good nationalist) in this struggle in Indonesia in the 20th century and ended up in detention for ten years. He was released by the Japanese and became the first president from 1945 to 1967. In a society as complex as Indonesia which is composed of 17,500 islands, 7000 uninhabited, Sukarno was very successful at trying to unite all the different ethnic and religious groups, up until 1959. Initially he collaborated with the Japanese who helped to spread nationalist ideas but then got into trouble with the Western World for going down this road. After the Second World War he did not get complete independence from Dutch rule until 1949. In 1955 Sukarno hosted leaders of 29 Asian, African and Middle Eastern countries, in Bandung which to the West was like a red rag to a bull because it metamorphosed into the Non-aligned Movement. Calling for neutrality between the two cold war warriors, they also supported decolonization, wherever it applied and for third world countries to get hold of their own resources and to benefit from those resources. By 1959 Sukarno had decided that their form of parliamentary democracy was not working, so by 1960 he invented 'Guided democracy'. At this time, he veered to the Left supporting the communist party of Indonesia (PKI) to the alarm of the military set up and the Islamists. He even went further taking an anti-imperialist stance and becoming good friends with Russia and China.

If Noam Chomsky is correct about this time in history (Year 501) the attempts to overthrow Sukarno and other Left-wing type regimes around the world, started in the 1950s, with possible assassination attempts on

Sukarno's life, organised by agencies of the USA government. However, their real concern was that the PKI may become an elected government with real power in Indonesia. This never happened because on the 30th of September 1965, an alleged Communist coup attempt killed six Indonesian generals. This allegation was based on some dubious assumptions. In fact, it was Sukarno's palace guards who did it to protect their president, from a perceived CIA plot according to Olive Stone & Peter Kuznick. (26)

 This was the excuse that General Suharto, as head of the army, wanted and used to kill hundreds of thousands of peasants, maybe at least a million, many of them PKI members and landless peasants. He did this with the help of Islamic extremists, and a million people were also imprisoned for decades. The legendary John Pilger even asserted the British got involved in this whole disgraceful slaughter through selling arms around the globe, ironically under a labour government (27). US diplomats supplied thousands of names of perceived communists to Suharto, to be killed. Suharto finally overthrew Sukarno and locked him up and one of the biggest robberies in history started with the whole economy opened up to the Western world with Suharto taking huge slices of the cake, for himself and his family…. while most of the population lived in poverty. Suharto had grown up in a small village called Kemusuk in the Godean area, from a humble background. During the Japanese occupation period he had served in the army for the Japanese and then after independence, for the Indonesian Army and then rose to the rank of Major General, under Sukarno. The Sunday Observer has also noted that the secret Information Research Department (IRD) a British 'black propaganda' unit in the foreign office, employing 360 people, revealed the IRD's major campaign in

Indonesia in 1965 that helped encourage ant-communist massacres which left hundreds of thousands dead. The IRD prepared pamphlets purporting to be written by Indonesian patriots, but in fact were created by British propagandists, calling on Indonesians to eliminate the PKI, then the biggest communist party in the non-communist world'. (Sunday Observer 15 May 2022)

As I have noted above it had been observed by the Ruling Elite in the USA, even in 1954, that Southeast Asia had large rewards for basic commodities still unused after centuries of colonial plunder. The wellbeing of the indigenous people was of secondary importance during colonialism. The escalation of the war in Vietnam under LBJ may not have just been about communism but also about resources to be plundered. This escalation was of course a disgrace to mankind, albeit LBJ had been warned that the whole thing was going badly for the USA, by several advisers. 'In August 1964 Johnson and McNamara used a fabricated incident in the Gulf of Tonkin as an excuse to escalate the war'. (28) He escalated the war very slowly so as not to alarm the American public or drawing in China which he seemed to fear the most, especially when the US started to bomb North Vietnam, using napalm and white phosphorus which burned to the bone, causing horrific and painful deaths. An 'evil act' is a 'crime against humanity', full stop. Like Laos et al, between 1964 and 1973 millions of bombs were also dropped on this very small country, first thought of as a communist threat to the USA under President Kennedy. 1965 seems to have been a pivotal year in the rejection of bombing Vietnam, not only in the USA but around this wonderful little world in the vastness of the mighty Universe, which is not understood by most people on this planet. When these first acts of protest started to happen against the war, especially in the USA, LBJ thought it was a communist conspiracy, which it was not. He berated Richard Helms for failing to prove it. A huge organisation called

'Chaos' was set up by the CIA to monitor 300,000 people in the USA. This was nothing new due to the existence of a witch hunt against anyone who was not patriotic to the Flag of the USA and a perceived communist threat throughout previous decades. Dr Martin Luther King Jr was one of the first targets of this insanity, apparently saying the USA was 'the greatest purveyor of violence in the world today' which of course was true and still is, to a certain extent virtually all over the world, maintaining their hegemony, at any cost - just like the Roman Empire did 2000 years ago, in their known world.

In the first James Bond movie called Dr No and starring Sean Connery as Bond, which was released in 1962, (and to my mind the best actor to play the part and now sadly dead, at 90) there is a great line in the movie with him meeting his nemeses, accompanied by Honey Rider. (When in theory he could be hundreds of feet below the sea). Dr No explains to Bond the wonders of the huge fish, etc in front of him in a specially curved aquarium, he had made - Bond says – 'just like you Dr No, minnows believing they're Whales', meaning they have grand illusions above their station in life. It seems to me this is an extremely good metaphor for some presidents of the USA et al, who think they are Dr No, but, as individuals have very little power, but do control a very dangerous system that can blow up the planet. LBJ used the levers at his disposal to try to make the 'Great Society', and indeed he did carry out some reforms to improve society for everyone. But he got bogged down in these reforms and decided not to run for a second term at the end of 1968.

Richard Nixon won in 1968, narrowly defeating Hubert Humphrey and having run for the presidency himself but having just lost out to Jack Kennedy who had shaven before the TV debate (Nixon had not), which apparently made all the difference to the voters - he was also vice president for eight years under General Dwight Eisenhower. Chapter nine of Stone & Kuznicks' amazing book about the USA just about sums up what I have written above because it is called 'Nixon and Kissinger: The Madman and the Psychopath'. Apparently, Kissinger perceived Nixon as a very cold man, a very unpleasant man, a nervous and superficial person who hated to meet new people. He also found it very strange that a loner like Nixon who hated people, became a Politician. The dynamic tension at times became so intense between them that Kissinger called him 'that madman'. Nixon referred to Kissinger as a 'Jew boy' because he fled Germany in 1938 and a 'psychopath', but one who shared the same vision of USA hegemony. The year that Nixon got elected was the year that in many countries around the globe young people revolted against the brutality of the capitalist system itself.... albeit this was not new as I describe above. The problem that capitalism has as a social system, and will have to its dying day, is that it will not work without 'wage slaves' who are forced to sell their 'labour power' in the 'labour market' and not revolt, so must be kept poor in relation to the ruling class. The hippie movement started up in the 1960s was so despised by the ruling classes all over the world and still is to this day, as the system will not work without a docile labour force to be exploited. Richard Nixon was very concerned that the Universities were the hotbed of radicalism, (very much like current times) so had to be controlled like everything else under capitalism. Ironically, Henry Kissinger was an academic and Harvard professor who thought Nixon would be a disaster as president. As he noted: 'the man is unfit to be president'. Richard Nixon basically only got elected because he pretended that he had a plan to end the Vietnam War, which was not true. The real plan seemingly was to bomb North Vietnam into submission and I presume into the Stone Age? Stone & Kuznicks' take on these events is quite revealing about the symbiotic relationship between home events and foreign policy being carried out often by subterfuge. LBJ tried to get North Vietnam to the negotiating table by stopping the outrageous bombing. During this period however, there was a lot of political chicanery at home, but by fair means or foul, Nixon was duly elected.

Richard Nixon was not interested in domestic affairs once he became the president, so got Kissinger on board, a Harvard professor to help him with his objectives - as he wanted like all presidents to go down in history, on the world stage. William Rogers was in theory secretary of State, but Nixon and Kissinger decided to run most foreign affairs from the White House and Rogers could look after 'the blacks' in Africa and was kept out of the loop most of the time. Kissinger had decided that during the transition period he should get the RAND organisation to come up with a set of policy options on Vietnam. RAND picked Daniel Ellsberg, an expert on Vietnam who had already prepared papers for Robert McNamara but refused to include a nuclear option. This research later became the famous Pentagon Papers. Ellsberg's second report called NSSM 1, posed several questions for the Joint Chiefs of Staff to mull over. The Joint Chiefs of Staff told Nixon it would take eight to thirteen years in South Vietnam to crush all opposition; costing many lives and dollars. The madman decided (I presume) that this was bonkers, so he had to end it on his terms 'with honour'. How many people had to die in the process was irrelevant to his logic which included using nuclear weapons if the need arose. This shocked J. Robert Oppenheimer to the core. Over time Nixon persuaded the South Vietnamese to take over more of the fighting on the ground, from the Americans. These peaked at 543,000 fighting USA soldiers, which included the great Oliver Stone. However, the bombing of South Vietnam was still on the agenda and was intensified and included the bombing of the North and sanctuaries in Cambodia. The latter was done secretly until the New York

Times exposed what they were up to in Cambodia, in April 1969. Nixon bragged that attacking Cambodia was the real 'Nixon doctrine', because they could damage the country without having USA troops on the ground, so none would die in that part of Southeast Asia. The nuclear option nearly became a reality when the North did not buckle under the onslaught of USA power called 'Operation Duck Hook', because Kissinger did not believe that a fourth-rate power like North Vietnam could not be brought to its knees through brute force. Invasion was on the menu, as was mining Haiphong harbour and bombing dykes to destroy food supplies. Lucky for North Vietnam, Nixon called off Operation Duck Hook mostly due to the anti-war movement in the USA and around the globe. Albeit on the 13th of October 1969 nuclear SAC bombers were armed to the teeth secretly, escalating the game up further on the 25th, signalling to the Russians that he wanted them to intervene with Hanoi to negotiate. They were unaware that China and Russia were in a dispute of their own on their borders at the time, which could have turned into a nuclear war according to Stone & Kuznick, in their amazing take on these affairs. These were very dangerous moments for us all with a madman and a psychopath in charge of USA foreign affairs in the White House, scheming the end of the world as predicted in the great satire *Doctor Strangelove*...see above. The Soviets were so angry with China that they wanted the USA help to knock out China's nuclear facilities. Not only were young students etc getting upset at what was going on in Vietnam and Southeast Asia but also 100,000 scientists, who signed a famous resolution, were also upset throughout the nineteen sixties; especially over the use of chemical weapons destroying crops and so on and did not want science being used for criminal activities. In the last analysis what Nixon and Kissinger did not really understand about the war in Vietnam was that they could bomb the place into the Stone Age (which they tried to do) and win many battles but in the long term they could never win the war. What Vo Nguyen Giap, the North Vietnamese Military leader, explained after the war was that the Vietnamese people were never going to be American slaves, which should really be the motto of the whole world. Ignorance of Southeast Asia was Nixon's problem as it was for most people in the USA, the high and mighty as well as humble middle classes, partly caused by Nixon himself who hounded the experts who knew anything about Southeast Asia out of the State department in the 1950s, because he held this department responsible for their ignorance over China. Ironically, at least a few North Vietnamese troops fighting the Americans educated themselves about USA culture and disseminated this information to their friends about fighting American colonialism. Another factor that helped sway the war against Nixon was when Seymour Hersh exposed the 'My Lai' massacre of 500 innocence civilians, including children - with many women who were raped, before they were killed. The killing went on for so long that the soldiers involved even took a lunch break. This horrendous crime was kept quiet for a whole year, although 50 officers, including a few senior ones, knew about it. Ron Ridenhour was the hero of the day who wrote a two-thousand-word report which he sent to thirty members of congress. Americans were so shocked by this story that some mothers thought that the Army had turned their sons into murderers, which in many cases it had, often killing civilians at will. The brain washing of servicemen is all part of this insane process that you must hate your enemy to want to kill them, which is not unique to the USA, but a worldwide phenomenon. The birth of the insane nation state has taken this phenomenon to new heights. The invention has been responsible for more deaths in the last century than all human history combined. Man in one form another may have been around for 2 million years or more, according to Richard Leakey and in our form for at least half a million years, according to Anthony Giddens. Paradoxically the brutality of the My Lai massacre did not affect everyone but only hardened the hearts of 65% of the USA population when polled, who were not concerned about this crime. Nixon, however, turned to drink and watching the brilliant movie 'Patton' repeatedly. George C Scott, one of America's greatest actors played Patton and was the first actor in history to refuse to accept an Oscar on philosophical grounds, as each performance is a one off and nothing more, according to him. Nixon's story was basically about a man on the verge of a mental breakdown who wanted to ape Teddy Roosevelt with small but significance actions that electrified America in his day, so Nixon said at one briefing 'let's go and blow the hell out of them'. The campuses erupted, with students and professors going on strike and at the Kent State University, four protesters were killed and nine wounded, while seven hundred other campuses also acted against the war in Vietnam. In this case the pluralistic model of liberal democracy was starting to work, albeit at a terrible cost in Southeast Asia, under the Madman and the Psychopath.

The trouble for all societies that have developed over millenniums and now in their current form is that they can be used and abused on a gigantic scale, as under Hitler in Germany or under Nixon & Kissinger in the USA in the 1960s and 1970s, just mentioned. Science has developed in recent times (along with the idea of the Nation State) - mostly for the benefit of mankind, like medicine, electricity and so on – but also it has been used for cruel and despicable purposes, especially in warfare, with chemicals that can kill you as well as those that keep you alive. Nuclear bombs and their derivate that can destroy the planet and all of mankind, are the most dangerous things in history that have ever been made, by man...now used by the biggest bullies in the playground and ostensibly protection against the biggest bullies in the playground at the same time. (Hence the excuse for 'deterrents') This was the reason that many scientists in the USA were so up in arms about Nixon and Kissinger's' outrageous behaviour in Southeast Asia, including Cambodia and Laos, while in office; in essence they were using their skills and knowledge for nefarious operations, against

Asian people. Nixon, like Hitler, basically became the LAW and did not think the 'fourth amendment' applied to him when asked by David Frost, the English journalist who was part of the whole rotten British establishment. Frost died a very rich man, on a cruise ship, years later. The contradiction at the heart of the Western idea of liberal capitalist democracy, is of course a complete sham not only at home (as in the USA and the UK for example) but also because it is mostly about freedom to make money at any cost anywhere in the world. In Vietnam and elsewhere the assumption was that the Americans were fighting terrible socialist/communist ideas, while at the same time pretending, they were giving them democracy. In Chile Salvador Allende was elected in November 1970, the first Marxist and medical doctor to be elected against all odds because of USA propaganda on a huge scale, in a close three-way race. This was a terrible crime according to Nixon and Kissinger. On the 11[th of] September 1973, he was overthrown with the help of the CIA. In theory he shot himself, instead of being taken prisoner, with a gun given to him by Fidel Castro. He was replaced in a coup d'etat by General Augusto Pinochet under whom thousands died, many were tortured and hundreds of thousands fled for their lives. I met one of these wonderful families in Bristol, in 1996, who had a successful café/restaurant on Gloucester Road, in Bristol UK. The crime Allende committed was to nationalize major industries, expand education and improve the living standards of the working class...amazingly even to this day this is a terrible crime in the USA and the UK. On the 4th of December 1972 Allende gave one of the most powerful 90-minute speeches to the United Nations assembly ever, in Washington: decrying the crimes of multinational corporations' exploitation of Nation States and for stealing resources like copper in Chile, and in the process sealing his own death warrant. Albeit what he was arguing for was the truth as stealing resources is a sort of war that has been going on for 500 years all over the globe. Noam Chomsky called this whole process the 'fifth freedom': to rob and exploit other people's resources. In previous epochs, over 10,000 years or so ago, the world was much smaller, for example the Roman Empire was big but not as huge as the Spanish or British empires. A few years after the successful overthrow of Allende, 'Operation Condor' was set up killing first the Chilean ambassador to the United States, Orlando Letelier a few blocks from the White House with a car bomb and probably killing 13,000 dissidents living outside Chile, if Stone & Kuznick are correct. Ironically, Pinochet, a modern-day neo-brute, (after Aristotle) was praised by the tyrant and neo-brute Margaret Hilda Thatcher, until her dying day for at least in theory helping her gain the Falklands back from Argentina in the 1982 conflict……stolen from the Spanish in 1833. Thatcher also claimed that Castro had killed more people than General Pinochet's regime, which was very unlikely, after overthrowing the cruel and brutal Batista's government in Cuba in 1959.

For any sane person on Planet earth, with Nixon's complete hatred of communism and any form of progressive ideas whatsoever, it seems strange why he wanted to visit China in 1972 - which was organised by Kissinger in 1971 on a secret mission to Beijing…….the objective being to have some leverage over the Soviet Union and upstage the democrats. No USA president had ever visited China after Mao took over on the 1st of October 1949, because it did not exist in the minds of the ruling Elite in the USA; only Taiwan was recognized as the legitimate government of China under Chiang Kai-shek. Apparently, the visit in February 1972 was a huge success and in May the same year he visited the Soviet Union; Richard Nixon was now a world statesman. Only Jimmy Carter has not visited China since this visit - so now we can empirically note that over ONE billion people on the Planet do exist after all and they all want to buy stuff; how amazing? Wary of what Nixon was up to in 1972, the Soviet Union warmly welcomed him and signed the Strategic Arms Limitation Treaty, which in theory restricted each side to two anti-ballistic missile systems, which did not mean a lot, but at least it was a start and of huge symbolic importance. Nixon told Congress on his return that he was the new messiah, not completely true, but in theory the cold war was not as hot as it had been before, for the previous 25 years of total insanity. Sixty-five million years ago the dinosaurs were wiped out by an asteroid hitting the planet, from outer space - now ancestors of the first mammals can destroy the Planet themselves; isn't progress wonderful? Nixon was known as 'tricky Dicky' and several other names (which he gained for many reasons), but it was the agreement over Okinawa in 1971 that must be one of the most devious in USA history. In theory it gave back the Island to Japan for a price but kept an American base on the Island for strategic purposes in the region. It then got the Japanese to pay for the bases to be there and informed them they would not keep nuclear weapons on the Island. But unknown to everyone apart from Prime Minister Eiskaku Sato, Nixon subverted the agreement and let the Americans reintroduce nuclear weapons on the Island. For historical reasons, the dynamic tensions between Japan, the USA and China were always going to be there for decades after the Second World War, what with China becoming a communist State in 1949 (also getting the bomb), Japan invading China in the 1930's when millions were killed because they thought of the Chinese as 'inferior beings', trade disputes between Japan and the USA and so on. The decline of the USA seemed inevitable, so in 1971 Nixon and his economic advisers changed the rules of the game. This was the best policy when you are losing, as he said. He suspended the convertibility of the dollar to gold, overturning the international monetary system; he imposed wage-price controls and a general import surcharge. He reduced federal taxes and domestic expenditure in favour of the rich and racked up debt for the State and the individual. In this respect Nixon was the architect of what was to come later, under virtually all USA presidents.

Daniel Ellsberg, however, saw through Nixon's lies about the USA involvement in Vietnam, pretending that he was going to bring it to an end. He gave the Pentagon Papers about the secret history of the Vietnam War, made up of forty-seven volumes copied from the McNamara study, to the New York Times. In Ellsberg mind the war was a 'crime', an 'evil' and mass murder, which it was, and the Washington Post took over where the Times had left off. He also gave copies to nineteen newspapers and then went into hiding, but after 13 days gave himself up to the FBI. Nixon and Kissinger went out of their way to destroy Ellsberg, calling him the most dangerous man in the USA, using dirty tricks and breaking into his psychiatrist's office in California with the help of some Cubans who trashed the place. These were dangerous times for Nixon, leading up to the November election in 1972 as Hanoi was getting the upper hand in South Vietnam. Worried that he may lose the war before the election, Nixon contemplated measures so extreme that even Kissinger objected, like destroying power plants, the docks, and dykes and so on, and evoking the possibility of using nuclear weapons. After Nixon got re-elected in 1972, he unleashed a massive twelve-day Christmas bombing against Hanoi and Haiphong, one of the heaviest of the war. The international outcry was deafening, and peace talks resumed. The United States troops were withdrawn, although 150,000 North Vietnamese troops stayed in the South and respected the cease fire again according to Stone & Kuznicks' take on these events. President Nixon was the only President in USA history who engaged in sustained military action against three nations without a mandate from the government bureaucracies of the elite, and the American public. *Ride the Thunder* (2015 movie) denied that the USA were ever the bad guys in Vietnam and purported they did not commit crimes against the locals, and so on - according to the actor playing John Ripley, a true American hero like Audie Murphy in the Second World War, but this time in Vietnam. In theory this was a true story from a Right-wing perspective critiquing Jane Fonda, Donald Sutherland et al. But what concerned me about this movie was how the North Vietnamese were the bad guys (which may have been true in the movie) without explaining the true historical overview of colonialism, in Southeast Asia…. that even some one as brave as John Ripley was not aware of? Even the legendary actor Robert Mitcham visited the troops in Vietnam and got involved in the controversy over why the USA troops were there in the first place and believed that they should not have been withdrawn.

As many people in the world know of Bob Woodward and Carl Bernstein, incredible investigative journalists working for the Washington Post. Under the editorship of Ben Bradlee, and with a little help from 'deep throat', they investigated the break in at the Democratic headquarters in Washington in June 1972…which led directly to Watergate and the cover-up that followed, and eventually to Nixon resigning on the 9th of August 1974, facing almost certain impeachment. The movie about this whole process with Robert Redford and Dustin Hoffman, called *All the Presidents Men* - which I have watched several times, was brilliant. Amazingly, even to this day, whenever we see a movie about journalism at its best, Woodward and Bernstein get mentioned; like *The Dark Reflection* which was/is a true story about another cover-up in the airline business, which I saw very recently (mid 2021) and it was a very disturbing one at that. It showed how toxic oil fumes from the engines can get sucked into the air pressure system inside the aircraft and as someone who has flown around the world a few times on a shoe string this movie was very worrying indeed!

Gerald Ford took over from Nixon, pardoning him, but according to Lyndon Johnson, Ford could not walk and chew gum at the same time. Kissinger stayed on as Secretary of State and national security adviser but was very concerned that the USA was on a downward spiral (with a trade deficit instead of the 70 years long surplus) which most intelligent men say is now happening to the USA again with the rise of China (sic) - as all great empires have fallen in the end. Albeit because the British are 'wood' from the neck up (according to Rupert Murdoch, mentioned by John Le Carrie in *The Pigeon Tunnel* and this author) we may have a Monarchy for the next five thousand years, by which time we will probably be by then the poorest country in the world? Like all ruthless empires, that have committed horrendous crimes, a few mentioned in this project, very few have ever given their victims reparations or post war aid. The USA had promised Vietnam billions at the Paris Peace Conference but reneged on the agreement pretending the protocols did not exist. They also imposed an embargo on all of Indochina, froze Vietnamese assets in the USA and vetoed their membership in the United Nations.

A constant theme of bourgeois democracy.... (Liberal Capitalist democracy) is that in the end, when the new president, prime minster or whoever takes over and becomes the new captain of the 'ship of State' (after Plato), everything will be much better or improved for all. This happened in the USA, Britain, Japan and most of Europe for 30 years after the Second World War. However, since the middle of the 1970s and especially during the 'reign' of Regan and Thatcher, the class nature of the system has broken through to expose the sham it really is. In the USA, Jimmy Carter was elected in November 1976 and became the president in January 1977, a millionaire peanut farmer and Sunday school teacher. Carter's big idea was to restore trust in Government and heal the wounds of the Watergate scandal, the Vietnam War and gender and racial issues. This idea is a constant theme throughout USA political culture, but the issues are rarely resolved. Ironically even Alexis de Tocqueville, a French aristocrat who admired the USA, understood that black people had an extremely raw deal in life nearly 200 years ago while writing these observations in his best-known works (n two volumes) called *Democracy in America* and realized that this could be the source of future problems. I read them while in higher education in the mid-nineteen-eighties and was very impressed. Jimmy Carter knew very little about foreign affairs so was ill equipped to fulfil all his ideals about promoting human rights, cutting defence spending, the hypocrisy of having nuclear weapons while denying them to other nations. In theory he believed they should be abolished. He also thought that being involved in other Nation's affairs was wrong. These ideas went slightly astray when Zbigniew Brzezinski, National Security Adviser, started to gaslight Carter's inner soul, virtually from day one in the White House. This is not to deny that Carter at the beginning of his presidency did achieve some of his goals, like the Camp David accords. He also made headway in arms control procedures and renegotiated the Panama Canal treaty. But finally, the power of the Brzezinski narrative beat Carter down, bragging that he was the most successful Pole ever to have power in the last 300 years of USA history and could 'stick it to the Russians'; for example, linking détente to human rights abusers in the USSR. By this time in history this was very hypocritical when racial abusers were still highly prevalent throughout USA society, their prison population being on the rise and so on. The prison population is now 0 .7 of the total USA population and the highest in the world, making it a very profitable business to make lots of money out of incarceration. The Soviet Union was also at this time in history, backing progressive forces in Africa and elsewhere, often supported by Cuba, (especially in Africa), pushed the socialist model of development. This was a terrible crime in the eyes of the Western powers, especially in Ethiopia and Southwest Africa. Emperor Haile Selassie of Ethiopia had been overthrown in 1974, in a military coup. He was also facing an invasion from Somalia, and then got lots of help from the Soviet Union with a 'billion dollars' worth of military equipment and 17,000 Cuban assistants. Mengistu used brutal force on his opponents, after overthrowing

Selassie who had been on the throne for 44 years and whose lineage went back to the Queen of Sheba, according to him, which may have been a myth. Carter accused the Soviet Union of expanding their influence abroad, through military assistance and military power, with Brzezinski shouting from the side-lines. The top of the hierarchy in the USSR were concerned about getting involved in countries that were not following progressive forces in society. Human Rights often backfired on the USA, for example when Andrew Young, Ambassador to the UN, told a French newspaper that there were hundreds/thousands of political prisoners in American jails, while the USA was always blaming the Soviet Union for Human rights violations. It would seem that nothing much has changed with reference to Navalny and Assange in 2022.

Also, between 1968 and 1973, when the British Empire was in decline, they forcefully evicted two thousand natives of Diego Garcia in the Indian Ocean, part of the Chagos Islands – so that the Americans could use it as Military base. Carter also continued to back the Shah of Iran with weapons and urged Iran to start a domestic nuclear programme to save its oil reserves. The Shah had visited the White House in 1977 and during their discussion the USA agreed to sell six to eight light-water reactors to Iran with others from France and Germany in the pipeline. Their friendship continued up to the very end, with Carter and his wife visiting Iran and asserting that Iran was an 'island of stability'. How wrong can ONE man be; two years later the Shah fled for his life. Even Marshall Law could not stop the discontent in society. The Americans, thinking that the USSR may get involved, drew up a plan for the Americans to take over the Iranian oilfields. This was a huge failure of the whole intelligence network of the USA, who did not understand how millions felt about the Shah and his human rights violations. Ayatollah Rullollah Khomeini, who had been in Iraq and France for fifteen years, had kept up an invective against the Shah and American backers before flying back to Iran after the Shah had left in February 1979.

Khomeini formed an Islamic republic, based on Sharia law. The Shah ended up in the USA, which angered the new Iranian regime. His life continued until December 1979 when he died in Egypt. In July 1980, 66 Americans were taken hostage in their embassy. Of these, 52 were held for 444 days. Fearing Soviet intervention in Iran, Carter rushed 25 warships to the Persian Gulf and 1,800 marines. He also blocked Iranian assets in the USA and cut off oil imports from Iran, trying to inflict as much pain as he could on the new enemy.

As things turned out, the USSR was invited into Afghanistan (some say invaded) with the help of Brzezinski, as a ploy to bog them down in a conflict as were the Americans in Vietnam, which sadly happened. Afghanistan which had hardly changed as a country since Alexander the Great's days and the several invasions by the British in the 19th century. The pure daily hypocrisy of the Western world is nearly beyond belief and very few can see through it, apart from Noam Chomsky and some left-wing sociologists. So, when Saddam Hussein for example, was a good guy, people like Donald Rumsfeld actually met him in Iraq and the USA supplied him with financial aid. This continued during the eight years of the conflict with Iran from 1980 to 1988, (costing about a million dead). The USA did not want Iran to win. Whether the USA encouraged Hussein to pick a fight with Iran seems to be open to conjecture, but after 9/11 he became public enemy number ONE along with Osama Bin Laden, (who was a good guy in the 1980s). The Iran hostage crisis did not turn out well for Carter. They sent in the military without success. This was called 'Operation Eagle Claw' which ended in disaster with ruined military planes and the hostages no closer to freedom. This was the death knell for Carter, as he was perceived to be weak and not in control of events in the run up to the election in November 1980. Whereas Jimmy Carter was an intelligent man (who has now written 30 books and is a noble peace prize winner), his successor

Ronald Reagan was nothing but a B movie actor, with extreme right-wing views like those of Mrs Thatcher in No 10, who got elected in Britain in 1979. How Reagan beat Carter, who was leading the election in some of the polls, resembles a thriller straight out of Hollywood. Carter wanted to sell arms to Iran, if Iran released the hostages, as had been agreed under the Shah. Reaganites smelled a rat, and called it an 'October surprise'. In 1980 they did their own deal with Iran asking them to hold the hostages until after the election and then they would sell arms in exchange for them, through Israel. The trick pulled off here seems to be that the Reaganites offered more arms than Carter. The American hostages were released on the 21st of January 1981, Reagan's first day in office and arms started to flow to Iran for several years via Israel. This later in the 1980's turned into a huge scandal. Mrs Thatcher was the first foreign dignitary to visit the White House after Reagan's election victory and they got on like a house on fire, according to Lord Carrington the British foreign secretary, because they were both so 'vulgar'. The main reason they got on so well was that they both believed they were fighting pure evil in the form of socialism wherever they found it, and both believed in the wonders of 'blind faith' and the so-called market system. Even Jimmy Carter on meeting the new president to brief him on the task in hand for the next four years, was quite shocked at how uneducated he seemed to be. This has been a constant theme in the USA for over a generation where the democratic president is normally well educated and the republican ones extremely uneducated and very dangerous to the world. According to Stone & Kuznick's portrayal of Reagan, he was in a small way, very much like Trump (my analysis) as not only did he lie but also drifted into a world of make believe like pretending he filmed holocaust survivors in Germany at the end of the Second World War, which was just not true. Whenever there is a 'vacancy' in someone's brain as there must have been with Reagan, especially on foreign affairs, there are always plenty of takers to fill it. Jeane Kirkpatrick, a conservative democratic political scientist from Georgetown and a strong anti-communist, was made the ambassador to the UN and persuaded Reagan that supporting right-wing dictatorships all over Latin America and beyond was the way forward for USA foreign policy. This was hardly a new idea in the realms of American history, was it? *Turning the Tide* by Noam Chomsky was the first book I read written by the great man (and one of the most quoted men in history) in the mid nineteen eighties, and I was completely shocked by the major themes of the book and read it within a day and several times since. It is a tour de force on the crimes of USA foreign policies over decades, especially in Central America, which under Reagan reached new heights of cruelty, explained in detail by Chomsky from many sources. The new/old arms race under Reagan had begun under Carter, when the USSR arms expenditure had been declining from 1972. The rhetoric around this, however, was a complete fabrication of the truth. Reagan was fighting the evil empire that had to be destroyed at all costs, with the help of the tyrant Mrs Margaret Hilda Thatcher. Before 1917 the USSR was not an evil empire, according to this sort of nonsense, although the history of Russia was a bloody slaughterhouse of crimes over hundreds of years, before Stalin was ever born. *The Romanovs* (1613-1918) by Simon Sebag Montefiore is an excellent (book) source of knowledge to understand the brutal nature of Russian society for over 300 hundred years.

Nicaragua had been invaded by the USA in 1912 over banana wars, hence where the term a 'banana republic' comes from, I presume. By 1937 the brutal dictatorship of the Somoza family had taken control of the country until they were ousted by Daniel Ortega's Sandinistas in 1978-79, the new devil in town who had been in prison, where he was mistreated from 1967 until 1974, then exiled to Cuba. According to Chomsky the Sandinistas did not treat the Miskito Indians very well, but in some cases better than they had been treated under Somoza and a lot better than the thousands of indigenous people murdered in Guatemala and El Salvador by US clients.

This was one of the main accusations that the Reagan administration used for setting up the contras, in essence a bunch of right-wing thugs out to destroy any gains that Ortega was trying to make in Nicaragua. This theme seems to be repeated, throughout the last 243 years American independence from Great Britain, (now apparently called Global Britain...a rebranding exercise by Boris Johnson and his bunch of Right-wing Nationalistic lunatics). During this time the USA managed to take over from the Spanish Empire, as they progressed to being the biggest bully in the playground and still are.

'Reviewing the human rights situation in Nicaragua, the Americas Watch report finds that Nicaraguan government atrocities, which it believes it was able to review in full, are far slighter than those of the US-organized terrorist army and have sharply declined since 1982, in contrast to those of the contras, which can only be sampled given their scale and the lack of resources. Even in the case of the Miskitos, not the prime target of the US-sponsored terrorists, Americas Watch finds that most serious abuses of Miskitos rights have been committed by the contra groups, and the contras' treatment of Miskitos and other Indians, has become increasingly more violent, while that of the government has notably improved'. (29) The legendary John Pilger reported from Nicaragua in the early 1980s when Reagan's contras were committing crimes galore, like killing '3346' children, many thousands of parents and slitting the throat of a midwife because she had learnt skills to help her community, the fifth to die this way in her valley (Hidden Agendas P, 26).

The biggest bully in the playground, to get away with his crimes, must invent basically fairy stories for the uneducated majority to believe in, or as Noam Chomsky would have it, we need 'a docile intelligentsia and well-behaved ideological institutions' to get away with it. The problem arises when the better educated, like the hippie movement in the 1960s, stops believing in fairy stories. There was no logic to believing that Cuba was ever a threat to the USA, likewise Nicaragua or even little Grenada, in 1983 a British colony, which became independent in 1974, was but still part of the Commonwealth, and whose government was overthrown by Maurice Bishop in 1979 and took a Left-wing stance so becoming perceived as a threat to the USA. In October 1983 Bishop was killed by supporters of his deputy Bernard Coard who resented attempts to mend bridges with 'the US'. Later that month 6000 US troops invaded Grenada. According to Reagan 'we got there just in time' to save it from Soviet penetration and the communist threat to the world. Mrs Thatcher was not told about the invasion, so was most upset about it, considering that she, single-handedly, saved the locals in the Falkland Islands from the Argentine junta, in 1982. The Falkland's conflict of 1982 was a real problem for Ronald Reagan as the Junta in Argentina were firm friends of the USA, helping to fight the terrible threat of communism wherever it popped up. Galtieri and his Junta were just taking back what was really Argentinian land as he perceived it, which was true. It was taken by force on the 3rd of January 1833, by the British. According to my research on this topic, when writing a book about Mrs Thatcher, even the CIA had thought that eventually Argentina would take the Malvinas (as they call them) back, just as India did to Goa in 1961. In the end Reagan had to come down on the side of Mrs Thatcher, well at-least for the 10 weeks of the dispute, which killed over 900 people to save 1800, probably the most stupid conflict/war in history. Just before the end of this conflict Ronald Reagan came to the UK on the way to a summit meeting in Paris. He addressed the House of Lords with the Commons in attendance, with the help of an auto-cue and even went out for a horse ride with the British Head of State....part of the richest aristocracy in the world, which most British people do not seem to be aware of?

As I have noted above and throughout this book, since 1917 and especially after the Second World War, communism was enemy Number One to the Western World. Under the Reagan period in office, the paranoia with the help of Mrs Thatcher went up a notch, even allowing cruise missiles on UK soil, aimed at the USSR. Thus, every action of the USA foreign policy must be understood in this way. Also, most textbooks about this period note how Reagan often fell asleep at briefings and for some of the time was maybe not aware what was going on in his name. This certainly applied to the Iran/Contra scandal, where originally the justification for arms shipments to Iran from America was that Hezbollah was holding seven American hostages in Lebanon. They were hoping that sales of arms to Iran would influence the people in power in Iran to release the hostages. In theory Hezbollah was a paramilitary group with Iranian ties. The Boland amendment in the USA Congress stopped the Americans from selling arms to the contras in Nicaragua who Reagan supported. So, in his second term, Lieutenant Colonel Oliver North came up with the idea that some of the money, extracted from Iran should go to the contras, fighting the nasty Left-wing Sandinistas in Nicaragua, thus by-passing Congress. In 1983 the USA launched Operation Staunch to try and stop all countries from selling arms to Iran, which proved extremely embarrassing when the above story leaked out in 1986. The other part of this saga was that if America did not sell overpriced arms to Iran after Iraq attacked it, (in 1980), that Iran would buy them from the USSR, a shocking idea to the Americans?

The crimes under Reagan in Latin America were nearly beyond belief, which Anthony Lewis in the New York times exposed along with America Watch, etc, where Right-wing dictators just butchered and slaughtered hundreds of thousands, often poor peasants, with the full support of Reagan's regime and Margaret Thatcher's government in the UK. Lewis believed against all odds that the USA were supposed to be the good guys on the block, which for most of the time as an independent country, was far from the truth. Lewis quoted the Boston Globe 's assessment of this anti-guerrilla campaign as falling "somewhere between a pogrom and genocide". He noted the fact that Reagan's embrace of "torturers and murderers" extended beyond the leaders of Guatemala and El Salvador to include recent visits to Washington from the dictators of South Korea and the Philippines and an upcoming one from Muhammad Zia-ul Haq of Pakistan, who since taking power in 1977 "had eliminated the political opposition and resorted regularly to torture". Lewis ended with a poignant reminder that has rung true throughout all the decades of the American Empire: "The shame marks all of us. When the economic follies of the Reagan Administration have been forgotten, its insensitivity to human cruelty will stain the name of the United States" (30). Reagan even believed that the contras were equivalents of the founding fathers of the USA fighting the ghastly British Empire. This whole period in Latin America and elsewhere was that an extremely small elite of very rich landowners was trying to stop the majority having their fair share of the spoils, in the process killing so-called Leftists and even nuns, as well as tens of thousands of peasants. Vice president George H. W. Bush could not understand the rational of why nuns would get involved in Left-wing causes…perhaps he had not read the bible?

Ronald Reagan, like Margaret Thatcher in the UK could not see anything wrong with attacking the poor in whatever form or way they could, Reagan sacking the air traffic controllers when they went on strike and suffering several other strikes in his term of office and Thatcher destroying the working-class trade unions in the UK: both inhumane and cruel people. The defence budget went up 51% under Reagan while slashing domestic programs by 30%, effectively transferring 70 billion dollars from domestic programs to the military. In the UK Thatcher broke what was called the 'consensus', which had been in place since 1945, thus crashing the economy and driving the unemployment rate to over 4 million; only the Falkland's war and the gang of four (sic) saved her bacon in 1983. The theory behind this was that the 'commies' were coming and the rich were not having enough of their rightful spoils. Reagan cut the highest income tax rate from 70% to 28% and slashed federal spending for the majority who really needed it. The other rational behind the build-up of arms, was to bankrupt the USSR which would be hard pressed to keep up with this insanity. Reagan and Bush senior were so mad they even thought they could win a nuclear war, even if the USA lost 20 million souls. When the history books are written about this period in time, including what happened under Kennedy during the Cuban missile crises of 1962, I think they will record that the whole world was on the edge of an abyss of destruction. During the Reagan/Thatcher era, I was studying a Social Sciences programme in the West Midlands and one of my excellent lecturers was Philip K. Lawrence who wrote *Preparing for Armageddon: A critique of Western Strategy,* which I have been lucky enough to read, a work which just sums up this whole period of madness under Reagan and Thatcher. He also wrote several other books and went on to get degrees in other subjects apart from modern history. The other book I read of his was another critique of Modernity called *Modernity and War: The Creed of Absolute Violence.* Two books very unlikely to be understood by Thatcher, Reagan, or Trump - I would have thought?

However, this phenomenon would have been clearly understood by the amazing Mikhail Gorbachev who came to power in the USSR after Knostantin Chernenko died in 1985. A very well-educated man, Gorbachev had travelled widely and wanted no more than to try and improve the living standards of all his citizens, the complete opposite of Reagan and Thatcher.

The problem Gorbachev had was that too much of the total budget of the USSR was being spent on defence. It was very hard for him to find out the true data relating to these events. His first objective therefore was to stop the arms race and get his troops out of Afghanistan, albeit the crazy 'Star Wars' initiative of Reagan's war machine was getting in the way. Gorbachev wrote his first letter to Reagan on the 24th of March 1985, which Stone & Kuznick note, could have been written by Henry Wallace, the great vice president under FDR.

In his letter Gorbachev said: 'our countries are differentiated by their social systems, and by the ideologies in them. But we believe that this should not be a reason for animosity. Each social system has a right to life, and it should prove its advantage not by force, not by military means, but on the path of peaceful competition with the other system. And all people have the right to go the way they have chosen themselves, without anybody imposing his will on them from outside'. (31) He also wrote another letter in October of the same year, noting that we are all living on the same planet, and we must learn to live together. Gorbachev was also aware that the 'Star Wars initiative' would not protect the USA from the USSR weapons, but the hidden agenda may have been a first strike by the maniacs in America, against the USSR, and for that matter by Thatcher in the UK. Amazingly after calling the USSR the Evil Empire in 1983, Reagan met Gorbachev in Geneva, Switzerland, in November 1985 for talks about the possible reduction in nuclear weapons. Apparently, they got on well at a personal level but disagreed on many issues, one of which I presume was that the USSR now was not an 'evil empire', but that the USA had been for years….my take on it! What Gorbachev feared was that Reagan was just another mouthpiece for the military industrial complex, like he was when an actor promoting General Electric. Gorbachev was so far ahead of the field that he wanted to get rid of all nuclear weapons, testing and so on, before the end of the 20th century, from around the globe. The devastating nuclear accident at Chernobyl was a god send for anyone who wanted to do away with nuclear weapons, an incident which may have killed at-least 8000 people and affected hundreds of thousands of others. When Reagan and Gorbachev met in Iceland in October 1986, Reagan was caught off guard because what Reagan was prepared for was not what Gorbachev had brought to the table. As 'Gorbachev offered to cut strategic offensive arms in half, eliminate all US and Soviet IRBMs in Europe while allowing Britain and France to maintain their arsenals, freeze short-range missiles, stop nuclear testing, allow on-site inspections as the Americans demanded, and limit SDI testing to labs for the next ten years' (32). In the end nothing was achieved, albeit it was the nearest any one had been to eliminating nuclear weapons from the face of the earth. The Americans insisted on keeping the Star Wars fantasy on the table. Gorbachev was also aware that he was dealing with a person in Reagan who had very limited education and was surrounded by right-wing advisors who had their own agendas. First, they believed the USSR was so desperate to have a deal that they would agree to anything; secondly, they were hoping that this agreement would also hurt the USSR on the world stage and finally that Star Wars would allow the USA military superiority. After the Iran/Contra scandal hit the fan, it was basically all downhill for Reagan in his second term, during which he ran up the national debt to record levels and left office more confused than when he entered it. Margaret Thatcher even dedicated one of her three autobiographical books to Reagan, and Gorbachev became her second Platonic lover. Gorbachev at the end of the Reagan era even noted that the cold war was over and gave one of the greatest hour-long speeches ever given at the UN, about winding down the need for arms in Europe, getting out of Afghanistan and so on. He was a voracious reader of everything, including Western literature, by people like Francois Mitterrand and notably Willy Brandt, who was one of the most important post war leaders in Europe, and who was given a Nobel Prize for peace in 1971, for helping to heal the rifts between the West and the old USSR and its satellite States in Europe. I presume that Gorbachev was using Willie Brandt as a role model of how he could do the same thing with his life. While at the Wolverhampton Polytechnic in the mid-nineteen eighties as a mature student, I actually read the Brandt report, and was very impressed with it. Gorbachev may have also read it. The report written by the Independent Commission first chaired by Willy Brandt, wanted to rectify the uneven development between the rich North and the poor Southern Hemisphere. Mrs Thatcher did not agree with whole project, (socialist tripe, I presume)! After the end of the cold war, with the disintegration of the old USSR, the fall of the Berlin Wall etc, Thatcher and Reagan tried to claim victory through their actions - but as two of the biggest warmongers in History, who nearly blew up the Planet, most intelligent people now suggest that it was Gorbachev who really ended the cold war, albeit a terrible cost to Russia. Now the West is again whipping up hatred of Russia and China, for not being a so-called liberal democracy and a member of the 'rule-based order' (whatever that means) and which RT (Russia Today) in the UK were satirising (Early May 2021) on TV, and from what I have observed were completely 'on point' about the madness and complete insanity of this rhetoric.

Sadly, as of March 2022, RT has been taken off air in Europe, presumably for not sharing the Western narrative over the crisis in Ukraine……which it seems is really about 'rare earth resources' like Lithium and very little else?

While Gorbachev was in New York he met Reagan and Bush senior who had just been elected after Reagan, at the end of 1988, for one term only. All the available evidence collected so far suggests that the CIA and other agencies of the USA were just not aware of the dramatic events that would happen after 1988 effecting Europe and Russia. This was mainly due to Gates, Cheney and others with extreme right-wing views, albeit Gorbachev at the time was suggesting the elimination of tactical nuclear weapons out from Europe, a stance most Europeans agreed with, (including me after just graduating with a social science degree in June 1988). The United States, in reply, said the USSR should pull 350,000 troops out of Europe and that they would withdraw 30,000. Bush senior neglected the Soviet Union and concentrated on China instead where he had been the de facto Ambassador to China in the 1970s. While there, apparently, he had decided that the USA should not be too pushy, muscular but not domineering, to ensure stability. What went wrong here I wonder? This whole process of leaning towards China nearly came unstuck for Bush when Beijing cracked down on the demonstrations in Tiananmen Square.

Ironically, when running for president, some said that George H. Bush was a bit of a wimp, and that he was lucky to be alive. During the Second World War in an attack on a Japanese installation at Chichijima in 1944 he was shot down by enemy fire and lost his two crew members. He was rescued but some members of other crews were not so lucky and were killed by the Japanese when captured, allegedly having their livers eaten by Japanese soldiers on the same mission.

Gorbachev urged Eastern European governments to embrace the spirit of 'perestroika', meaning in Russian restructuring, along with 'glasnost' meaning increased openness and transparency. After the Berlin Wall had fallen, foreign policy advisor Anatoly Chernyaev's view on what was happening was recorded in his diary as 'this is the end of Yalta (and) the Stalinist legacy.... this is what Gorbachev has done'. Francis Fukuyama, working for the Rand Corporation in the USA, even had the cheek to write a book called *The End of History and the Last Man,* which was probably the biggest load of tosh ever written by an academic. I read it when it was first published in paperback edition. It basically noted that liberal capitalist democracy and capitalism, within very narrow parameters, were here to stay into perpetuity. For helping to facilitate the 'end of history', Fukuyama was promoted to professorships at George Mason, John Hopkins and Stanford universities. Gorbachev was hoping that this was not the 'end of History' but the end of NATO and the cold war and that NATO would not push its border all the way up to the Russian front as did Hitler before the invasion of the USSR in 1941. The verbal agreement Gorbachev was given on this proposition did not last long and over the next few years NATO did expand to the Russian border, which the new state of Russia, as an independent country, was and still is very concerned about. And so they should be, having been invaded twice in the 20th century by first the USA and the British et al after the 1917 overthrow of the old regime, and again by under Hitler's Third Reich in World War 2. Of course, previous to this was the invasion by Napoleon in the 19th century.

'Global Britain' is now flexing its muscles in the Black Sea near Crimea (or recruiting fruit pickers…see my letter in the Sunday Times - 19th September 2021) as I progress on with this project (June 2021) which is nearly beyond belief, but true. I presume this was engineered by the Right-wing faction in the Tory party and the nationalistic Boris Johnson, now thrown out of Number Ten at long last. On Channel 4 news in the UK Cathy Newman noted that the 'temporary replacement' Prime Minister Liz Truss was nothing more than Boris Johnson in trousers, so very concerning to all of us and the safety of the whole world!

Other problems that arose under George Bush senior's role as the president was a little trouble down in Panama where the good guy Manuel Noriega became a bad guy and drug baron, so had to be overthrown with 12,000 USA troops. This exercise was called 'Operation Just Cause'. This probably killed thousands to capture one man! In essence State terrorism, but when the West does something like this it is classified as something else. Saddam Hussein invaded Kuwait, probably with the acquiescence of April Glaspie (the ambassador to Kuwait, at the time). She said 'we have no problems with boarder disputes. This was because the USA wanted a better and deeper relationship with Iraq. But after it happened, Saddam Hussein became the bad guy with allegedly doctored photos showing that Saudi Arabia would be his next target, misinformation of the highest order. Under pressure from some in Israel, Bush senior started to call Saddam another Hitler, and a threat to the world. This is the norm now, whenever a perceived threat to the West occurs. but at least some understood that sanctions could solve the problem and an invasion would cause chaos in the region. It did, after the invasion by George W. Bush and Tony Blair in 2003. Chaos ensued because of the complexities that were created by the British and French after the breakup of the Ottoman Empire, at the beginning of the 20th century. Ironically, Kuwait hired Hill & Knowlton, the largest public relations firm in the world, to sell the up-and-coming war with Iraq, telling porkies and manipulating public opinion, especially in the USA for this course of action. On the 29th January the UN Security Council needed authorisation to get the Iraqi troops out of Kuwait. They did this with bribery and corruption by writing off massive debts owed by Egypt and other Gulf States and 2 billion dollars given to Syria and so on. The opposite treatment happened to Yemen for voting against the resolution, by cutting 70 million dollars of aid. Saudi Arabia also expelled 800,000 of its Yemeni workers. Cuba also voted against the 'all necessary means' resolution. Cuba had been enemy **Number One** against the USA, since January 1959. Yemen today (May 2021) is again in deep trouble, with the worst humanitarian crisis for many years, with as many as 14 million people practically starving. The problem Bush senior had was that this conflict was not popular with most Americans or Europe and Japan, who relied a lot more on the Gulf for their oil. The USA and the despotic rulers of Kuwait were hardly the paragons of democracy. The next tactic was to pretend that within the next few months Saddam Hussein may have some sort of nuclear device, albeit Scowcroft, Cheney and others had apparently forgotten which country had dropped two nuclear devices in 1945 and threatened several other countries since with weapons of mass destruction. Operation Desert Shield at its height, between 2nd August 1990 – 17th January 1991, had 700,000 troops to get the Iraqis out of Kuwait and reinstate their Royal family. Saddam Hussein stayed in power until he was overthrown in 2003 and finally hanged in 2006, for crimes against humanity. The Shias who are the majority sect/tribe in Iraq were not helped by Hussein whereas the Sunnis (roughly 35% of the population) were the Islamic group that Saddam Hussein belonged to. The USA was afraid that Hussein would make an agreement with Kuwait before the Americans could take physical action against Iraq, but this never happened. However, it is worth quoting Stone & Kuznick's take on these events of what happened at the time, in full. 'The United States pummelled Iraqi facilities for five weeks with its new high-tech weapons, including cruise and Tomahawk missiles and laser-guided bombs. After having crippled Iraq's communications and military infrastructure, U.S. and Saudi forces attacked battered, demoralized, and outnumbered Iraqi troops in Kuwait, who put up little if any resistance. U.S. forces slaughtered escaping Iraqis along what became known as the "highway of death". They deployed a new category of weapons made from depleted uranium, whose radioactivity and chemical toxicity would produce cancers and birth defects for years. Victims may have included U.S. soldiers, who suffered from what became known as Gulf War Syndrome. But enough of the Republican Guard escaped the slaughter to ensure that Saddam would retain his hold on power' (33). An 'Evil Act' can be a 'crime against humanity' whoever is committing it, as far as I am concerned and so it is for most decent people in the world, I would have thought? These crimes were committed against an independent Nation State with the prime objective of driving Iraq back into the stone age, and getting rid of the terrible Vietnam disgrace once and for all and creating a 'New world Order'. The sanctions already in place for over ten years or more may have killed half a million children….to the Americans this was just collateral damage. Even with the Cold War dead after 1991, the Hawks in the 'Military Industrial Complex' over time had to invent new bogeymen to kill.

The old Soviet Union and other parts of Eastern Europe, as I have noted in other parts of this project, took a nosedive into destitution for tens of millions of people with the help of Boris Yeltsin and academics from the USA and elsewhere. At home Clinton tried to reform the health service but the republicans spent 50 million dollars on frightening the public into thinking that it was a crazy idea, albeit the great Michael Moore (documentary maker) praised the NHS in the UK. Clinton went on to have an affair with an intern. He denied this originally but in his second term was impeached for perjury but acquitted of all charges by the Senate. In his second term the federal budget was in surplus for the first time since the 1960s.

Meanwhile, with the breakup of the old Yugoslavia, formed after the First World War and suffering massive crimes under the Nazis, civil wars broke out between different ethnic groups. Under Clinton and Blair, NATO bombed Yugoslavian military infrastructure from high altitudes, without permission from the UN Security Council as China and Russia opposed such action, but it was supported by NATO. The air strikes lasted from the 24th of March 1999 to the 10th of June 1999 until an agreement was reached that led to the withdrawal of Yugoslavia armed forces from Kosovo. This apparently was a 'humanitarian' intervention to stop Serbian repression in Kosovo according to Tony Blair. It could be said Blair only wanted to be another pop star like Mick Jagger, given his penchant for mixing with them.

Certainly, the late George Michael made some very acerbic comments on his meeting with the then PM. Blair carried on with the Thatcherite economic agenda, something very similar to that of Bill Clinton in the USA, albeit Gordon Brown in the UK had to mitigate against the outcomes of Mrs Thatcher's shocking crimes, or millions could have died of starvation, in a so-called first world country?

The problems in the Balkans stemmed from the second half of the 19th century when the five great powers were hovering over what they saw as a future breakup of the Ottoman Empire, the rise of Nationalism in the region and competing religious beliefs. For example, in the Second World War Croatia ended up as a puppet State of Nazi Germany and fascist Italy where terrible crimes were committed. During my back-packing trip to the Far East in 2006/2007, researching my somewhat 'over the top' travel book, in India, which was my first port of call - I actually met Riza Haziri from Croatia on a sleeper Train from Mumbai to New Delhi. He had been a football coach in Melbourne. We got on like a house on fire over the few days I was with him. He was shocked by the poverty in India, but informed me that a sister and his father had been killed in the breakup of the old Yugoslavia. I was lucky enough to visit Croatia a few years later; unfortunately, I did not know where Riza lived, so did not meet him again – but I enjoyed the place and its very friendly people immensely.

One of the many strange paradoxes about modernity in its capitalistic form is that no one seems to be concerned about the possible consequences of State or Human agency on future events, as long as a few are making loads of money and the perceived enemy is being destroyed. For example, in Afghanistan when the old USSR had troops there, for nine years the West, with the help of Saudi Arabia et al, financed a guerrilla war with billions of dollars against the USSR. The fighters became known as the Mujahideen, basically insurgent groups fighting the ghastly Russian troops. Albeit a contributor on a Radio 4 BBC programme (7th August 2021) called Any Answers asserted that the Russians were trying to bring Afghanistan into the 20th century, which we can only presume was against USA and others wishes? Will Podmore in the Morning Star (6th September 2021) gives us a far more objective reflection on this time in Afghanistan. He notes it was the Afghan Government/people of 1978 who were trying to drag Afghanistan into the 20th Century, (before the old Soviet Union got involved in December 1979) by promoting a mass literacy programme, introducing free medical care, freeing 13,000 political prisoners, having mixed schools etc and by the late 1980s, half of all University students were women, half of all doctors were women and most teachers were women. He also notes that President Carter got involved in arming the Mujahideen six months before the Soviets got involved in the country…and as I note above this was against USA orthodoxy. I should just note (add) a little form of sanity into this debate from none-other than Rehmad, who helps run a small take away south of Nottingham with other Afghans and belongs to the ethnic Pashtun group, who had lived in the UK for 14 years. He informed me on the 2nd October 2022 (evening) that the old Soviet Union did more for Afghanistan in about seven years of rule than USA et al ever did in twenty years of occupation? I highly recommend to history buffs that for one of the best documentaries to watch about Afghanistan was shown on PBS America in May 2023, in the UK called *Afghanistan – The Wounded Land,* which did try to be objective, I think, to explain the complexities of a very old tribal societies and the emerging ideas of the 20th century which clashed with the old especially in the 1960s, which is very rarely mentioned by journalists in the Western world! Or for that matter, how the Western world were backing the Mujahideen in Afghanistan but in Iran the new Islamic state in Iran after 1979 became the enemy of the Western world?

Once the Soviet Union decided to pull out of Afghanistan, the West lost interest in the place, albeit millions lost their lives and millions of refugees were the outcome of this whole sorry saga. The bloody civil war that followed these events between various Islamist factions, one of which it seemed consisted largely of Afghan refugees recruited from Madrassas – Saudi-sponsored religious schools in Pakistan. Ironically even the University of Nebraska, funded by USAID got involved in printing propaganda books, which were designed to whip up hatred of the Soviet Union when they were published in Pashtu and Dari languages (two of largest ethnic groups in Afghanistan). The Talibs (students) formed the Taliban and seemed to have been the main source of this propaganda and in 1996 they seized Kabul and continued using the same violent Jihadist texts. Girls were banned from school completely, so were not aware of such horrendous propaganda. The same year the Taliban took Kabul, Osama bin Laden was welcomed back to Afghanistan. He returned as head of Al-Qaeda (the base). His father was one of the richest men in Saudi Arabia and his primary objective for some time had been to get rid of the USA forces from all Islamic lands. In theory his group/faction was responsible for bombings in the Middle East at this time, killing American servicemen and others. Whether this was true or not is open to conjecture, albeit in January 1996 the CIA opened an office called the Counter-Terrorist Centre for the sole purpose of eliminating Osama bin Laden. However, the rulers of Saudi Arabia blamed the Saudi Shiites tied to Iran for the above-mentioned bombings. The paradox to this story was that Unocal thought that the Taliban faction were maybe the good guys as they could stabilize a war-torn country. Unocal, an oil company from California whose genesis goes back to the 19th century, wanted to build an oil pipeline infrastructure called the Trans-Afghanistan pipeline from Turkmenistan to Pakistan with the help of the Taliban and set up an office just across the road from Osama bin Laden in Kandahar. It was not until two years after the bombing of two U. S embassies, in Nairobi in Kenya, and Dar es Salaam in Tanzania, killing more than 200 people (the USS Cole also being attacked in a suicide mission), that Bill Clinton ordered Osama bin Laden to be killed at his base camp in Afghanistan. Bob Woodward disputed this in his book on George W. Bush. After these terrorist attacks Unocal pulled out of the pipeline deal but others were interested in exploiting the Caspian region. Gore Vidal said that the invasion of Afghanistan had nothing to do with Bin Laden but making it safe for Unocal/Union oil processes and USA big business. Hamed Karzai was the first president following USA intervention and was a CIA confidant who had previously worked for Unocal.

President Clinton had squandered the so-called peace dividend and had spent billions more on defence, out-doing the republicans on this issue at the time. Whatever one president spends on defence is never enough according to their opposition, a constant theme that virtually runs throughout the last hundred years of USA foreign policy. The Project for the New American Century (PNAC), made up of neo-cons, were harking back to Henry Luce's (a powerful right-wing publisher) vision of unchallenged USA hegemony, presumably in perpetuity, something the Roman Empire was very keen on too. In fact, as I note in this project, Roman aims were very similar to those of the USA. Since the end of the Second World War America has emerged as the most powerful nation in the world. 'Nothing must challenge our power and let us get ready for the next invasion or conflict with whoever' seems to be their mantra. According to PNAC, Saddam Hussein was to become the next 'bogeyman' whose country was to be destroyed by sanctions. There was an on-going search for weapons of mass destruction, resulting in the deaths of at least half a million children in Iraq. This did not seem to bother Clinton/Albright or Tony Blair. Blair, a so-called Christian, along with George W. Bush, became in the eyes of some akin to war criminals when they invaded Iraq in 2003. George W. Bush had become president in 2000, beating Al Gore by only a few hundred votes in Florida. Dick Cheney became Bush junior's vice president and sage who directed most of his actions, especially on foreign policy and had also been George H. W. Bush's secretary of defence. Stone & Kuznick note that the 2000 election was one of the most scandalous in USA history. George W. Bush went to war with John McCain in the primaries, saying for example, that his wife Cindy was a drug addict and that McCain had fathered an illegitimate black daughter.

The Supreme Court came to the rescue of George W. Bush when they voted 5-4 to stop a re-count in Florida (where Jeb Bush, the younger brother of George, was the Governor, and Katherine Harris certified the results). Many intelligent people and authors have said over the years since this scandal, that Al Gore was robbed of the presidency. If he had become the president, we cannot be sure that the 9/11 outrage would not have happened in New York in 2001, but he may have handled it with a lot more decorum than Bush junior did (See also below)? According to Molly Ivins & Lou Dubose, Bush was an extremely dodgy businessman and politically to the **right** of Ronald Reagan and Margaret Thatcher on economic affairs. The great Bob Woodward's take on *Bush at War* makes the Bush administration seem very much like Boris Johnson's chaotic government in the UK (after 2019), without any form or structure. In essence no one was sure what to do about the 9/11 outrage when 15 out of the 19 hijackers were from Saudi Arabia, albeit Osama Bin Laden had become the latest bogeyman to be attacked. Bin Laden was in theory in Afghanistan at the time. Condoleezza Rice even admitted at one point in their preparations for war against Afghanistan, that they did not have a plan for what happened if the Taliban was defeated. The problem Bush had was that Colin Powell, the wise old

General and excellent diplomat who got the President of Pakistan on side, was cautious, while the wild men like Rumsfeld and Cheney were gung-ho warmongers and the last thing the George W. Bush administration wanted was another type of Vietnam war. In the end the Northern Alliance, which Musharraf (president of Pakistan) called a bunch of tribal thugs and others, were paid 70 million dollars to help defeat the Taliban in 102 days, following the terrorist attacks in the United States. Amazingly this initial foray was called 'Enduring Freedom'. If it was not for Bradley Manning and Julian Assange and his big idea called Wikileaks, we would not know some of the true crimes that the USA, British et al were up to in Afghanistan and Iraq. Basically no one would have known about the notorious Task Force 373, a shadowy troop of US killers, who were responsible for killing children (perhaps by accident) and targeted Taliban commanders. Leigh & Harding noted: 'these events, and hundreds like them, together constitute the hidden history of the war in Afghanistan, in which innocent people were repeatedly killed by foreign soldiers. The remarkable level of detail provided by the war logs made this information available for the first time' p, 124. (Logs sic). Amazingly even the BBC (12th July 2022) has now got in on the act and produced a truly remarkable documentary about how the Australian and the British SAS were involved in killing innocent Afghans, calling them 'death squads' in the Helmand province of Afghanistan.

Twenty years later the USA were still in Afghanistan and talking of withdrawing their troops for good by September 2021 (which they did), and talking to the Taliban of what should come next; how ironic indeed! Apparently, the Americans have spent **ONE TRILLION dollars** on their war according to Joe Biden, but it could be maybe double this amount? Thousands of USA servicemen have lost their lives; 457 Brits and perhaps 240,000 Afghan people (including 70,000 civilians) have also lost their lives, over the twenty-year period…. a form of madness beyond comprehension!

The leaving process itself turned into a nightmare, something very similar to the exit from Vietnam in 1975. The exit in Afghanistan was nightmarish, with a few people hanging on to a C17 transport aircraft and falling to their death at the airport in Kabul as people scrambled to escape. The country was left in the hands of the Taliban with no resources to run the place and now living in one of the most desperate economic situations in the world.

Noam Chomsky was interviewed by many people after the 9/11 attack on the World Trade Centre in New York and put into a small book form a scathing account about how the Mujahideen (freedom fighters against the USSR in the 1980s) was financed mostly by Saudi Arabia. He asserted how the Taliban are in fact an offshoot of the Saudi version of Islam (albeit the ideology goes back to the 19th century, in response to the British Empire's barbaric behaviour in India) and noted, just before the West attacked Afghanistan, how millions were starving in the country. It should not pass notice that Charlie Wilson, a senator from Texas, pressed congress to help fund the Mujahideen as well – this process being made into a brilliant movie starring Tom Hanks.

The ironic fact about Osama bin Laden was that when he was in Sudan, their government had a vast intelligence database on him, and also on two hundred members of Al-Qaeda whom they wanted to hand over to the American government. The FBI wanted them extradited to the USA but the State Department refused because of their hatred of the Sudanese, 'the worst single intelligence failure in this whole terrible business' (Chomsky 9 - 11). This quote from Chomsky just about sums up this whole shocking debacle which was hardly mentioned in the mass media over the last 20-year period. Certainly no one from any of the government agencies wants Jo Public to know how incompetent they were, and nearly 3000 people died in the twin towers because of this underlying fiasco. Also, the many conspiracy theories do not help us to get to the root cause of why it was not picked up by NSA et al in the first place. Albeit *The Good American*, (documentary by Friedrich Moser 2015) certainly tries to explain what went wrong, by talking to William Binney and several others about their time at NSA, over a 40-year period. Binney, a mathematical genius, basically designed systems that predicted future events. 'Thin Thread' was the tool that Binney and others invented that encompassed the whole world, based very much on a model of the globe and the Universe, picking up patterns of connected 'nodes' out of the billions/trillions of transactions taking place everywhere. So, for example when Boris Johnson was having an affair with Jennifer Arcuri, he may have made many calls to her to get her into bed (which he did apparently when married to Marina Wheeler), but because no one needed to know the seedier side of this story we only know about it now because she sold her story to the Daily Mirror for £70,000. Apparently, NSA also got hold of Bin Laden's cell phone, for at least two years, after he first came to the attention of the USA in 1993. The Foreign Intelligence Surveillance Act was adapted to try and prevent all individuals, at least in the USA, from being spied on; we can only presume that before and after Edward Snowden's bombshell exposure this idea was dropped? With all good documentaries, like Friedrich Moser's, there are good people like Binney and bad ones like Maureen Baginski, General Hayden, and Sam Visner et al. According to this masterpiece it seems that it was General Hayden who set up 'Trail Blazer' and closed down 'Thin Thread', three weeks before 9/11. If this had not happened then more than likely 9/11 may never have happened? In a nutshell, 'Thin Thread' was an in-house State set-up and 'Trail Blazer' was about outsourcing and making money for people like Sam Visner and Baginski, Signals Intelligence Director at the time.

Dominic Lawson in the Sunday Times (22 August 2021) puts a strange twist on the 9/11 events, which may or may not be true? When I first heard this story on BBC Radio 4, 20 years ago, I thought I was dreaming; apparently, in extreme Islam, if you kill infidels like the 19 young men who attacked the twin towers did, you will end up in paradise where '72 virgins' will be waiting for you. Lawson noted that most of these young men were probably virgins themselves so could not wait to get to heaven. Part of this underlying problem, according to Lawson, is that for example in Saudi Arabia, half a million men there have more than ONE wife - hence cutting down the available young women for the rest of the population, raising the levels of sexual frustration in society. I would like to remind the reader, that this is Dominic Lawson's take on these events!

The coordination problem Bush junior had was that there were so many different agencies of State, with their own agendas and access to the president in different order of status; so very different to the Roman Generals in Gaul and elsewhere, of 2000 years ago, who were sure of their objectives from day ONE. 'Crush the bastards before they crush you and enlarge our empire' seems to have been their raison d'etre. Although I don't think the Roman Generals had a rendition programme, thought up by the CIA, to snatch so-called terrorists from all around the globe and torture them, with hundreds ending up being incarcerated in Guantanamo Bay on the east coast of Cuba. This happened to Mohamedou Ould Slahi who was from West Africa and was only released after 16 years, probably because he wrote a book about this huge stain on USA society with the help of an amazing lawyer.

What I found so amusing after reading Bob Woodward's book and other stuff about this period in history was that after the fall of the old Soviet Union and then Vladimir Putin's rise to power, George W Bush was on first term names with Putin; also, Russia was helping the USA with the preparations for war against Afghanistan, as was Iran for a short period during which they became the good guys as well as the Russians. Now, Joseph R. Biden (46th president of the USA) is calling Putin a 'killer', while under the George W Bush presidency, Iran, Iraq and North Korea became the 'Axis of Evil'. Bush was decrying North Korea for starving its people while ignoring tens of millions of Americans in the same boat, just as in the UK now and under past cruel and brutal Tory governments. In the UK now maybe as many as '8 million' people are going hungry according to the Morning Star on the 8th June 2021. George W Bush gave a huge tax cut to his rich friends/class and brought in the Patriot Act. When I first read about this in the British Guardian, I could not believe that the brutal Orwellian nature of the beast could happen in the 21st century as confirmed by Edward Snowden, and has grown into an out-of-control monster.

You would have thought that the USA should have learned lessons from British history about Afghanistan, as we first marched into the country in 1838 with 20,000 troops made up of British and Indian brigades and were involved with the place on and off for over 80 years, opposing the rise of Russian influence called the great game in the 19th century. Alexander the Great also invaded the place over two and half thousand years ago. I presume the arrogant British thought they were just repeating Alexander's efforts in the region? The truly amazing American movie called the *Outpost* and starring Scott Eastwood, Orlando Bloom et al playing real war heroes, was about a small group of American soldiers fighting in an exposed valley between mountains in Afghanistan and really showed not only their bravery in an impossible situation but, according to the script, at least some of the young men were aware of these events I have described. Many were highly decorated in this fight with the Taliban but it is very unlikely that George W Bush or Tony Blair would ever allow themselves into such a situation? As in all wars, in recent times; Politicians send troops to war but don't get involved in the fighting, whatsoever.
.

What comes next in this story is nearly beyond belief, because at least a few in the Bush junior administration understood another war with Iraq would open a Pandora's box in the Middle East, which it did and in theory the West had no mandate to carry one out. The dispute started much earlier than March 2003, when Saddam Hussein would not allow weapon inspectors back into the country. Bill Clinton ordered Operation Desert Fox with 650 bomber and missile sorties over a three-day period......still refusing to let in the weapon inspectors. The 'war on terror' and weapons of mass destruction theory was the big idea that prompted George W Bush and his warmongers around him to go into Iraq. Albeit George W had told Bob Woodward at his ranch in Crawford Texas, he wanted 'to achieve world peace'. *Perpetual war for perpetual peace* by the great Gore Vidal (which I read in Australia in 2014 and must be re-read) seems to ring true here. Vidal was one of the most important American intellectuals of the 20th century and probably of all time. One of the first actions that Bush did to remove Hussein was to give the CIA nearly 200 million dollars in covert money to help the opposition forces in Iraq, just as he did in Afghanistan, with USA help if needed. As late as August 2002 Brent Scowcroft was warning on TV that an attack on Iraq could turn the Middle East into a cauldron and thus destroy the 'war on terror', and he had been George H W Bush's national security advisor during the first Gulf War. Colin Powell, the day after Scowcroft had appeared on a Sunday morning talk show, was also warning Bush junior of the possible consequence of going to war in Iraq, basically both singing from the same hymn sheet. According to George W Bush, Saddam Hussein was starving at least some Shiite people; considering the Hussein tribe were from the minority Sunni group, this may have been true. In addition, sanctions from the West would not have helped this problem along. However, there was very little evidence, if any, that Saddam Hussein had an operational relationship with Al-Qaeda. This story line was Western propaganda made up to justify the invasion of Iraq and steal its oil and overthrow Saddam Hussein. In George W Bush's speech to the UN on the 12th of September 2002 Bush suggested that he would work with the

UN, and Powell stayed behind in New York to work on Nations that might not go along with future actions of the USA (like Russia and France) who had vetoes in the United Nations assembly. The next day Saddam Hussein said he would let the weapon inspectors back into Iraq, after four years absence. According to Bob Woodward's take on these events of the time, Bush et al were afraid of another strike on the USA, which was possible, albeit a lot of their direct problems arose from having helped the Mujahedeen in Afghanistan when the Russians were there, as well as from their support for ruthless Sheiks in the Middle East. This is a fine example of what is called a blowback phenomenon. George W. Bush's idea that the Americans may have to have a pre-emptive strategy, whatever happened at the United Nations, was also very concerning. Congress voted to grant the president full authority to attack Iraq unilaterally in October, on the 10th and 11th 2002. On November 8th, the UN voted 15 to 0 on resolution 1441 for Saddam Hussein to give up all weapons of mass destruction. Hans Blix and his team of weapon inspectors arrived in Bagdad on the 27th of November 2002 and went to work. The conclusions steered a middle ground, although Iraq submitted a 12,000-word dossier to the United Nations saying they had no weapons of mass destruction whatsoever. This being true, Bush et al were creating their own reality based on Alice in Wonderland stuff and lies by Ahmed Chalabi, an Iraqi in exile. Chalabi was feeding the lie that Saddam Hussein had weapons of mass destruction and possible access to nuclear weapons to Cheney, Rumsfeld, Rice and the neo-cons. This lie was repeated by Colin Powell at the United Nations on the 5th of February 2003. The same stuff was also being fed to the New York Times and other news agencies, all repeating the same theme. However, before this event a gallant whistle blower called Katherine Gunn working at the GCHQ spy agency in Cheltenham UK, had leaked a memo to the Sunday Observer via Yvonne Ridley and a friend from the United States. The said memo requested that the UK help the USA to get dirt on several diplomats to blackmail them into voting at the UN for war in Iraq. Marcia & Thomas Mitchell wrote a brilliant book about this story called *The Spy who Tried to Stop a War* which was turned into a movie called *Official Secrets* starting Keira Knightley as Gunn. In the movie based on the book, Gunn kept saying that Tony Blair et al were lying and 'intelligence was being manipulated to go to war'. Martin Bright and Ed Vulliamy (from the Observer who supported her in court) along with Gunn and Liberty, were the real heroes of this amazing true story. The British State prosecuted her, but at her trial the prosecution dropped all the charges against her…. because Lord Goldsmith, the Attorney General, had changed his mind about it being legal to go to war, when it was not. While Gunn was doing study work for the truth and millions of people were protesting on the streets of the world against the war, another little-known organisation called the Knight Ridder, was also searching for the truth about these events led by John Walcott in the Washington Bureau with another two brilliant journalists called Warren Strobel and Jonathan Landay.

These two journalists compared themselves to Woodward and Bernstein and in the film *Shock and Awe* were played by James Marsden and Woody Harrelson. The film also starred Rob Riener as Walcott. Riener also directed the movie with the help of Joe Galloway, but the American Establishment was not happy that the truth was being told. Its chronological logic is very similar to what *Official Secrets* did in that these two brilliant journalists would not give in to the lies and propaganda that was being published by other agencies, with many clips of Bush, Rice, Rumsfeld et al telling lies on live TV and whipping up crude crass nationalism. The two journalists, from Knight Ridder interviewed many sources along with Joe Galloway (war correspondent played in the movie by Tommy Lee Jones, another great American actor) which just confirmed what they already knew - that this whole operation was a put-up job and nothing else. Albeit their stories were not always printed because the agency itself was not the New York

Times etc... so it was up to independent editors around the country as to what was published. France and Russia announced they would veto any second resolution, thereby assuring its defeat in the United Nations. The war called Shock & Awe by some was one of the biggest mistakes ever made by the USA and the coalition of the willing. The New York Times apologised for going along with the American Establishment and the journalists at Knight Ridder were proven correct. Dick Cheney seems to have been the main driving force behind the war in Iraq, and the power behind Bush junior's world view, who had made a fortune from being the CEO of Halliburton and an insider in the Washington cabal for decades. The chaos that a few were warning about in 2002 came true in Iraq. Saddam Hussein was captured and hung, at least a million people were killed in the chaos, the rise of ISIS happened, and 3000 USA troops are still there at the time of writing, with a few hundred in Syria. Ironically, according to Ivins Dubose about 6000 people are killed in the USA at work every year. This is twice as many as died in '9/11' and 165 people die of occupational diseases every day. However, the American government pays very little attention to this fact (34).

President Obama, basically a highly intelligent lawyer and decent human being, was given a poison chalice when taking office on foreign policy (Like many before him). For example, issues such as his vice president Joe Biden (now the president) sadly voting for the war on Iraq in 2003. Afghanistan was still up and running, so all he could do was go along with the military advisers, like Johnson and Nixon in the days of Vietnam. Obama wanted his troops to protect the civilian population instead of killing large numbers of militants and to get rid of the terrible corruption in the country. He also said he would close Guantanamo Bay but never did. He ended up killing dozens of so-called terrorists with drones and many others? If the Washington Post is correct 'between 1,350 and 2250' (quoted by Stone &

Kuznick p, 572) people, mostly innocent civilians, were killed by drones mostly inside Pakistan within the first three years of Obama's presidency?

On the 2nd May 2011, after a ten-year hunt, Osama bin Laden (in theory the head of Al-Qaeda without phone lines on his property) was ostensibly hunted down and killed in Pakistan by the US Navy Seals. Apparently at an award ceremony for this event, film producer Mark Boal, who wrote *Zero Dark Thirty,* was in the audience, unbeknown to the military? This was an excellent movie based on true events, or at least partly, showing the terrible torture carried out on so-called terrorists from all around the world in order to achieve the objective of killing bin Laden. The main thrust of the movie is about a CIA female agent called Maya but based on a real person of very high status in the organisation who became obsessed with hunting down bin Laden. The methods of torture employed by the CIA had very little relevance to his eventual capture.

The Arab spring uprising in the early 2010s caught the Western World off-guard, starting in Tunisia and spreading across the whole middle east, in response to corruption and economic stagnation. Considering that most of the corrupt ruling elites in North Africa was propped up by the Western world, Obama et al were caught in a dilemma of their own making. In one of the most important documentaries ever made about these problems, called *Killing Gaddafi* directed by Jacques Charmelot (and now on Amazon Prime). In this documentary he notes in essence an occurring theme of Western zeitgeist, which is one minute a leader/dictator can be a bad guy, then good guy, and then a bad guy again, like Gaddafi. In fact, you could not make it up what happened to this Arab leader who overthrew King Idris in a coup d'etat on the 1st of September 1969 and transformed the whole country to a better standard of living with health and education free, by gaining control of the oil and gas reserves. This was like a red rag to a bull to the Western elites who turned Gaddafi into a bad guy/terrorist. The blowing up of Pan Am 103 in December 1988 over Lockerbie with the deaths of 270 people, which including 11 local residents, was blamed on Gaddafi. Albeit, I don't think even to this day that anyone knows for sure who the culprits were? In 2003 Gaddafi accepted Libya's responsibility for the Lockerbie bombing and paid compensation to the families of the victims, (but said he never gave the orders to blow it up) to get UN sanctions against Libya lifted. This led to Tony Blair et al making Gadhafi into a good guy, but only a few years later in the Arab uprising/spring event he became a 'genocidal dictator' who declared war on his own people? This was done mostly by 'propaganda and lies' about the Gaddafi regime, according to this brilliant documentary. However, according to Denis Kucinich an ex-mayor of Cleveland and a Representative from Ohio from 1997-2013 NATO basically committed 'war crimes' against Ghaddafi regime to overthrow him?

When I first read *Rogue State* by William Blum (in Australia in Perth - 2014) I was so shocked to the core, especially after reading the last chapter, that I was shaking drinking a cup of coffee outside the State library for at-least an hour. When I first read *Turning the Tide* by Noam Chomsky in about 1987/88, I was also shocked by the frank details in the book about USA atrocities, often by proxies, in Latin America (it nearly made me physically sick), all read within a 24-hour period…. but Blum's version of events against USA citizens and immigrants, just shook me up completely, especially the evictions and arrests revealed in the last chapter of the book. I now have the paperback 2014 edition and have read it several times since the first time in Australia and half of Noam Chomsky's books. The list of events he gives is far too long for me to document in this book; however, the themes are basically that nothing is beyond the bounds of government agencies to do whatever they want against their own citizens. The war on drugs probably being the most stupid action of the State - where at-least half all prisoners now in prison are only there because of some minor drug offence; Chomsky in fact once noted years ago that this was more about social control of black and poor people than selling drugs per se - planting evidence, raiding property for no specific reason, sending in SWAT teams to terrorize people, stop and search on a massive scale and so on.

Why I am giving you this information is the sad case again of a black man being killed by police in Minnesota on the 25th of May 2020, which is nothing new in the annals of American history going back hundreds of years, with riots ensuing this event all over the USA. This time it was a man called George Floyd, a lovely kind black man, (so it seems) who was 46 years old with a 6-year-old daughter. He was killed by Derek Chauvin, a white policeman, who held him down with his knee on his neck for nearly nine minutes until he stopped breathing. Three other policemen were looking on. The Morning Star (British Left-wing newspaper and very good) reported that the Minnesota police had probably had training from the State of Israel, under FBI instructions (conferences, etc) on how to handle so-called anti-terror organizations, or in this case a black man who was not harming anyone, that we know of? This technique is used in Israel against Palestinians who are protesting against the State of Israel. This possibility is disputed by some. With 100,000+ dead so far from Covid-19 in the USA and the 'new cold war' against China (Niall Ferguson on Sky news 1st June 2020) emerging from the ether, 40 million unemployed in the last few months, Trump was in real trouble if he wanted to be re-elected in November 2020…. so of course, he lost. What does he do? He blamed left-wing groups/anarchists and told state chiefs to 'crack down' on protesters and 'dominate' the situation or they would look all like 'jerks'. According to the Guardian newspaper on the 2nd of June 2020, 'this last weekend saw the most wide-spread civil unrest in the US since the assassination of Martin Luther King in 1968. There have been several deaths in protests around the country, and at least 4,400 arrests' (by the 3rd this figure has gone up to 5,600). During these events Trump seemed so alarmed, or at least the guards who protected him did, that he was obliged to hide in a 'bunker' in the White house, I presume like Hitler did in Berlin, in 1945? 'Toughen up' seemed to be the mantra that Trump espoused to agencies of State control including putting the national guard on the streets and in time, the armed forces if things got out of hand. The theme of a Trump response is to crush or be crushed, also when the 'looting starts the shooting starts'…. stoking up the rhetoric to these whole events. This theme is similar to that of the UK over generations of Tory rule which was to be tough on crime and lock everyone up who questions cruel ruling class policies. Trump is just following suit with this idea, which Nixon did in 1968, to be strong on 'law and order'. Cornel West a philosopher and civil rights activist, writing in the Guardian (3rd June 2020), adds fuel to the fire of the George Floyd dispute and previous ones, as he notes during protests in Charlottesville, Virginia. These were against hundreds of masked armed Nazis with live ammunition, in which the police stepped back and remained still and silent 'as we were mercilessly attacked. Without the intervention and protection of antifa, the anti-fascist protest movement, some of us would have died'. Heather Heyer lost her life in that dispute and Trump called 'antifa' a 'terrorist' organization that needed to be crushed by the 101st Airborne Division. In fact, he was trying to ban it. This seems very similar to Germany under Hitler and Boris Johnson in the UK, (for example: the Unions and recent legislation concerning the police and protesting) that all opposition must be crushed, at all costs. Max Keiser on RT recently noted (end of May 2020 and Putin's propaganda channel according to Luke Harding) that Trump, Boris Johnson and Bolsonaro of Brazil were 'macho boneheaded idiots', which is not far from the truth, in the epoch of madness. I should also note that Max

Keiser is probably one of the most intelligent men on TV. Last weekend (as above) also saw unrest all over the world, mostly among young people. Even in the UK over 100,000 people took part in demonstrations against the death of George Floyd and in support of 'Black Lives Matter' movement. In the UK they were mainly peaceful. However, in London police on horses were charging down Whitehall and several policemen got injured, but when I saw this on TV, I did think what the hell were horses charging down that specific part of London for? In Bristol where I lived for 20 years, a statue of Edward Colston was torn down and dumped in the harbour, the reason being that he was a 17-century slave trader who enslaved at-least 84,000 black people from Africa, taking them to the new world where as many as 19,000 may have died. Some were thrown overboard to lighten the ships. The statue was put up in the 19th century, in honour of so-called philanthropy in the city of Bristol. This was partly due to the fact that the working class was getting restless towards the end of the 19th century, so these so-called 'great men', could cement a sense of community. It concerns me that this past history is little known as is much of European colonialism, denoting a gap in the school curriculum.

The 1870 Education Act was the first to provide education from a young age in the UK, a response to the USA and Germany catching up economically fast with the UK? As Bilton et al assert 'The provision of a highly developed system of education is a response to the general technical requirements of industrial production - the need for a labour force in which skills and talents are developed to the full and matched to the complexity of jobs in a modern industrialized world' (35). By the year 1900 only 1.2% of the population was going into Further and higher education. During the next 54 years it had only increased to 5.8% of the population. In fact, until the level of education improves in the UK, we will never ever get any progressive change, or curtail the power of the extreme Right-Wing press to influence the majority. As Herbert Marcuse correctly asserted in the 1960's, the ruling class and their media power 'portrayed the demise of independent reason amongst workers because of the power of bourgeois ideologies and institutions'. (36) For those who are better educated and not brainwashed and read the Guardian and journalists like George Monbiot, environmental activist and good egg, who really tore into the narrative of the British Empire (17th June 2020) somehow being a force for good, which it never was. It built railways, taught some of the locals how to speak English and administered vast tracts of the globe, but that is about all. As Monbiot noted, 'Don't edit the past'. Britain has been deceitful for decades over these issues……for example with the lies that Boris Johnson has told most of his life suggesting that we cannot edit out our history, especially about the so-called 'great men', now often dead and honoured with a statue, like Churchill. However, most children are not taught about the concentration camps in Kenya in the 1950s (as there were in South Africa at the time of the Boer War), where in 48,000 people died…black and white. The sheer brutality carried out on a million Kikuyu people in Kenya, whose land the British stole, led to many of them being put into these concentration camps where probably tens of thousands died, when they put up a resistance to the crimes of the British settlers. John Pilger writing about these events several years ago thought that about ten thousand indigenous people of Kenya died and 32 Europeans. In a TV documentary on British TV shown in 2021, it was suggested that 15,000 indigenous people had died. However, since this time some historians have suggested that maybe as many as 100,000 people died at the time of the Mau Mau uprising in Kenya between 1952 – 1960. The discontent had been on going probably since the 1920s…. hence the discrepancy in the numbers. The policy was 'divide and rule', as it was all over the empire for hundreds of years. According to George Monbiot's article many men were castrated, one was roasted alive; others were raped, some mauled by dogs and electrocuted. A part of this process took place when Sir Evelyn Baring was Governor of Kenya, and what is notable about this now, is that Baring's granddaughter is married to Dominic Cummings, Boris Johnson's former chief adviser. I like to call Cummings a modern-day Rasputin as he lived in Russia after 1991 trying to set up an airline. Since first writing this he has now left Downing Street for pastures new and was taking revenge on Boris Johnson and Matt Hancock, in 2021/22. The reason most people know very little about these terrible crimes in Kenya was because they have been censored since the days of Baring. Only in 2012 were many of these secrets discovered, because a group of Kikuyu survivors sued the British government. This process of covering up crimes committed by the English ruling class continues according to Monbiot, and it seems that 'Baring's family fortune was made from the ownership of slaves and the compensation paid to owners when the trade was banned'.

As this book is progressing in June 2020 the 'Black Lives Matter' protests seem to be increasing all over the world. Some radical intellectuals are suggesting that we have seen nothing like it since the mid-1960s. I would have thought that the ruling class in the USA and the UK are probably getting very worried. If not, I have just put an advert in the Morning Star (daily paper of the Left, circulation about 10,000 a day) that you should 'Start your own Spartacus/Edward Colston moment, by reading the books of Brian V. Peck …. Consult the neo-Oracle at Google/Amazon…for more infor'. The triple whammy that has been created by the covid-19 virus across the globe, a worldwide huge recession and in the USA the death of George Floyd has caused a firestorm, which has 'ignited protests and riots from New York to Los Angles and the south, and then in London, Berlin and beyond' (The Sunday Observer 7th June 2020). That was about last weekend this weekend. This weekend (13/14 June

2020) we have seen in the UK, the rise of the extreme Right in its many forms, just as in the USA under Trump, getting in on the act to protect statues and causing mayhem. According to a Sunday Times journalist (14 June 2020) called Gabriel Pogrund, a 'Far-right thug yelled scum and attacked me' in London with skinheads chanting the national anthem while pelting police with bottles and flares. The mixture was very toxic as 'Black Lives Matter' was going on at the same time in central London so the police in theory had to try and keep the different factions apart. 'The two groups were kept apart by a massive police presence, helicopters circling overhead and sirens screeching as hundreds of officers in riot gear, on horseback and in vans blocked all exits from Parliament Square and barricaded off Whitehall'. As the Sunday Times (14th June 2020) suggests, this whole process 'seemed like a symbol of a divided Britain, a country with so much pent-up rage that people came out during a pandemic, despite the highest death rate and worst economic downturn in Europe'. This I should also add mirrors the same problem in the USA under Trump which Joe Biden is now trying to heal with huge stimulus packages to boost the economy. In theory he will also have a much more mature take on foreign affairs? However, this is not believed by RT (was Russia Today), on at least some of their excellent programmes that I have watched.

SOURCES

(1) Noam Chomsky - Hegemony and Survival 2004 - p,6

(2) Noam Chomsky - Turning the Tide...US Intervention in Central America and the Struggle for Peace - 1985 p, 46.
(3) John Pilger - Freedom Next Time - 2006 p, 19
(4) Turning the Tide - Noam Chomsky – 1985 p,127
(5) Ditto -p45
(6) Michael Woodiwiss - Gangster Capitalism - The United States and the Global Rise of Organized Crime 2005 - p, 122.
(7) Ditto p, 123
(8) Ditto p123
(9) Noam Chomsky - Turning the Tide - 1985 p,67.
(10) Seumas Milne: The Revenge of History – The Battle For the 21st Century – 2013 p, 43
(11) Noam Chomsky & Gilbert Achcar: Perilous Power 2007 p, 111
(12) Michael Woodiwiss: Gangster Capitalism - The United States and The Global Rise of Organized Crime – 2005 p,124
(13) Ditto p,124
(14) Ditto p,124/125
(15) Noam Chomsky: Rogue States – 2000 -p, 82
(16) Ditto p, 8
(17) Ditto p,166
(18) Ditto p, 164/165
(19) Ditto p, 8
(20) Oliver Stone & Peter Kuznick – The Untold History of the United States - 2013 p, 305
(21) Ditto – p, 241
(22) Oliver Stone & Peter Kuznick – The Untold History of the United States – 2012 p, 242
(23) Noam Chomsky – Optimism Over Despair - 2017 p, 138
(24) Oliver Stone & Peter Kuznick- as above p, 312
(25) Ditto – p,323

(26) Ditto – p, 350
(27) John Pilger – Hidden Agendas – 1998 p, 139
(28) Oliver Stone & Peter Kuznick: as above p, 328
(29) Noam Chomsky: Turning the Tide – 1985 p, 75.
(30) Oliver Stone & Peter Kuznick: as above p, 429.
(31) Ditto – p,447
(32) Ditto – p, 451
(33) Ditto – p, 478
(34) Molly Ivins & Lou Dubose: Bushwhacked - Life in George W. Bush's America 2004 p, 53
(35) Tony Bilton et al – Introductory Sociology – 1987 second edition p, 380
(36) Ditto – p, 583

OTHER SOURCES

The Internet
Hannah Ardent: The Origins of Totalitarianism - f/p 1951 Paperback edition Penguin
BBC4 - British TV Channel
BBC2 - British TV Channel
Hombre – 1967 movie starring the legionary, Paul Newman.
Michael Woodiwiss - Gangster Capitalism - The United States and Global Rise of Organized Crime.
The Guardian many editions
Sunday Observer: Several editions
Sunday Times Rich List
Sorry We Have Missed You – A Movie by the great Ken Loach.
Oliver James: Affluenza – 2007

Parasite - The Movie. From South Korea and about the class system in South Korea as satire.
Noam Chomsky – Optimism Over Despair
Plutarch – AD 46 – AD 119.
William Blum – Rogue State – 2014 Paperback edition....Chapter 5 called 'Torture' is very relevant to this chapter as is the movie called Rendition (2007) directed by Gavin Hood, apparently based on a true story.
PSB America TV channel
JFK: The Movie by Oliver Stone.1991
Noam Chomsky – Year 501 – 1992
Dr No the first James Bond movie released in 1962, starring the great Sean Connery.
Anthony Giddens: Various textbooks.
Ride the Thunder: A movie about Vietnam and the heroism of John Ripley and others.
Oliver Stone: Chasing the Light - Hardback edition 2020.
All the President's Men: Starring Dustin Hoffman & Robert Redford...an excellent movie about the breaking into the democratic headquarters and the outcome to these actions, in the 1970s.
David Frost interviewing Richard Nixon on TV and now a movie about these events.
The Dark Refection: a very disturbing movie made in 2013/2014 about fumes in aircraft.
Alexis de Tocqueville: Democracy in America
Charles Moore: Authorized biography about Mrs Thatcher in 3 volumes.
Patton the Movie starring the great and amazing George C. Scott, as Patton – 1969/70.
John Le Carrie – The Pigeon Tunnel - Stories from my Life hardback edition – 2016.
Noam Chomsky: Turning the Tide 1985

Philip K. Lawrence: Preparing for Armageddon: A Critique of Western Strategy
Philip K. Lawrence: Modernity & War: Creed of Absolute Violence
Willy Brandt: The Brandt Report
RT (TV) in the UK from Russia and studios in London and Moscow.
Al-Jazeera TV from the Middle East and the UK
Francis Fukuyama: The End of History and the Last Man – 1992
Bob Woodward: Bush at War – 2002
Morning Star – Left-wing newspaper published in the UK.
Gore Vidal: Perpetual War for Perpetual Peace
Official Secrets: A movie about Katherine Gunn at the GCHQ Headquarters in the UK in 2003
Shock & Awe: A Movie about two journalists plus at the Knight Kidder an America Media Company leading up to the invasion of Iraq in March 2003: trying to get to grips with propaganda and lies of politicians and other news agencies, agreeing with them…+ the interview on BBC2 where Amol Rajan spoke to Carl Bernstein & Bob Woodward for 45 minutes, an incredible emotional watch for an old man like me who is just a little younger than these two great men. …on the 18th May 2023.
Zero Dark Thirty – A movie about the hunt for Osama bin Laden.

Sky News in the UK
Sunday Times several editions.
Simon Sebag Montefiore: The Romanovs (1613 -1918).
John Pilger: Hidden Agendas – paperback 1998
The Sunday Times: 15th August 2021 - Rod Liddle…stats on casualties in Afghanistan.
Afghanistan Opium Trail 2007 documentary…an excellent bit of objective journalism as far as I could, see?
Morning Star – 18th August 2021.

This is not a Movie: A documentary mostly about the great crusading Irish/British journalist called Robert Fisk…. PhD…. like John Pilger, Fisk went out with his notebook to find the truth and expose lies…even interviewing Bin Laden three times and praised to the roof tops by Noam Chomsky….in ….i.e.

Noam Chomsky: 9 – 11…an open media book - 2001

Sunday Times: 22nd August 2021 – Dominic Lawson…. albeit a MI6 spy?

Jihad – A Holy War documentary showing on Amazon Prime, about the Mujahideen fighting the Soviet troops, 'atheist infidels'…. who were made up of mostly rural young men…with a lot of the money raised being spent in Pakistan on expense toys?

Morning Star: 6th September 2021

Colonia Dignidad (Dignity Colony) a movie inspired by true events about a dangerous religious cult in Pinochet's Chile, where according to the movie even the Germany Ambassador was in cahoots with the brutal Pinochet regime supported to the hilt by Mrs Thatcher. This movie was/is a warning from history about where the election of politicians like Donald J. Trump and Boris Johnson may have led us, had they stayed in power.

A Good American: by Friedrich Moser 2015 documentary about the amazing William Binney et al.

Luke Harding: The Snowden Files paperback 2014…a must read before you die…..which I have read 3 times+ the movie based on this book by Oliver Stone.

BorderTown: One of the most important movies ever made about the NAFTA agreement and the true brutal and callous nature of modern-day capitalism and what can happen and did to hundreds/ perhaps thousands of poor 'wage slave' women.

Paul Fussell: Class – Style and Status in the USA – 1983.

'Vice' the Movie about Dick Cheney and directed by Adam McKay – 2018.

BBC TV: 12th July 2022 SAS Death Squads exposed: A British War Crime.

The Vietnam War…showed on PBS America in the UK in August/September 2022….and probably one of the best documentaries ever shown about this conflict, starting with the French arriving in the 19th century…. interviewing people from both sides of the War, including the great Joe Galloway.

Killing Gaddafi: directed by Jacques Charmelot

War on Iraq a book by Scott Ritter and William Rivers Pitt

David McClure: The Queen's True Worth – 2020….in this book McClure notes how the Obama's have made a fortune (now probably more than £48 million…p7) from writing two books, about while Barack was the President of the USA.

Narrative of the Life of Frederick Douglas an American Slave – printed by Amazon.

Frederick Douglas: My Bondage and My Freedom - printed by Amazon.

Frederick Douglas: The Life and Times of Frederick Douglas – Oxford University Press.

CHAPTER TWO
A SHORT HISTORY OF CHINA IN UNDER 13,500 WORDS.

I qualified as a lecturer in June 1991, from Cardiff University, and had no success at gaining employment in the UK. After several years I got interested in teaching English abroad, again without success and turned down by the British council et al, probably because I originally came from the wrong class. But I did read several books on China, which fascinated me, probably just as much as it did Christopher Columbus, who read Marco Polo's adventure in China, who was in awe of the place. Christopher Columbus did sail out of the Spanish port of Parlos for the Far East on the 3rd of August 1492, with three small ships, the Nina, the Pinta and the Santa Maria where his main objectives were the riches of gold, pearls and spices. However, as most of us know but Columbus did not know at the time – that if you attempt to reach the Far East, North and South America are in the way. In the Americas the locals were very friendly and helpful to the new invaders. Unfortunately, they did not understand how cruel their new masters would become over the next few years according to Noam Chomsky. Nothing new, of course, for anyone who has read the history of imperialism.

Marco Polo was even getting resurrected again by no other person then President X1 of China on a visit to Italy in March 2019, when promoting the new Silk Road to the West, and saying that it was the 'first bridge' between Italy and China. This visit to Italy by President X1 so it seems upset the USA and European establishment, who I presume are very suspicious of his motives? Marco Polo may have spent 20 years in China between 1275 - 1295 and spent a lot of his time in Hangzhou the capital of the Southern Song dynasty, with six million inhabitants. At the time Venice only had

160,000 inhabitants. The awe of the place must have been beyond belief for Polo and other explorers that went to China, with products made only there and nowhere else and because, let us be clear, communication was very slow at the time. In fact, no faster than a pace of a horse as it was at Laguna Isla in the Falkland Island, at least up until the 1980s. According to James Kynge in *'China Shakes the World'* the first that Britain learned of the Mongol invasion of Europe was that the price of fish rising. This was because 'fishing fleets along the Baltic coast, abruptly deprived of sailors required to face the horse-borne enemy approaching from the east, had remained at their moorings. That had reduced the supply of cod and herrings to Harwich, and prices had gone up accordingly. (1)

On a chapter of so few words about one of the oldest civilizations on earth we must start at the beginning as there is a real possibility that the Far East which includes China and now what is called Thailand was the first in the world to create static society and not the middle east, so is probably over 12,000 years old especially around the yellow river, where myths were created about males and females who were formed out of the mud. I am basing my premise here on what the great Jean-Jacques Rousseau had written about in the 18th century regarding the genesis of static civilization, for example; fencing land off to grow food, own it through property rights, and exploit people. Contrast this to the fiction of John Locke (1632 - 1704) who once told us that private property was the 'true state of nature', countering the argument that Thomas Hobbes (1588-1679) made in Leviathan that life in the 'true state of nature' was nasty brutish and short. A very unlikely scenario I would have thought. Freedom can only arise when we are all free and not serfs, 'wage slaves', subjects and peasants, or really free like the Gazelle-Boy of the Rio de Oro, who was brought up by Gazelles and lived with them. Ann Widdecombe, an ex-Tory MP and a fleeting MEP for a few months before we left the EU (in theory on 31st October

2019...'actually' left 31ˢᵗ January 2020), likens Brexit to 'slaves turning on their owners'. She also said that throughout history 'oppressed people turning on their oppressors, slaves against their owners, the peasantry against the feudal barons, colonies against empires, and that is why Britain is leaving…. we are off'. I presume, as I was born below the 'working class (2.) in Port Stanley Falkland Islands, a vassal country which still is part of the British Empire, that I might compare myself to the late great Frederick Douglass et al. Or indeed Spartacus, whereby I might see the world as he saw it, over 2000 years ago (see Plutarch AD 46 - AD 120 about the real evidence of this great man and above)?

First this chapter is not meant to be anything like the incredible John Keay book about China published in 2008/2009 which is so focused on fine details about all aspects of life in this great country only a genius could write it. As I am no genius but have always tried to use great role models like: Cicero, Plato, Marx's, Rousseau and Voltaire and many others as knowledge kings to ape and nothing wrong in that. But rather this work is more of a thumb nail sketch of some of the major events that have happened in China, over the last ten thousand years.

According to Jonathan Fenby and co-authors in *'The Seventy Wonders of China'* silk production may go back 8000 years and jade production 6000 years. (3) The history of Chinese civilization seems to be analysed, in most books on the subject, especially those written by western authors, in epochs/ dynasties, '36' in its history according to Martin Jacques. Will Hutton, who seems quite critical of all things Chinese in his book called *'The Writing on The Wall - China and the West in the 21ˢᵗ Century'* published in 2007, albeit admits that for thousands of years China did have a very sophisticated society. In fact, I just do not believe that Mao's rule directly or indirectly caused 70 million deaths, mentioned by Hutton from other sources. (4). Mao never believed it, that is for sure, according to Jonathan Spence in his biography about the Chinese leader; it seems that in Mao's mind, it was propaganda coming out of Hong Kong, (part of the British Empire at the time) which may not be far from the truth? (5) For more real evidence of this phenomenon just read the extreme right-wing press in the UK, especially at election times, about how they treat labour leaders, albeit they do lie and cheat most of the time 24/7 and 'gaslight' the uneducated majority. Martin Jacques just notes millions lost their lives under Mao in his brilliant book about China, called *When China Rules the World,* one of the most important books ever written about China in recent times. (6).

Western academics (not all) did a similar hatchet job on Stalin, conflating maybe deaths attributed to Stalin millions killed in the Second World War, this number perhaps being as high as '27 million' (depending on the sources). Again, in Cambodia, where Pol Pot in theory killed 2 million people, no contrast is made with all the people that were killed by America bombs illegally authorized by Richard Nixon and Henry Kissinger (Christopher Hitchens) during the Vietnam war, which may have been high as 600,000. In a recent BBC Four TV programme called Wild China (October 2019) it was suggested that China has always been self-sufficient in food, meaning mostly rice production - I presume, which may have not been true under Mao?

If Michael Sherington is correct in *'The Seventy Wonders of China'* it was the Han people who can be equated with the Chinese and their unique civilization and making up 92% of the population of China, albeit there may be as many as '50 different ethnic groups'. Who cultivated the land at-least 5000 years ago around the Yellow River basin, (may have grown rice for 8000yrs according to BBC Four TV - October 2019), but Robert Ash in the same book suggests that around this time, or even later in history, a slash and burn philosophy was carried out on the land for many centuries. (7). Never forget that once a system starts, in agriculture or whatever it tends to continue regardless; for example, as an ex-girlfriend of mine from Botswana once told me that at a specific time of year the locals farmed, growing crops whether they needed them or not. This acceptance of established culture also applies to very primitive semi-feudal countries like the UK, where it seems Monarchy could be in place for the next 10,000 years, or into perpetuity unless we are lucky enough to overthrow the whole rotten British Establishment this century. Maybe the education system itself could flourish and become progressive, with critical thinking at its core, so that everyone can understand Private Eye (probably one of the most important magazines in the world, a publication which pokes fun and satirises the ruling class and their henchmen) once a fortnight. Boris Johnson, during his premiership (2019+), seemed to be trying to stop the working class from going to university and get educated in any form, thus Friedrich August von Hayek's brutal philosophy took hold again, like it was under the neo-brute and tyrant Margaret Thatcher.

Where Will Hutton seem very pessimistic about most aspects of China's history and the future of their society? Michael Woods is the complete opposite in his brilliant short movies made for the BBC, now on DVD which I own, called *'The Story of China'*. He starts his analysis by saying that China is the 'oldest Nation on earth' and is rising again in the 21st century. But not new, because throughout its very long history on several occasions it has been the most powerful Nation on earth in economic terms. The whole idea of Chinese philosophy starts with the family. The Chinese look back through their generations for their own values and so on and through the eyes of great philosophers like, Lao-tzu and Confucius, who they see as guiding lights of aspiration and knowledge. (8) The ideas of Confucius are very profound and seem a million miles from the beliefs of Donald Trump &

Boris Johnson. Confucius's beliefs seem very similar to those of Socrates, in that the mission of Rulers should be to restore civilisation through virtue, and that they should set an example for the whole of society, by ruling correctly and 'protecting the people' and preserving the State. Education is also at the core of this process, as in the example of Socrates who questioned everything, and Confucius who said intellectuals must 'speak truth to power'. (9) this being repeated over two and half thousand years later by Noam Chomsky. Even to this day education is appreciated by all, and working hard to gain qualifications in the whole of south Asia is a must do process, whereby in contrast in the UK, for example, education is not appreciated by most, and rigged by the ruling class to keep the majority uneducated, stupid and 'down'. In fact, my conclusion is that the educational situation is a disgrace in the UK, especially in England, and for any country that pretends it is civilized it is beyond belief! However, like the wars in the Peloponnese regions between different city states and beyond, similar things happened in China over thousands of years including civil wars with added problems of floods where millions died. New dynasties like the Ming rose and fell. Zhu Yuanzhang was the founding emperor of the Ming dynasty, which lasted for 300 years. Zhu was born a peasant so understood the codes of the countryside, but also believed that the Ruler had to 'force people to be good' with a strong State to support the system.
The first Emperor who united China's seven warring kingdoms, including the Han at the age of 34 was called Qui Shi Huang. He was the founder of the Qui dynasty and lived at roughly the same time as Alexander the Great ruled modern-day Greece. Born in the kingdom of Chin, and through brute force and guile (with a new form of strong bow made on an industrial scale) he became like Caligula a living God, or so he thought? He also started the Great Wall of China and was buried not far from the famous Terracotta army whose spirits were, in theory, to protect him from all the people he had killed in battles and elsewhere during his life. The impression given in

an excellent documentary about the First Emperor of China I watched on Amazon prime TV (11 September 2021) was that Qin ran the new State through a system called legalism/ideology, a form of totalitarianism to control thought - he also had books burned and was obsessed with the notion of immortality. Towards the end of his life advisers suggested that having lots of sex could extend how long we have on earth, which may be true, and he was also given mercury tablets towards this end, which may have killed him in 210 BC?

A constant theme of static society and history seems to be that man is never satisfied with his lot, or at least the Ruling groups that have emerged over thousands of years (see above) have not? Hence, the need to trade and often plunder other people's resources is a theme throughout history, as is the idea that we need a philosophy to live by, and in China there are several. At the time of the Tang epoch (618-907) many foreigners were allowed in, including 25,000 in the capital Xi'an, in the centre of the country. Many more, quite possibly over 100,000 - Christians, Jews, Moslems and Zoroastrians - were based at Guaanghou and Quanzhou at the junction of China's key southern routes. China at this time was so far ahead of the rest of the world 'that it needed nothing from it'. 'The golden Tang period was a true golden era. The most sophisticated and open society in the world. China boasted more than two dozen cities with population of over half a million at a time when large urban centres in Europe counted their inhabitants in the tens of thousands' (The China Dream p, 4-5). (10) However, like the USA in this epoch under the neo-brute Donald J. Trump as president, (after Aristotle) who got voted out in November 2020, China's love of openness came to an end and the fear and paranoia of foreigners became the norm by the end of the Tang epoch, because of rebellions, massacres of foreign merchants, corruption, natural disasters, higher prices and increased inequality, which all helped with the rise of anti-foreigner sentiment, which became the norm - and even Buddhism was banned and persecuted.

Much of this whole process lasted for centuries, with China developing its own peasantry, farming and a canal system, opening rivers for trade and so on, and being less warlike than its European counter parts, who were always fighting one another and plundering other countries resources. According to Hutton (2007), and taken from other sources, in this case none other than John Maynard Keynes 'suggested that Francis Drake's Golden Hind, completing the circumnavigation of the globe in 1580 with a cargo of gold stolen from the Spanish and worth 100 billion dollars in today's prices, effectively paid off all of England's international debt and provided the risk capital for the City of London's first trading and banking institutions, and was thus the economic foundation of the British Empire'(11). No mean feat, but to my knowledge this fact is never taught in schools, which it should be because Chomsky's famous axiom about the 'fifth freedom' (sic); was as relevant then as it is now?

'Man is never satisfied with his lot' can of course go much deeper in the class structure. James Kynge noted in 2004 that with the rise of China in modern times, the demand for scrap metal became intense and manhole covers started to disappear from roads and pavements around the world, to satisfy the need for metal in China. (12) A story that I cannot remember reading in the British press at the time. Ironically, it was Napoleon, who once remarked 'Let China sleep, for when she wakes, she will shake the world', something it is very unlikely that Trump would have ever read, but now she has 'awoke' it is turning into the worst nightmare for the USA and its poodle the UK. Get rich schemes in their many forms are/were the driving force, and still are behind most trade transactions around the globe, and especially in trying to penetrate the Chinese markets. This has been the case for hundreds of years, particularly by the European powers. The size of the population has always been the big thing that these powers were always trying to exploit, from its first encounter with this sleeping giant to the present day. 150 million in 1600 doubling to 300 million in 1800 and now over 1.3 billion, which would have been millions more, had they not had a ONE baby policy for many years. Michael Woods (as above) in his excellent TV series for the BBC (now on DVD) explained all aspects of Chinese history and culture in the *'Story of China'*. This should be on the English curriculum because it is so good, going back to the inception of this great Nation, which Martin Jacques calls a 'civilization-state'. China had been 'the greatest civilization in the world', but when the Europeans arrived, in the form of the British, Dutch and Portuguese et al: things started to go downhill for the indigenous Chinese, mainly in the British case because their thirst for tea was paid for by opium, getting millions hooked on this dangerous drug. Christianity had arrived with the Portuguese who wanted a trading deal with China, but they also got Matteco Ricci, (albeit the first missionary may have landed in China in the 7th century), an Italian Jesuit priest. Two dangerous drugs in a deadly concoction, at first the Chinese thought that Christianity was a 'strange theology', which it is, but now 70 million people in China are hooked on it, according to Michael Woods. Ricci did however also enlighten the Chinese with his other knowledge of geography and the need to study maps of the world.

Will Hutton in *'Writing on the wall China And the West in the 21st Century'* (published in 2007) does paint a grim future for China if they stay in the same mode of behaviour as a nation state, as he finds it; which by 2021/22 is now maybe out of date? However, there is probably more than a grain of truth in his deep analysis of how China got behind the West over several centuries and then how a few powerful Western countries exploited their weakness. The main underlying reason seems to be that China for most of its existence has always thought itself superior to all other civilizations, which would not have been the whole truth, considering the power of Rome 2000 years ago along with Egypt and other civilization that had grown up in the Middle East over millenniums. Hutton thinks it was the war like nature of the European world that first started their progress into the future, creating 'the invention of the public realm'. Ironically, this was the main reason that the new EEC trading partnership was started up after the Second Word War in the mid-1950s, to stop wars - which some-how in the UK, has now been forgotten about, especially by the British Tory party, who instigated the insanity of BREXIT? According to Hutton: 'The unintended consequences of preparing for and waging war were far-reaching'. To pay for wars, taxes had to be levied and loans raised, serviced and repaid: and, bit by bit, this created a new on-going, interactive relationship between governors and governed; taxpayers wanted something in return. Nor was it just a matter of more pressure to raise money because there was more war. The European aristocracy and merchant classes alike were harder to take over and repress because they had distinct power bases, initially from the structure of feudalism and then, between 1500 -1800, increasingly from the profits of long-distance oceanic trade'. (13) Paradoxical feudalism is still very relevant today in the UK, as I note above, and some say like Bilton et al (1987) note that Monarchy is a bulwark against any form of progressive thinking and action, which it is! Hardly a day goes by in the UK where we are not bombarded with pictures and articles in the mass media about the Royals doing good deeds, meeting other Heads of State, (for example Donald J. Trump in June 2019, costing the State at-least £40 million pounds), breeding and so-called working: which to my mind does not fit well with one of the most cruel and brutal and powerful ruling class in the world, or was? Apparently, it was Edward the 1st who first got wind of the need to inform parliament to give exceptional 'grants of supply'(14). In other words, from now on Kings had to tread very carefully, especially between the ruling groups where the taxes mainly came from. As we know from history, when the dynamics got too stressed Kings and Queens could lose their heads, which they did in Britain and France. 'War also spurred the creation of financial institution and power centres beyond the state that required superintendence by independent institutions'(15). This is one of the main themes running through Hutton's book between the European countries and China: Capitalism in the West brilliant but Capitalism in China within the parameters of a 'one-party state', terrible? Ironically, it appears that the UK is now drifting in to a cruel and brutal 'One Party State' run by conmen, crooks, gangsters and plutocrats, after the 2019 election in Britain, where the Tories gained an 80-seat majority in the House of Commons, albeit only 29% of the population that could vote, voted for the Tories, truly amazing, roughly 15.5 million did not even both too vote and the Tories won dozens of seats normally controlled by Labour, called the 'red wall'. Now Boris Johnson is boasting he now runs a party for everyone, nothing could be further from the truth, as Johnson, like Trump, has, in the eyes of many, told so many lies that it is beyond belief, and he seems not care to hoot about the majority, and ended mired in sleaze and corruption.

Many small businessmen that I have met over decades, like Del Boy from 'Only Fools and Horses' in the UK (British TV show very popular in the 1980s and 1990s), perhaps sum up everything we can understand about how they operate at an individualistic and psychological level, which is that some day in the near or far distance they will become millionaires. Most never make it and live in a fantasy world (first hand evidence with my own eyes and other senses and reading a book like 'Out of my Depth' by Ann Darwin …. May 2020 sic), just like how the business world has seen China as another route to riches over centuries. Which included the Chinese lobby in the 19th century; 'after 1869, the opening of the Suez Canal - contemporaneous with the development of steamships - made the Suez-Bombay - Colombo - Singapore - Shanghai route the jugular of the British empire. Not only did Manchester cotton markets and other durable goods manufacturers demand that the British government secure their market access in China, but the highly influential grandees of the City of London - blue-blooded pioneers of international financial services - insisted that their turf be protected. China needed financing, and London must profit by it'. (16) This applied not only to China but many places around the globe, because Britain was the first country in the World to create an Industrial base, the ruling class had more money than sense, so as Mark & Engels had predicated in the Communist manifesto (1848) markets had to be found somewhere by the capitalists to sell their wares and invest their spare money. Lenin even remarked on this phenomenon many times in his works, especially at the beginning of the 20th century, about the rich and powerful in Britain. When businessmen saw the potential of making a fast buck on the railways in the UK in the 19th century, they went mad; very similar phenomena were predicted about building railways in China not only by the UK but America as-well. 'The first great investment gold rush in China concerned railways. At first the Chinese court was very suspicious of railways but under intense pressure they finally agreed in 1887 and the first trunk lines were built in the 1890s; by the first decade of the 20th century 5000 miles of track were laid. American, Russian, Belgian, German, French and British companies and businessmen poured in millions of dollars of investment'(17).

Very few empires in history have been so ruthless in their objectives as global phenomena as the Europeans and Japan who looked down on the Chinese as an inferior race in a similar way as the English French Spanish and so on, did wherever they went, and the 'ruling class' still do in the UK on its own downtrodden subjects. Japan got a lot of its beliefs and culture over thousands of years of civilization, from the Chinese. According to Martin Jacques, the reason for Japan's thinking was a shock to the system in 1853 when the Americans and the British turned up in Tokyo Bay to demand, in 'Black ships', that Japan 'should open itself to trade' and be forced to sign trade agreements that were not completely in their interest. But amazingly this was the moment that the Japanese ruling elite understood they must industrialize and catch up with the West. The real problems for the Chinese started during what is now called the Qing Dynasty (1644 – 1912), when in the late 1800's the English turned up in China to try and sell stuff to Emperor Qianlong with a 700 strong party of businessmen, soldiers', diplomats etc. This was not the first attempt at market penetration into China; in his attempt Lord Macartney had been rebuffed and sent packing via Canton. However, the opium trade had already started by this time, exporting dope from India into China, which proved highly profitable. In 1829 the Chinese stopped this trade to the fury of the British/English ruling class, one of the most cruel and brutal in world history (repeated but true)! As relations deteriorated the British launched its First Opium War (1839 -1842) bombarding the south of China into submission. The treaty of Nanjing as it was called forced the Chinese into signing this agreement along with the stealing of Hong Kong (see also below), opening the first five treaty ports, and paying reparations; China's century of humiliation had begun (18). Up to 1915 China was forced to sign another 13 agreements that were not in their interests, all made mostly by European countries but also including Russia the USA and Japan in 1915.

As I was noting above and the main theme of this chapter: there was hardly a consumer good from underpants to cigarettes that the USA, UK et al did not get excited about selling to China, as well as Railway construction. Again, as one of the major themes of this chapter needs repeating repeatedly - it was the size of the population that really got the capitalists so overawed with pure greed, even to this day, with over 1.3 billion people to exploit. Ironically even the British Navy got in on the act, protecting the Chinese eastern seaboard from pirates. Which sounds slightly out of place when one considers the British Navy itself was for hundreds of years virtually piratical, plundering other countries ships, especially the Spanish, for booty. Also, during this period, then as now, there was savage rivalry between the USA and Europe over trade. The reason for protectionism in hindsight seems obvious now as during the period between the wars in Europe, Shanghai was the second busiest port in the world. Throughout the 19th century and into the 20th century the old order in China was coming under dynamic strain, from inside and out, and by 1911 the dynastic system that had lasted for thousands of years was over. Britain played a major part in this process as did other states, one reason being that from the inside the UK was using opium as a source of payment for exports and getting millions hooked on this deadly substance, because after the Napoleonic wars we were running out of gold and silver. Also, because of the weakness of China from an industrial standpoint, the West and Japan were able to force the Chinese state into signing agreements against their will. 'The Celestial Kingdom that claimed to rule "all that was below heaven" and held foreigners in contempt had to concede that the destructive trade in opium had to continue, that to pay every pound of Britain's war cost and more, that it ceded Hong Kong to Britain, and that it allows British merchants freely to operate in its five leading ports' (19). In essence China, at least on the east coast and Manchuria in the north, was being sliced up like a melon, by foreign powers, including Russia, France, Germany, Japan, and Britain even seizing Kowloon, adding it to Hong Kong as part of the British Empire. These crimes were, of course, horrendous for China and are still remembered to this day as a 'century of humiliation'. But China itself had several rebellions in the 19th century, most notably the Taiping Uprising between 1850- 1864, which may have killed up to 40 million people. The Taiping ideology was it seems to have been a strange concoction of evangelical Christianity, primitive communism, sexual Puritanism and Confucian utopianism which had been triggered by famine, floods and British crimes, according to sources in Martin Jacques book about China (20).

From 1912 to 1949 China was virtually taken over by warlords and neo-brutes, dishing out brutality on a grand scale, especially to the peasants often under so-called nationalistic flags (an old trick played by the ruling elites to this day, especially in the UK and the USA), the most successful being Chiang Kai-shek who by 1927 had established a semi-unified Chinese Republic. Albeit he could not modernize the economy and beat back the Japanese invasion that had begun in 1931 and which, by 1937-38, had captured Shanghai, Nanjing and Canton and probably murdered over 200,000/300,000 peasants (Martin Jacques…'Nanjing massacre' in December 1937 et al), which even horrified the Nazis at the time!

According to Hutton (2007) if the Nationalists had been more skilful, they could have defeated the growing communist insurgency by 1935. The Communist's famous Long March was retreating to the 'rural redoubt of Yan'an in the provincial west of China and the sustained attack on their organization in the cities; less than 10% of those who began the march ended it'(21). The success of the communists seems to be that they recruited 'intellectuals, students, workers and businessmen who were fleeing the Japanese and who saw communism as the most effective way of modernizing China and winning the war'(22). According to Jonathan

Spence, in his excellent biography of Mao (1999), Chiang Kai-shek wanted to destroy communism before beating the Japanese. Mao was also miles ahead of the West in his early life, if Spence is correct, when it seems he believed in free love, (a contradiction in terms if you are my age, good people of planet earth). He was a small businessman, very well educated, well read and a lifelong learner, like myself (albeit he had doubts about his own achievements when comparing himself to other people, like academics). Qualities many modern citizens of the USA, especially Republican Presidents including Trump, seem to lack, making them, some might say, the complete opposite of Mao: uneducated, unread and stupid? (23)

After 1941 it was obvious to most, even a blind man and perhaps Donald J. Trump had he been alive then, that Japan would be defeated in the Second World War (after a lot of initial success), and China would be free from at least one colonial power. There is no doubt about it; Mao was a very rare breed of homo-sapiens in that he tried at least (at first) to learn from History, what would and would not succeed in a revolution. For example: the "mass line" big idea/concept embracing 'all correct leadership is necessarily from the masses to the masses', Mao wrote. 'This means take the idea of the masses (scattered and unsystematic ideas) and concentrate them (though study turn them into concentrated and systematic ideas) then go to the masses and propagate and explain these ideas until the masses embrace them as their own' (24). Land reform was another big idea that had to be taken very slowly and in a relational way, as in the 1920s and 1930s when the communists had tried forced collectivism the peasants resisted it. As Hutton noted: 'Land would be redistributed from rich peasants to poor, but property rights would be respected' (25).

By 1945 the cruel Japanese had been defeated and a civil war broke out between the nationalist under Chiang Kai-shek and the communists under Mao, partly caused by hyperinflation of 6000% in 1948. The Nationalists had no strategy for winning popular support and were defeated. Chiang Kai-Shek and his followers fled to Taiwan and on the 1st of October 1949 Mao declared the establishment of the People's Republic of China in Tiananmen Square, albeit Chiang Kai-Shek called Taiwan the Republic of China claiming the whole of China as his, which is still a flash point between the mainland and this large Island of 23 million people which in theory is protected by the USA. This could be a flash point between USA and China, which could lead, along with other factors outlined in this book, someone like Trump blowing up the world? (Even the BBC Radio 4 on the 1st of October 2019 suggested that China and the USA may go to war one day). Faced with a similar situation to the Soviet Union, after the Second World War, China had to reconstruct its economy and improve life expectancy through education, better housing, infrastructure, health care, etc. At the time 85% of the economy was based on agricultural production, so land reform was Mao's number one priority, and controlling the hyperinflation he had inherited. As Hutton asserts again: 'An agricultural surplus would be created to finance the first five-year plan that would deliver economic modernization. Mao, who in Yan'an, and before he had dissected the Chinese class system in elaborate detail as a guide to the communist strategy to win the war in the country, now undertook the same analysis at the national level. Everybody in China was given a class position by which his or her fate would be determined. Radical egalitarianism had begun' (26). It was through this system that land reform was carried out very much on a hierarchical basis, and for the first five-year plan between 1952 and 1957 was quite successful, with an average of 9.2% economic growth.

China did get involved in the Korean war. Japan had occupied Korea between 1910 to 1945 and treated the Koreans appallingly, for example using tens of thousands of women as sex slaves. The background to the Korean problem and war is well documented by Oliver Stone and Peter Kuznick in their amazing book called: *The untold History of the United States*. 'In the North, the Soviets installed General Kim 11 Sung, who had led guerrilla forces against the Japanese in Manchuria during the war; the Americans installed Syngman Rhee in the south' and both turned out to be ruthless operators. 'Border skirmishes occurred frequently. The Joint Chiefs had warned repeatedly against getting drawn into a war in Korea - a place of little strategic importance bordering on the Soviet Union and China - and recommended that it be excluded from the United States defence perimeter'. (27) But under the auspices of the United Nations, they did and nearly came unstuck when in 1950 the North invaded the South because the North had T34 tanks supplied by the USSR, whereas the Americans and their allies had light armaments. The North also thought they were fighting to reunite the whole of Korea, in essence 'fighting for the unification of Korea', with the help of USSR power. Most of Korea was taken apart from a small section in the southeast of the peninsular. It was only after General Douglas MacArthur got in involved with very clever tactics that the United Nations troops (mostly Americans, albeit the very famous actor Michael Caine was with the British troops in Korea, and troops of 17 other countries) started to gain ground and crossed the 38th parallel in October 1950. General Douglas MacArthur, who saw the successful allied occupation of post-war Japan, did not think China would get involved. When they did at Christmas 1950 with 200,000 troops initially, he must have been shocked and was slowly pushed back to the 38th parallel, an arbitrary line drawn on a map by two Americans in 1948. The North set up a communist state and the South a freewheeling capitalistic state. According to a very important BBC Four TV documentary (23rd October 2019), where this information comes from, General MacArthur wanted 24 atomic bombs to drop on the yellow river in China. President Harry Truman refused this offer and when MacArthur criticized him Truman fired him. However, after June 1951 the USA virtually destroyed North Korea with bombing, likewise most of the South had been destroyed by the war....the reason George Blake became a Russian spy (sic) in the first place. The death of Stalin in 1953 helped to seal the agreement between the USA, USSR and China, very much like the First World War it came to a stalemate, fighting over hills and getting nowhere. The armistice was signed on the 27th of July 1953, but has been a festering sore ever since, which even President Trump tried to settle, because North Korea has nuclear weapons, a crime in the Western belief system. After the conflict, the USSR helped North Korea to reconstruct itself and the Americans helped the South. No one knows for sure how many Chinese were killed in the war, but the best estimates are between 150,000 and 400,000, some say a million…. I presume because the Chinese government committed 3 million to the conflict which it seems was done to impress Stalin. Over 33,000 Americans lost their lives, in a very dubious adventure of cold war politics.

Ironically, anyone who has studied sociology in depth should be aware that most of us have been designated a class position (see above) from birth. Living in places like the USA and the UK, these positions are very hard to escape from (even Oliver James in Affluenza admits this axiom of the UK) where you were born if you were born very poor, like me. As I often try to explain to newly educated people I meet occasionally: I was born below the 'working class' with a plastic spoon in my mouth in the Falkland Islands (British colony - 8000 miles from the UK), and had only 6 years formal education. Prince Charles, (now Charles 111) named 'Brian' in Private Eye (sic), was born 'upper class' with two silver spoons in his mouth and worth millions and still 'upper class', whereas I am still very poor but educationally have escaped from my birth status and 'station in life', a terrible crime in the UK......just ask King Charles?

On re-reading William Blum's excellent Rogue State for about the 6th time (I first read it in Western Australia in 2014), I must quote a very small section of chapter 17 called 'A concise History of United States Global Interventions 1945 to the Present' and very relevant to what I have just been writing above, subtitled 'The American Empire' China 1945 - 51: 'At the close of World War 2, the US intervened in a civil war, taking the side of Chiang Kai-Shek's Nationalists against Mao Tse-tung's Communists, even though the latter had been a much closer ally of the United States in the war. To compound the irony, the US used defeated Japanese soldiers to fight for its side. After their defeat in 1949, many Nationalist soldiers took refuge in northern Burma, where the CIA regrouped them, brought in other recruits from elsewhere in Asia, and provided a large supply of heavy arms and planes. During the 1950s, this army proceeded to carry out several incursions into China, involving at times thousands of troops, accompanied by CIA advisers (some of whom were killed), and supplied by air drops from American planes' (28).

The adventure into Tibet by China in 1959 is often perceived by the Western Elites for both middle class and proletariat consumption as something that should not have happened as the indigenous Tibetans were living in some sort of Shangri-La, with a form of Buddhist belief called Lamaism in Tibet starting about 1040, but which in reality as a system of Feudal serfdom. Until China cracked down on Tibetan rebels and the Dalai Lama fled to northern India, around 98% of the population was enslaved in serfdom, a form of theocracy imposed by corrupt and incompetent leaders.

Something like the UK in the 21st century (joke, of course) but apparently Prince Charles now gets over £22 million a year (June 2020.... now Charles is King his oldest Son William gets this booty) from the Duchy of Cornwall, and millions from State coffers while millions go hungry in the UK. Tibet had actual been a part of China for centuries going back at least to the time of the Mongols, known as the Yuan dynasty. However, like all regions of the earth where man and language has evolved independently each little area had become an autonomous island with its own culture and beliefs. Some have also said that Tibet was a vassal state of China, like the UK is to America in the 21st century. The Dalai Lama's rule did not start until the 17th & 18 century after the decline of the Yuan dynasty, which had lasted centuries. The Ganden Phodrang was the Tibetan regime or government that was established by the 5th Dalai Lama with the help of the Gush Khan of the Khoshut in 1642. Lhasa became the capital of Tibet in the beginning of this period with temporal power being conferred to the 5th Dalai Lama by Gushi Khan in Shigatse. At the time of China's intervention into Tibet of March 1959 a million Tibetan's serfs and slaves assisted the Peoples Liberation Army's smashing of the secessionist serf-owners revolt. A practise that I was not aware of until I read it in the Morning Star (letter by Nigel Green - 27/28 June 2020) about Tibetan culture, at least valid up until 1959, was the process called living burials. 'Lamist superstition, made it allowable, sometimes mandatory, to bury little boys beneath important buildings or images so they would stand forever'. Cruelty seems the one thing that all ruling classes have done to others across the globe for millennia. Rudyard Kipling's great yarn *The Man Who Would be King was* published about 1888 and made into a movie in the mid-seventies of the 20th century. It was directed by the legendary John Huston, who wanted to make it 20 years previously, and starred Sean Connery as Danny Dravot and Michael Caine as Peachy Carnehan with Christopher Plummer playing Kipling and Saeed Jaffrey as Billy Fish. Having never read the book or known a lot about Kipling per se, albeit he was born in Mumbai in India where I visited in 2006. He won a noble prize in Literature in 1907 (he must have been a lot more intelligent than me...well his dad was a professor). This literary confection sums up neatly how the majority can be hood winked by clever con-men. In this case two ex-service Brits who had served in the British army in the 19th century decided to go north through the Khyber Pass through Afghanistan into Kafiristan, where Danny Dravot becomes a God/ruler. The adventure is a great yarn, and I was very impressed with it when I saw it decades ago, and it was very recently shown on British TV as a memorial to the great Sean Connery, who ironically came from a very humble background in Edinburgh to become a King himself of the movie business. But I have to say I do not understand why actors are so revered when acting is just like any 'trade'...say a bricklayer or whatever. The message in the story to me was very clear that people who are uneducated and we could say easily led and question nothing, like the majority in the UK, can be easily manipulated by the ruling King/Elite, who can 'get away with murder', figuratively speaking.

Oliver James in his famous book Affluenza published in 2007 notes that only 7% of English children have private education, but they dominate the top Universities like Oxford and Cambridge and it is the British class system (and their parents) itself that helps this whole rotten society along, and they should be grateful to that whole edifice rather than to their own efforts, like mine for example. When this book was reviewed on BBC Radio 4 in 2007 several professors were put up against James because it was so controversial at the time. According to Oliver James the Affluenza virus is caused by the desire of acquiring money and possessions and looking good in the eyes of others and wanting to be famous, if you have these values, you have caught the virus, like Donald J. Trump has and Boris Johnson; I never did. The other side of the coin is what he calls Affluenza distress caused by trying to achieve these goals. The reason I have used this book as a source in this project is for two reasons, first James starts his research in New York where Trump comes from and it contains interviews of people from New York who are seriously psychology damaged by the Affluenza virus, where everything is just a commodity to be used and abused daily. Secondly, he interviews several well-educated women (gals) in Shanghai who have caught the virus but who are not distressed. The mystery deepens. The reason seems to be that most Chinese people are very optimistic and have positive thoughts every day. In the West this is far from the truth. Albeit when James was researching this book about 14 years ago only 30 million people were called affluent, now I presume tens of millions more are in this bracket. Now if I do not make it today I will tomorrow, and it is also a collective effort, which it is certainly not in the West. A man like Trump pretends he made it on his own, like a small per cent that have, but he had a lot of help from his father, with perhaps 600 million dollars, according to his niece. However, most of the wonderful Shanghai girls understand clearly that everything in modern China now is about making money and very little else and jealousy can take hold but not for long. Often through peer pressure, which is very prevalent at the level of friendship and interaction between these women, which often just adds up to what have you got, like a new Mercedes Benz, and I have not got. 'Do not do unto others what you do not want done to yourself'; Confucius famous 'Golden Rule' hardly seems relevant to modern day capitalism in China, but it seems it is making a comeback. A very similar aphorism was said by Kant over two thousand years later in the 18th century……. Confucius also believed in modesty. Albeit the respect for the old seems to have gone the same way as the UK and the USA, you do not exist and to hell with any thoughts of helping them on public transport and so on. The young woman he interviewed born outside of Shanghai thought this was outrageous, but even she had to adapt to the new culture/zeitgeist now encompassing the whole of China, especially the big cities. Trying your hardest is the most important thing you can do for yourself, your parents and society as a whole, 'no one will castigate you, and you are under no pressure to castigate yourself, so long as you have tried your hardest'. (29) Strange as it may seem for young Western women even when one of the girls was studying in the USA, she felt she could not sleep with a young American man because it would have let Chinese society down in the eyes her culture. The key factor, that most people in the Western world do not understand about the paternalistic nature that imbues the whole of Chinese society, albeit the Han big idea was a myth originally. Noam Chomsky praises this sort of phenomenon in *Year 501* as he notes 'one phenomenal success has been township and village enterprises for the most part factories owned by rural farmers which now account for close to 20% of China's GNP employing more than 100 million people' (30).

The 1989 student revolt or pro-democracy event as the western journalists called it, in Tiananmen square by mostly students but not all, seems to have been misjudged by the Ruling Elite, I would have thought, and probably got out of hand. Where according to several documentaries on the BBC TV on the 30th of September 2019, killings did actually take place, with eyewitnesses like the personable Kate Adie confirmed on the ground. She was one of the very few western journalists actually there, with a TV crew. She, of course, got into terrible trouble with the brutal Thatcher government in the 1980's when reporting live for the BBC from Libya when Reagan and his henchmen tried to kill 'mad dog' Gaddafi, as they called him, with weapons from aircraft? According to these documentary's the Chinese troops closed off the square, so the students could not escape and then started shooting them with AK47 rifles at random with live ammunition and rubber bullets, and tanks crushing people under their tracks, which may have been a 'war crime', according to these documentaries. After the event thousands were arrested and some may have been shot albeit that the ruling elite said this did not happen and was erased from history: very similar so it seems to the crimes of the USA and the UK, over decades and centuries, very few would have heard of the crimes that the ruling class in the UK did to China in the 1900 century. Kate Adie seemed to think that the whole exercise was about pleas for a better future and society, like most protests around the globe. In the UK in 2019 well over a 1000 people were arrested and charged for protesting about climate change. She also suggested that 10,000 troopers were sent into Tiananmen Square, mostly uneducated young men who were easily brainwashed by state propaganda, suggesting that the revolt was an existentialist threat to the state and a counter revolution? I would have thought it was impossible to aggregate the total killed: Kate Adie thought '2000', a student said '4000' and Private Eye (No 1575) thought '10,000'. Oliver Stone & Peter Kuznick thought '3000' died and '10,000' were wounded and George H Bush resisted any form of punishment and let 43,000 Chinese students in the USA to remain in the country beyond their one-year visas. Will Hutton's explanation of these events are much broader, covering a lot of the universities in China, but he seemed to think that only a few hundred were killed which included 223 soldiers. Ironically, Kate Adie said that 'human nature wants freedom', an axiom for thousands of years, but we are not going to get it without world revolts against naked and brutal wage slavery everywhere, Kate (?). This means the philosophy of 'existentialism' was some of the biggest tosh (sic) ever invented by man, as was the big idea that the sort of society constructed by man in the west, and now to a certain existent in China, is the end of history...see for example Francis Fukuyama. Normally the western world is very quiet about the riots in South Korea in 1980s in the city of Gwangju in Jeolla Province, which was an uprising against the new military strongman General Chun

Doo Hwan that killed hundreds of Gwangju citizens, I heard this on the BBC World service, probably for the first time on the morning of the 28 May 2020 and mentioned in *Rogue State* by William Blum.

This culture of get rich in its many forms seems to be the only reason that capitalism exists and why in countries like the USA and Britain it can be very dangerous, as it is in its globalist form. For example, during the prohibition period in the USA crime went hand and hand with law enforcement. Many movies and TV drams have been made about this period in USA history, one of the very best was called *The Untouchables* starring Kevin Costner as Eliot Ness, Robert De Niro as Al Capone and Sean Connery as Jim Malone, the latter winning an Oscar for his role, and now sadly dead at 90. In the UK scandal only raises its ugly head on very rare occasions, because of the power of the ruling class, which includes the Tory party and the powerful mass media pumping out lies and propaganda 24/7. Because the working class are so uneducated in the main, they believe what they are told especially by the extreme right-wing press, virtually believing that the whole rotten system is fair and above board, which of course it is not...see also above. Another example worth mentioning was a robbery in the early 1970s which was bigger than the great train robbery of 1962, for the amateur gang who carried it out. In fact, it was so surreal it is nearly beyond belief, set up by the British Establishment to get very embarrassing pictures of Princess Margaret (the queen's sister) taken in the Caribbean, out of a bank vault in London. If the movie (now on DVD) made about it is true, it was quite shocking (The Bank Job - Royal Scandal of the Century – 2007). Michael X, the black guy who took them, was virtually blackmailing the establishment, so he could commit also sorts of misdeeds in the Capital. The gang who carried out the heist were not aware of reason for the robbery, drilling through/underneath a food bar to get to the vault next door, but one, in the first place. According to the movie made about these events, the alarm system had been switched off, so the chance of being caught was quite slim; albeit that the British Establishment was monitoring the whole event, at the time and an amateur ham radio enthusiast, also got in on the act, purely by accident. What made the story so scandalous and very dangerous, for all of us was not only the main story line but also the sub-plots which included a porn king who was paying off the police force in London and kept a book on everyone he paid for services rendered, which was also in the same vault as the photos of Princess Margaret, including pictures of another upper middle-class person taken by a Madam, in Soho. The leader of the gang became suspicions of the model who asked him to carry out the robbery in the first place, so took measures not to get caught after the robbery…. after finding the explosive pictures of the princess, in vault 118. According to the movie at least one of the robbers got deliberately killed by the police, working for the porn king, and Michael X the black guy who took the originally photos killed a British agent in Trinidad and was hung for it in 1975. Two other robbers died in a mysterious way, either by the state or outsourced to hit men? The whole saga was covered up by the British Establishment a short time after the event with a 'D' notice, an idea to keep state secrets from everyone for decades. The leader of the gang with another two of the robbers (which included a model having an affair with an M16 agent, and who helped to set the whole thing up) came to an agreement with M15/M16 that they would get new passports and not be prosecuted if they handed over the scandalous photos of princess Margaret to Lord Mountbatten of Burma - they also handed the book with all the crooked policeman names in over to an honest cop. And as I said, this was a very disturbing true story/movie about how the British establishment operate at the highest level of State, on behalf of the ruling class whose cruelty is beyond belief and has been for centuries, as it was in China. Why this is so important to explain to the whole world, who may not be aware of past atrocities of the British elite, is that while researching and writing this book in 2019/2020/2021/2022 a constant theme about China in the West is the so-called clamp down on demonstrators in Hong Kong. This, supposedly, is over the idea of democracy, which the British never gave them, and the treatment of the Uighur people in Xinjiang province, which may be true if considered a threat to the whole of China? The impression given in the Guardian's (12th January 2020) Long Read by Gulbahar Haitiwaji, who grew up in Xinjiang province but because of discrimination in the work place her family moved to France in 2006, is as follows. She went back to China in 2016 to sign a document concerning her 'forthcoming retirement'. After going to the oil companies' office, the firm she had worked at for 20 years, to sign some documents (we presume) she ended up in Kunlun police station; it is not too clear how this came about. This is when the story, if true, does get a little disturbing as a policeman showed her a photo of ONE of her daughters with a little flag that represents the Xinjiang province taken in France. Apparently, the province was taken over by China in 1955 as an 'autonomous region', which has caused dynamic tension ever since between the Uighur people and the Han rulers. In 2009 the tension got so explosive that '197 people' died in an uprising. Haitiwaji's daughter was accused of being a 'terrorist' and Mother ended up in a re-education camp for several years. Her treatment was quite cruel, including being chained to a bed for '20 days' with military discipline and lessons on how to be a good Chinese citizen in the Han tradition. On the 2nd of August 2019, after nearly three years in this camp and a short trial, she was 'pronounced innocent'. However, a few days before this article in the Guardian appeared a letter by Michael Murry which was titled 'Beware anti-China propaganda war' appeared in the Morning Star (7th January 2020), which I believe was an axiom for all intellectuals who want 'to expose lies and tell the truth' (Noam

Chomsky) albeit even if there is a grain of truth in Gulbahar Haitiwaji story. The West is becoming terrified of what China is achieving and the fact China might overtake the USA economy in this decade. In this letter Murry even suggests that what the West is up to, apart from my thesis and those of a few others in this book, is to and try cause so much havoc it may collapse like the old Soviet Union. China is presented as another Iraq, a new Hitler, another threat to the USA and so on. In essence how can we be sure that any of this is true and not just propaganda of the Western powers? When Lui Xiaoming the Chinese ambassador in the UK was shown a video of so-called of Uighur people being put on a train and in theory being taken to a re-education camp on the Andrew Marr show in 2020, he said he would investigate it…but I must admit I was very suspicious of it as the BBC is up to its knees in lies and propaganda propping up a very ruthless ruling class in all their news coverage for years. Andrew Marr, one of the better educated and well-read journalists in the UK. But he and his wife fit neatly into an 'upper middle class' position in society, probably earning over £10,000 per week, while the average wage slaves in the UK are very lucky to pick up £400/600per week with millions earning a lot less. How can such a man even begin to understand the worries and concerns of ordinary working-class people and their daily struggle? Steve Cattrell in another letter in the Morning Star (14th January 2021) asserts that 'we must not join propaganda war' basically saying that we should treat stuff coming out of the West about China with severe caution because some of it may have come from an eccentric Christian evangelist Adrian Zenz who suggested China has interned over a million people in Xinjiang, something debunked by articles on the Grayzone website. On the same page (Letters) W J. Brunt said that perhaps we should still take the charges seriously of incarceration and re-education camps because of reports from Amnesty International and the Red Cross. Therefore, we should always be on the lookout for who is wielding the axe and what their reasons are. As I have noted before in other projects of mine, most people have never heard of Noam Chomsky, or if they have - have probably never read the great man, who some say is making up his critique of USA foreign policy as the wrong narrative when he is one of the very few who are 'exposing lies and telling the truth'... about the outright cruelty of the ruling classes (Power Elites) all-round the globe, especially the USA and NATO.

The latest crime China commits against the West, so it seems, is that the Chinese communist party is enacting a 'new security law' for Hong Kong, some saying it creates a 'death knell' for so-called basic freedoms of the ex-British colony whereas in fact there was no freedom for most under the British Empire that was supposedly going to last for 1000 years, similar in 'vision' to the NAZIS. Trump in the USA and Johnson in the UK whipped up crude, crass nationalism for personnel reasons back home, anything to deflect from the shambolic nature of their responses to covid-19. According to McGregor (see below), China is hoping to stamp out opposition to these new polices in the ex-British colony without killing off its vital role as a financial centre of prosperity. The Morning Star in the UK may have hit the correct note about this process, which you would not read about in most of the British press, as they noted 'the new draft national security law is aimed at restoring security after months of violence last year that saw a spike in anti-Chinese rhetoric and the targeting of business and individuals in the territory that were deemed pro-Beijing' (2nd June 2020). In fact, as they go on to say it is very unlikely that the way the British media like to portray these riots as pro-democracy affairs is maybe not quite correct. It is much more likely to be far right separatists bank rolled by the US regime through an organisation called the 'National Endowment for Democracy', a shady organization set up at the time of Ronald Reagan, which has interfered in regime change all around the globe. 'Earlier this year they were believed to have been behind a bomb attack on a hospital a day after masked anti-China protesters torched the site of a quarantine centre treating suspected Covid-19 victims'. Martin Jacques takes on the British in Hong Kong, in a much more honest rationale, was that there was a form of apartheid set up under the British whereby the Chinese had to carry night passes, and a nasty form of racism was rampant, which may have been taken up by the Chinese, with the idea that dark skin people were inferior to everyone else. This is certainly what happened to Jacques wonderful wife Hari, who sadly died in a Hong Kong hospital. She was dark skinned and probably discriminated against, so she thought, before she died.

An expert on China called Richard McGregor a senior fellow at the Lowry Institute in Sydney seems to think that because of covid-19 that China may be going through a downturn in the economy like all other countries that have been affected by this virus. As he noted in the Sunday Observer (31st May 2020), 'with an ailing domestic economy, can China still purse its global plans?' Wherein the USA and the UK the fallout from the virus is starting to look horrendous, with tens of millions unemployed in the USA and millions in the UK, in China because of its huge population the economy has suffered a brutal contraction, leaving a jobless rate of about 20%, according to McGregor. Which may mean that tens of millions or hundreds of millions have lost their jobs and those still in employment have had their salaries and wages reduced. With Europe the USA and Japan in a deep recession export cannot take up the slack.

As China goes from strength to strength, although most countries are suffering short term economy downturn, because of covid-19 it seems that whenever a dissenter in China or Russia questions the legitimacy of the ruling Elite the West exploits-it to the full. Millions like me in the West are dissenters but no one wants to hear our voice, pretending everything is all hunky dory, which of course it is not when we have so much contrast of extreme wealth and poverty, run by plutocrats. In the UK the total wealth in society may be as high as £14 trillion, of which 10% of the population own 50%.

Professor Cai Xia is a dissenter, according to the Guardian (19th August 2020), who taught at an elite college in China for officials, and now has been expelled from the communist party and has left China. Her crime, apparently, was to critique President Xi Jinping, 'accusing him of "killing a country" and claiming that many more wanted to leave the ruling Chinese Communist party'. The school apparently sacked her because she made comments that were damaging the countries reputation and were full of 'serious political problems'. Ironically, Professor Cia Xia seems to be saying that the CCP is not a force for progress but the complete opposite, which is very strange indeed, is it not, when Donald Trump, among others, seemingly tried destroy its success in economic matters. Also, she suggests that President Xi is making China an enemy of the world. Again, this seems to be turning social reality on its head when we had such a dangerous man in the White House, out to blow it up. The real reason for this dissent seems to be that Xi changed the Chinese constitution in 2018, which gave him the ability to stay in power indefinitely, something I would think Trump would do if he could get away with it! In the UK, or as I like to call it now North Korea on Thames (as satire), it being one of the very few semi-feudal societies in the world that has had a King/Queen as head of state for 1000 years, forming part of one of the most ruthless upper class/ruling classes in the world, along with the rest of the very rich aristocracy, owning billions of pounds of wealth. A country where the people are not citizens but 'subjects'. Professor Xia seems to think that now that president Xi is so powerful everyone is afraid of him and his aides will not tell him the truth about anything - for example, dangerous phenomena like the Covid 19 virus. Albeit, president Xi may have known about it on the 7th of January 2020; but news of it was not released to the world until the 20[th of] January. What I find so very amusing about this specific article is that the professor is suggesting that Xi is whipping up nationalistic beliefs, in China which is what happened in the USA and the UK. Steve Bannon, who helped to get Trump elected in the USA in 2016, just was arrested for fraud (August 2020) for stealing from private funds raised for construction of the great wall of Mexico/USA border, along with three other friends. Bannon, who has atleast two master's degrees, has been working on this model of independent countries for at least 30 years, railing against globalization and promoting the nationalistic ideal, which I would have thought was not for the same reasons people on the Left have been rallying against neo-liberal globalization. He also supports Nigel Farage, ('King of Europe' according to Trump) Boris Johnson, Jacob-Rees Mogg and other politicians who are against the EU. In fact, trading on the world stage has been going on for thousands of years, as most educated people are aware of, and in countries like the UK, if we did not trade with other countries for food half the population would die of starvation. Joe Biden thinks the Brexit idea was mad, which it was, only 'extreme' people like Boris Johnson, Nigel Farage and Trump, could believe in it. Albeit there are factions on the Left who also believe we should be out of the EU, mostly because the whole European project since the Second World War has been about maintaining the capitalistic system at all costs. However, there are many different versions of the system in virtually every country, especially in Scandinavia countries which are all much more humane than the brutal British version. For example, very few British people would know that Winston Churchill in 1910, when he became Home Secretary, had secretly proposed sterilization of 100,000 "mental degenerates" and the dispatch of tens of thousands of others to state-run labour camps so as to save the "British race" from inevitable decline if its "inferior" members are allowed to breed-ideas (eugenics) that were within the bounds of enlightened opinion of the day, but have been kept secret in Home Office files because of their sensitivity, particularly after they were taken up by Hitler' (31).

Nationalistic themes seem to be the new norm, but on such a small planet with a population of 8 billion people, it seems slightly bonkers regarding global warming and the covid-19 pandemic crises, because in both cases they need a world solution to the problem with every one working together, albeit Boris Johnson and his bunch of henchmen seemed determined to get the UK out of the European project, which has been going on since the 1950s and was originally thought up to stop the mass slaughter of total war again. (UK taken out of the EEC finally on 1st January 2021.) However, if lovely and beautiful Barbara Finamore is correct in the Guardian (6th October 2020), President Xi Jinping is very keen to set China on a course to be carbon-neutral by 2060; in the UK it is set for 2050. At the present China is 'responsible for 28% of the world's greenhouse gas emissions, more than US and the EU combined'. They are still building coal fire powered stations and burning half of all coal output in the world in these stations and directly in factories that produce steel and cement. When Finamore moved to China in 1990 there was hardly any cars on the road, but smog was all over Beijing, especially in the winter because everyone burnt coal for domestic purposes and not far away was the largest steel mill in China. Cycling was the main form of transport, now cars rule the roost as the way of getting from A to B. Because of this China is the world's biggest importer of crude oil. Ironically China now leads the world in very clean technologies, and is by far the largest investor, producer and consumer of renewable energy. One out of every three solar panels in the world are made in China. And in virtually all fields of the green revolution, China seems to be leading the world in electric passage vehicles - from buses to two wheelers, and battery storage facilities. If these green projects continue in the same vein, in a few years' time fossil fuels may become extinct, just like the dinosaurs, but unfortunately not the British aristocracy, who may be around for another million years? Finamore seems to think that President Xi will keep his promise whereas not one word Boris Johnson or Trump says can be taken as the truth. Albeit Xi has stiff resistance from vested interests and local governments, whereas in the UK local government has been decimated and crushed after another 13 years of Tory government, and now the UK is one of the most centralized states in the world, with 'misrule' by the Boris Johnson Government taken to new heights of believability.

Carlos Martinez again gives an excellent analysis to me and others, writing in the Morning Star (11 November 2020) that 102 years to the day the guns fell silent on Flanders fields where at-least 16 million people died, but for what? 'Profits', John Reed said at the time. The insanity of the ruling classes fighting over empires and glory, the posturing that 'I am bigger than you and more famous'…when you think about it seriously it makes one physically sick and to think of how it is now glorified by the ancestors of the same crass ruling class that caused it in the first place, especially in the UK, every year at the grave of the unknown soldier in Westminster Abbey. Returning to Martinez, who is correct in asserting that the West, especially in the USA, but we can say in the UK and parts of Europe as well, are in panic mode over on-going economic stagnation, the covid-19 crisis, the poverty rate in the USA at 15% (the highest it been for 50 years), infrastructure falling apart because of lack of investment, and so on. The dynamics of these factors are surely stretched to the limits when the masses start to question their political leaders' legitimacy? In response, capitalist government look for ways to restore profitability whilst maintaining social stability. In the1930s European fascism took this to extreme ends, with barbaric violence and vicious racism in order to keep the working class in its place, and to generate economic growth through investment in the war machine. The 2008 financial crash led to the ruling classes in the USA and the UK bailing out the banks while pursuing brutal austerity policies for the majority. Now they must find a new enemy to fight which is China, having read what they thought would just be fabulous profits for western companies on the back of Chinese workers, for ever - they did not understand that China's long-term objective was to improve the standard of living for as many people as possible inside China. This is one of the main themes in Martin Jacques brilliant book on China. The problem the Western Elites have is that China is doing it on similar principles to the West but with a very strong central government in the driving seat and doing it very successfully. To the ruling Elites in the West this is sort of a crime, like when someone like me can become educated and write books, ...getting above your 'station in life' they call it, in the UK. And like the brutal 'ruling class' in the UK cannot tell me what to do any more, so the Western powers cannot tell China what to do any more. As Carlos Martinez notes, the other clear objective of China is to stop the hegemony of the USA controlling everything and to let all countries be independent. Often this is done with the help of China, which is like a red rag to the US bull. Whereas China is no threat to most of the world's population, it is to the rich and powerful in the West. Hence, the West are using all the tricks in the book to prevent the inevitable, encircling the whole country with weapons, as the brilliant John Pilger's documentary noted, to outright racism in its many forms, an old trick the brutal English ruling class have been doing for centuries. The 'Black Lives Matter' movement is just one of many forms the majority can take to stand up to their so-called masters and set people free. Further evidence of what has just been written above is a report published on the 26th august 2021 by the Communist Party of China (CPC), in its English translation of 28,000 words celebrating 100 years of existence. The trust of the document according to Carlos Martinez in the Morning Star (1st September 2021) is that it is building on its basic premise of all this time. Adapting Marxism to China's specific conditions in the 21st century, while trying to do well in the world and increase wealth to all its citizens, at home.

Martin Jacques also makes some very important points about the huge investments China is making all over the globe, winning friends in the process, albeit the 45 million+ Chinese diaspora around the world is causing tension even in countries like Italy, where Right-wing political parties whip up the hatred of foreigners which is very similar to what the Tory party/government has been doing for decades in the UK. The Chinese are very good businesspeople, which also can in some cases cause stress with the locals, especially in the Far East.
I will complete this chapter with a few words from Noam Chomsky's latest book *The Precipice,* when being interviewed by C. J. Polychroniou about the narrative that Trump was creating when president about Iran and China etc. As he notes when Trump said 'China is killing us' stealing our jobs and so on, what does he mean? No one put a gun to the head of Tim Cook CEO of Apple and said invest in China or any other large companies that now have moved to China. They did it willingly as labour is cheaper there and these huge businesses can make massive profits. If, however China is violating the intellectual property regime (TRIPS) how legitimate is the whole organisation, in the first place and who gains and who loses? The rise of Huawei's cheaper and superior technology may give them an unfair advantage in establishing 5G networks, which is the reason the USA and the UK are trying to stop it…which is a very good example of why the USA is losing its marbles over the rise of China which is very similar to that of the Japanese in the 1960s/1970s/1980s?

SOURCES

(1) James Kynge: China Shakes the World – 2007 p, x1
(2) Tony Bilton et al: Introductory Sociology - 1987 Second Edition p, 55.
(3) Jonathan Fenby et al: The Seventy Wonders of China – f/p 2007
(4) Will Hutton: The Writing on the Wall – China and the West in the 21st Century – 2007
(5) Jonathan Spence: Mao – 2000 edition paperback
(6) Martin Jacques: When China Rules the World – f/p 2009.
(7) Michael Sherington & Robert Ash: The Seventy Wonders of the China – f/p 2007
(8) Michael Woods: The Story of China: DVD collection.
(9) Ditto
(10) Joe Studwell: The China Dream -2002 - p, 4-5
(11) Will Hutton: as above p, 58
(12) James Kynge: China Shakes the World – p, X11+X111.
(13) Will Hutton: as above p, 54
(14) Ditto p, 54
(15) Ditto p, 55
(16) Joe Studwell: The China Dream - 2002 p, 16
(17) Ditto p,
(18) Martin Jacques: When China Rules the World -2009 p, 84.
(19) Will Hutton: as above p, 63-64
(20) Martin Jacques: as above
(21) Will Hutton: as above p, 70
(22) Ditto p, 72
(23) Jonathan Spence: Mao – 2000 edition paperback
(24) Will Hutton: as above p,75

(25) Ditto
(26) Ditto p, 78
(27) Stone & Kuznick: The Untold History of the United States 2012 p, 236
(28) William Blum: Rogue State p, 163
(29) Oliver James: Affluenza 2007 p,132
(30) Noam Chomsky: Year 501 p, 108.
(31) Noam Chomsky: Year 501 p, 207/208

OTHER SOURCES

Jean-Jacques Rousseau: The Discourse on the Origins of Inequality (1712 -1778)
John Locke (1632 – 1704)
Thomas Hobbes: Leviathan published in 1651.
Gazella Boy of the Rio de Oro
Ann Widdecombe: An extreme Right-wing Tory ex MP & MEP speech given in the European Parliament.
Plutarch (AD 46 – AD119)
John Keay: China A History – f/b 2008 paperback edition.
Christopher Hitchens: The Trial of Henry Kissinger – 2001
BBC 4 (TV) Wild China
Private Eye various editions
The works of Friedrich Von Hayek, covering 60 years.
Noam Chomsky: Turning the Tide – 1985
Marx & Engels: The Communist Manifesto 1848

Private Eye

The Man Who would be King: story by Rudyard Kipling and made into a movie in the mid-1970s.

Morning Star: Various editions.

The Guardian: various editions

BBC News channels

BBC World Service radio

Francis Fukuyama: The End of History and the Last Man - 1992 paperback edition.

The Untouchables - a movie about Al Capone: starring Kevin Costner and Sean Connery.

The Bank Job…a true movie about the British Queen's sister, living the high life in the Caribbean and I presume a 'working royal'?

The Sunday Observer: various editions.

Morning Star: 1st September 2021.

The First Emperor: TV documentary now shown on Amazon Prime.

Private Eye - No 1575

Noam Chomsky: The Precipice - paperback - 2021.

CHAPTER THREE

ON THE ROAD TO ARMAGEDDON FOR THE WORLD OR 'HOW I LEARNED TO STOP WORRYING AND LOVE THE BOMB'……after Dr Strangelove!!!!!

I have reached the same age as Donald J. Trump and just survived pancreatic cancer (diagnosed June 2018) and have probably travelled to more countries than the last Republican incumbent of the White House (40 at the last count). I was also born below the working class (very poor with deep apologies for repeating it) in what Jacob Rees-Mogg and Boris Johnston (very rich Tory MPs in the House of Commons… Mogg may be worth £150 million) would call a vassal country. In fact, in this case, they wouldn't, because the Falkland Islands is a colonial outpost of the British Empire, so may not have the intuitiveness to understand their own contradictions, albeit they both went to Eton and Oxford? Whereas Donald J. Trump was given tens of millions by his father to start his own businesses, although he pretends, he is a self-made man. No one gave me anything, let alone a silver spoon, so, what I have learned through study at four Universities (some ex-polytechnics) over six years and in all my travelling is that the world is full of wonderful man-made and natural wonders with a plethora of different cultures and beliefs. In fact, what we see today in most places in the world is not only living history, and buildings that are often hundreds and thousands of years old - but also that over the last 500 years most countries in the world have been affected by European colonialism. India, for example, which I visited for a month in August 2006, was a very prosperous place before the English arrived and destroyed local industries, starving millions to death. As late as 1943 four million were starved to death. This occurred because during the Second World War economic and social policies carried out by the UK government resulted in the theft of trillions, according to George Monbiot. China, even to this day, is still ashamed of what the English Ruling Class did to them in the 19th century, pushing drugs on to the indigenous population, mostly grown in India, with the death of millions of Indians through starvation and the grand theft of Hong Kong that was only given back in 1997 and is now a Chinese special administrative region. Two years later in 1999 China had a warning from US/ NATO of what may happen in the future according to the great William Blum - saying that if you get too big for your boots, and challenge our hegemony, we will act, so they bombed the Chinese embassy in Belgrade, which they claimed was a mistake because of out-dated maps among other problems (1) …but was this true? What does appear to be true according to Private Eye (No 1490) (from other sources) is that a neo-conservative think tank called (HJS) Henry Jackson Society has been paid 'around £10,000 a month to spread anti-China messages on to "the radar of mainstream UK journalists and politicians"'…. from a Japanese government payroll. We could ask did Ian Duncan Smith (IDS - ex-leader of the Tory Party), and 6 other MPs receive payments from this organisation when IDS said on BBC Radio4 (11th February 2023) that if Erkin Tuniyaz the Governor of Xinjiang in China comes to the UK that we should arrest him and I presume send him to the Hague for 'crimes against humanity', slightly ironic indeed considering the crimes committed all over the world by the British Empire and the Tory Government in the UK today against the majority of the population?

As I have noted above like many other intelligent people, before me, for the last one hundred years or more the world has become a far more dangerous place, because of the industrialization of warfare, which now includes nuclear weapons as-well as the explosive mixture which is Capitalism itself, going from one crisis to the other in a globalized marketplace. So constantly trying to blame other countries and not themselves for the chaos, which is all around us, this also applies to internal conflicts. An example is the latest crisis of capitalism, which started in the USA with sub-prime mortgages going haywire with money being lent to millions of poor people, who after some time could not pay it back. This debt was then packaged up and called all sorts of wonderful names and sold on from one financial institution to another and when the bubble burst the last man standing took the hit along with many other banks, which had to be bailed out by the State. In the UK, the brutal Tory government/coalition 2010 - 2015 tried to blame the previous labour government for the crisis of 2008. The Tory government of 2015, who got elected with a very small majority carried on with the same rhetoric, albeit that 76% of the population who could have voted did not vote for the Tory party in the UK, in 2015! Isn't bourgeois democracy wonderful?

The sanctions imposed on China by Trump and vice-versa are probably just the start of the road to Armageddon, because as China becomes more of a capitalist country it will suffer the same problems as all other countries around the globe do. And according to Joseph Choonara and RT (Russia Today) it seems that it is now going through a debt crisis of its own - probably worse than the USA, whose state debt has now soared to over $21 trillion. Where in the past investment was engineered to make goods for export on high levels of exploitation and ever-expanding markets abroad, as these have declined China 'unleashed a wave of credit to continue the expansion' (2). This has helped the workers to ask for better wages and conditions, but it has also caused instability in the property and stock market. As Joseph Choonara asserts, with the help of Martin Wolf about these arising problems: 'In response to the 2008 financial crisis, China promoted a huge rise in debt-fuelled investment to offset the weakening in external demand. But underlying growth in the economy was slowing. As a result, the "incremental capital output ratio" the amount of capital needed to generate additional income - has roughly doubled since the early 2000s...At the margin, much of this investment is likely to be loss making. If so, the debt associated with it will also be unsound. In other words, the country is experiencing its own crisis of profitability, bowed down by over-accumulation and bad debt' (3).

The 'ides of March' (15th march), once given to Julius Caesar by a soothsayer on the way to the senate before he was murdered, with Cicero's approval, in 44 BC, should have been a warning to Trump and the world. Why? Because Trump imposed 25% tariffs on various goods, instead of the 10% that applied previously. The underlying reason for this course of action, according to Trump, was to 'open its markets' up. But ironically, as I have noted above, the rich Western powers especially the USA have always rigged the system in their favour, as did Great Britain regarding free trade as it was once called in its heyday, especially against India (Chomsky et al). The very impressive Joseph Stiglitz, who has a Nobel prize in Economic Sciences, and the John Bates Clark Medal informs us in 'Globalization and its discontents' (2002) how after the Berlin Wall came down in Germany and the fall of the old Soviet Union, their whole economies were transferred to capitalism from the old Command system, virtually overnight, and most State assets were stolen by the few. After this event, for example, according to Stiglitz in the USA, the government deliberately helped Paul O'Neal, head of Alcoa, form 'a global aluminium cartel. Cartels work by restricting output, thereby raising prices' (4). They restricted imports of aluminium from Russia by pretending that they were dumping these commodities on the USA market, below a 'fair market value'. Which was not true because: 'Russia was selling its aluminium at international prices' (5). Hence, 'the USA unfair trade laws are not written on the basis of economic principles. They exist solely to protect American industries adversely affected by imports' (6). Or as Noam Chomsky informed us in 1994: 'As the most powerful state, the United States makes its own laws using force and conducting economic warfare at will.' It also threatens sanctions against countries that do not abide by its conveniently flexible notions of "free trade". Washington has employed such threats with great effectiveness (and GATT approval) to force open Asian markets for U.S. tobacco exports and advertising, aimed primarily at the growing markets of women and children. The U. S. Agriculture Department has provided grants to tobacco firms to promote smoking overseas. Asian countries have attempted to conduct educational anti-smoking campaigns, but they are overwhelmed by the miracles of the market reinforced by U.S. state power through the threat of sanctions. Philip Morris, with an advertising and promotion budget of close to 9 billion dollars in 1992, became China's largest advertiser, which may well lead to deaths from cigarette related disease of 50 million Chinese (of whom many would be children under 20) according to the Oxford University epidemiologist Richard Peto. (7)

Hopefully, every country in the world has learnt the above-mentioned lesson, especially China; I would have thought that Mrs May, the British Prime Minister (who was still in office early 2019....and had left office by force on the 24$^{th\ of}$ July 2019) was not too stupid to understand this axiom? However, if this principal hegemony does not work, something else can always be made up. For example, that the Huawei telecommunications company from China, who directly threaten USA dominance in this field, are accused of violating 'sanctions by doing business with Iran through a subsidiary it tried to hide' (8) ….and stealing robotic technology from the US carrier T-Mobile. I of course do not know if any of this is true or false, nor, for that matter, do most of the 8 billion people on the Planet. But Meng Wanzhou, the daughter of the owner of Huawei, was arrested in Canada on December 2018 after a request from the US. Subsequent to this there were protracted extradition proceedings, with Meng eventually heading back to China, having reached an 'accomodation' with the US government. China condemned the US government's charges against, Huawei which is owned by its employees (1500 staff in the UK and 80,000 overall), as unfair and immoral, inferring it was trying to blacken the name of this company and others who are getting in the way of USA hegemony. Ironically, it seems that the UK government is caught in a catch 22 situation when it comes to this company and critiquing China in general. Albeit we are part of the 'Five Eyes' spying network of the: UK, USA, Canada, Australia and New Zealand, so have got to 'pretend' that if China helps with the new 5g system in the UK it may still be a threat to the West, by some back-door deception? This appears to be the reason with other massive investments in the UK, as much as 20,8 billion dollars between 2016 & 2017 and even Huawei wanting to invest another 3 billion dollars here, that the current Prime Minister is keeping silent (9). According to the BBC World Service (19 February 2019) the father of Meng Wanzhou said he 'would not do anything that harms his company' through attacks on the USA or by halting the huge leap forward in technology that this company has made, and its size.

What I always find so ironic about any information, for example partially true knowledge, disinformation, etc about stories like this one, is it is often very hard to find any sources telling the whole truth, hence the need reference multiple channels of information. For example, in a recent very long article in the 'I newspaper' (27th - 28th April 2019) called 'The Huawei invasion' it notes that Chinese equipment is already being used extensively by the Government to handle sensitive data. According to Dean Kirby and Cahal Milmo who informs us that 'thousands of civil servants, including officials at sensitive agencies responsible for criminal prosecutions and the records of every driver and vehicle in the UK, are using data devices made by controversial Chinese technology giant Huawei'. This is because equipment already in use with 4G and Wi-Fi dongles and wireless hotspots, were vulnerable to attack by individuals who could intercept data being sent over the networks. Another reason we should be concerned, according to a GCHQ (sic) source, is the standard of the equipment being made by Huawei, which may be 'shoddy'. It may pose a terrible risk to the 'five eyes' spying network, according to this aforementioned 'I' article, in that Theresa May allowed equipment to be supplied by this company. If this is true, or Western propaganda, nobody knows, I would have thought? 'The security in Huawei is like nothing else - it's engineering like its back in the year 2000. It's very, very shoddy', according to Dr Ian Levy, technical director of the NCSC who informed the BBC TV Panorama programme, in a recent broadcast.

But what we do know for sure according to Private Eye (1493) is the sheer hypocrisy of the British ruling class/British Establishment who have at-least three members involved in the management of Huawei. First Lord Browne the former BP boss who left his post as lead non-executive director at the Cabinet Office to run the Huawei board and other businesses. Secondly Sir Andrew Cahn, formerly head of the government's trade promotion arm, UK Trade & Investment, who joined the company's advisory board in 2011 and now sits on the main board. Thirdly John Suffolk who glories in the role of Huawei senior vice president and global cyber security & privacy officer. All deeply ensconced in the old boy network and the never ending 'revolving door', which ensured fat pay cheques for those who made it look respectable (10). Further evidence, if we need it, about this case and the surreal nature of British so called liberal democracy, happened in a NSC (sic) meeting of senior members of the cabinet and the security forces discussing Huawei and other issues I presume, in the spring of 2019? The Defence Secretary Gavin Williamson, or 'private Pike' as some call him, leaked what was said in the meeting to the Tory led propaganda sheet called the Daily Telegraph. Informing them that Gavin Williamson was among a small group of ministers whose warnings about Huawei's involvement were overruled by the Prime Minister. For this terrible crime of treason Theresa May sacked him, although he denies it was him. The saga continues. Which is getting very nasty indeed: as The Trump administration basically banned any trade with the Huawei Company without a special licence, and Google disallowed any of their software to be used on Huawei smart phones. Trump also put 25% tariffs on most goods coming into the USA from China as he was threatening before, (see above). The Sunday Times (12th May 2019) analysed this process in some detail in an article called 'Bull in a China Shop', with a picture of Trump being the Bull. This policy wiped 2 trillion dollars off the value of global shares at the time, and now virtually everything imported into the USA will have levies imposed on them, according to Tommy Stubbington. In the short term, the tariffs will mean higher prices for American consumers - who will end up paying the levies - as well as reigniting fears about the health of global economy. Perhaps more importantly, they mark a further breakdown in the global trading system that Trump has sought to reconfigure as he accuses China of "stealing" billions of dollars from America through its huge trade surplus. A rising tide of protectionism around the globe appears to be here to stay, experts say. Like Larry Elliot in the Guardian (20th May 2019) who noted that the weakening of global growth, which was already in progress, would only get worse with this tit-for-tat protectionist battle between the USA and China. As Tommy Stubbington continues, Trump seemed to think that imposing tariffs would force change to the trading practices pertaining to competition. Whereby China has a 400 billion dollar a year trade surplus with the USA, this constitutes theft according to Trump; 'no more' so he says via his twitter feed? China also steals intellectual property according to the Trump administration, which if we think about in an intelligent and rational way has been going on since the invention of the wheel, a few thousand years ago? Very few mainstream economists agree with this view and hold that trade deficits are largely caused by varying rates of saving and spending across different countries - not by trade barriers such as tariffs. Ironically, according to Professor Jim Rollo from Sussex University, Trump himself has been partly responsible for the size of the overall balance of payments problem since becoming President - by such policies as tax cuts and high spending and using tariffs simply ends up in tit-for-tat escalation that makes us all poorer. Trump's brain may only work in reverse gear, or everything he perceives is in the wrong order - because even the American car industry lobbied against tariffs, 'arguing that they would add thousands of dollars to vehicle prices and hit plants in America by driving up the cost of components. Considering that most Americans have lost the use of their legs and drive everywhere as a wider part of their culture over several generations, this is going to hit them hard. This also applies to many other consumer goods sold in the USA, like TVs. Manufacturers are also very concerned about the loss of export markets as China and other trading partners fight back, which may cost 400,000 Americans jobs, according to Tommy Snubbington. Not something that Trump had ever have noted to my knowledge, on his twitter feed, or anywhere else, for that matter? When reading thoroughly this excellent article you do start to wonder if perhaps Trump is from another Planet or Galaxy, because if subsidizing farmers with a '12 billion dollar' bung for growing soya beans that would normally have been sold to China, but this trade now wiped out by Beijing's retaliatory tariffs amid a sharp drop in agriculture exports, is deemed logical then surely 'The Donald' here stretches credulity to its limits? So, whether all this spare food is going to help the millions of hungry people in the USA or the UK (see above) is open to conjecture, I would have thought?

Returning to the Huawei saga, where even the executive vice-president in the UK Jeremy Thompson noted that the attack on his company from the USA is nothing to do with 'security' but trade. The restrictions brought in by the USA (see above) 'are likely to hit Huawei's European business, its second-biggest market, because it licenses many of its mobile phone services from Google in Europe' according to the Guardian on the 21st of May 2019. However, again it's Private Eye (No 1496) that spills the beans on certain aspects of this whole saga and the pure hypocrisy of the Western World. Deeply ingrained in many aspects of the certain government departments through conduit of Vodafone, Huawei is even celebrated as a great 'supplier of the decade'. Over the decades the firms have set up joint ventures around the world, including a "transmission innovation centre" in Milan, Madrid and Basingstoke, plus a joint "internet of things" lab in Newbury. The companies worked intimately on 5G and together boasted the first live connections with 4G'. (11) Ironically again according to this edition of Private Eye sourced from Edward Snowden, so it seems, it's an USA company that has a backdoor for spying called **Cisco** and not Huawei at all, as far as we know?

Even the IMF worried about the USA's 'bull in a China shop' which 'warns of further risk to globe economy as US trade war with China deepens'. According to the Guardian 24th May 2019 which asserts that Trump's actions: 'sent global stock markets sharply down yesterday, prompting a warning from the International Monetary Fund of increasing risk to the global economy. Shares fell sharply in Asia, Europe and North America on a day when investors became alarmed by the intensifying war of words between Washington and Beijing, by the poor news on the American economy, and by political chaos in Britain' (see above). Even Mike Pompeo is accusing Huawei of lying about their connections to the Chinese government and on the same day Panasonic cut their ties to Huawei (see below). Personally, I would not trust one word that Pompeo says as most of it is pure lies and propaganda from the Trump playbook (and John Bolton's), which while no one was around he admitted to. The problem here as I have noted above from other sources is that China - is not taking this lying down and are retaliating. 'Despite the warnings, markets fear that Washington is preparing for a protracted battle with China for global technology supremacy'. Whatever the right-wing lies pumped out by the mass media and think tanks, capitalism does not like competition, and this is one of the major themes I highlight in this project. Even in 2007 Will Hutton in his anti-Chinese book called *The Writing on the Wall China and the West in the 21st Century,* puts the boot into Huawei? 'The Chinese companies that can focus on their business undistracted are those whose majority ownership is in the private sector. Huawei is a privately owned multinational that is emerging as a fast-growing manufacture of wireless equipment and software with a strong commitment to R & D. But even it is not free from the long arm of the party-state. It operates with a 10-billion-dollar line of credit from the China Development Bank; has close links with the People's Liberation Army; and, to win business in China's protected telecoms markets, it is reported to have given controlling shares to the provincial telecom's companies with which its trades' (12). How shocking?

Again, Ed Conway writing in the Times (May 31st, 2019) suggests 'there'll be no winners in economic cold war'…. Globalization has painful side-effects but Trump's trade battles with China will not improve things. This specific article starts with what is basically a denial by the Trump administration of the complexity of a globalized economic world. Apple, for example, uses parts from all over the globe and for most products the final assembly takes place in China, but design, R&D etc. is based in the USA. 'Apple has become the world's biggest manufacturer yet doesn't manufacture a thing'. He also points out that when Apple shifted the assembly of the Mac Pro to Texas in 2012 it hit troubles straight away, even having trouble finding a specific screw in Texas, so it had to be brought in from China. Another problem the USA has, like most Western countries, is that for all the crushing of the working and middle classes into the ground over the last 40 years, is that China has a much more 'flexible' work force than the West (a Tony Blair mantra for at least most of his premiership, or as I called him in my book about Thatcher, a 'Tory Lite' prime minister and government). Ironically, as Conway informs us, 'when the president reignited the economic conflict earlier this month, pushing on with further tariffs on Chinese imports, Apple's share price tumbled. There are some obvious reasons. Tariffs could push up apples prices and it is possible that Beijing retaliates and effectively bans Apple from China, which accounts for one in every six dollars it earns'. Paradoxically Huawei sources some of its high-tech equipment from the USA, so if not careful could run into oblivion. Trumps ambition seemed to be to reverse the globalization process, which was very unlikely as the system itself is now self-generating in most parts of the globe for all sorts of products. 'It is right to be sceptical about the impact of 21st-century globalization. It has cut prices and improved access to technology, but with painful side effects. It has lifted millions out of poverty, but the benefits were unequally shared. It has contributed to rather than mitigated waste and pollution. It is right to debate its benefits and wonder how to reform it. But tearing it apart in economic conflict is not good for anyone' according to Conway. At a personal level I have recently got to know slightly a small businessman and his lovely wife, in the East Midlands in the UK, who makes and sells supermarket trollies to large and small retailers. They are made in China, shipped to the UK and assembled in the UK and sold to the retailers' supermarkets, all over Britain, a business that it is very unlikely Trump can stop?

This chapter is called: *On the Road to Armageddon for the World* and for good reasons as I have been explaining throughout this whole project. Occasionally something happens that is so unreal it is completely surreal, like the leaking of emails/telegrams from the British Embassy in Washington to London. The Ambassador Sir Kim Darroch told the truth as he saw it about the Trump administration being 'inept and dysfunctional'. 'Darroch also gave a scathing assessment of the White House, saying: "We don't really believe this administration is going to become substantially more normal; less dysfunctional; less unpredictable; less faction riven; less diplomatically clumsy and inept"'. Trump, being very thin skinned, hit back, by 'verbally bombing' London (well the British did destroy the White House in 1812} through his twitter account. As the Guardian (10th July 2019) informed us: 'Diplomatic crisis flares as Trump tweets out fresh abuse' calling Sir Kim Darroch 'a pompous fool' also 'wacky' and 'very stupid' and called Theresa May 'foolish'. Could it get any worse? Well, yes, it could as Sir Kim resigned from his post after the new prime minister in waiting Boris Johnson refused on British TV (9th July 2019) to endorse him. I should note here that Johnson thought Trump in the White House was wonderful, so I presumed intended to ape him when he became prime minister, by making the rich richer and the poor poorer, a scenario that played out, I would contend. In fact, what is so ironic about this whole pathetic saga over Brexit and this specific event is the reason we are supposed to be leaving the EU, is to break free from its rules and bureaucracy but at the same time we are just going to be another vassal state of the USA. 'Not even hostile States have behaved like Trump', Simon McDonald told British MPs (10th July 2019) and went on to assert to his knowledge the last time we had trouble with the White House, was in '1856, when President Franklin Pierce accused the British ambassador of recruiting Americans to fight in the Crimean war'.

Another fallout from the leaked emails/telegrams from Washington was, according to the Mail on Sunday where they were leaked to, the Iran agreement on nuclear weapons and other underlying themes. According to the leak, Trump only abandoned this agreement to spite Barrack Obama, whom he seems to hate, and he also pretended that Obama was not born on American soil, which was a lie. The sanctions he imposed on Iran seems to be really hurting the economic (i.e., BBC Radio4 et al), like most places where sanctions have been introduced. Only the biggest bullies in the playground are allowed nuclear weapons and to act like a thug, which is less than ten...probably 8 or 9, nations? In fact, the UK government was so upset with these leaks, they were going to prosecute anyone who published them, but because we are supposed to be living in a free society, freedom of the press and the rest of the pure hogwash, this story has disappeared from the radar, at least in the papers I read and the radio stations I listen to. In fact, as Julian Borger informs us from New York: 'Iran has faced a steadily tightening US-driven oil embargo and severe banking sanctions since May last year, when Trump withdrew the US from the 2015 nuclear deal with Iran known as the Joint of Action (JCPOA). The embargo has triggered a stand-off in the Gulf that has escalated in recent months, with sabotage attacks on foreign tankers, blamed by the US on Iran, Iran said it seized a foreign-owned vessel suspected of being used to smuggle oil out of Iran' (13). This specific saga did take what I would call a surreal turn when the Americans engineered the British to hijack the Grace 1, an Iran oil tanker off Gibraltar, full of oil bound for Syria (perhaps not). Originally this was denied as an USA inspired event but according to Simon Tisdall in the Sunday Observer (21st July 2019) it was a 'dangerous trap' that Britain fell for to punish Iran. 'The consequence of the Gibraltar affair is only now becoming clear, the seizure of Grace 1 led directly to the capture by Iran's Revolutionary Guards of a British tanker, the Stena Impero, in the straits of

Hormuz'. This whole process is tied up with the sanctions against Iran, and the USA leaving the 2015 nuclear deal, which the Europeans involved did not want. So, Britain caught in a trap trying to please Trump and the Europeans at the same time, and if this situation had got very 'hot', say for example after 2020 election in the USA, Britain could have got involved in another fruitless war like the invasion of Iraq in 2003? When the 'more than economical with the truth' Boris Johnson was in Number 10 (many sources including Peter Oborne) it was a real possibly, not worth thinking about? With Johnson in Number 10 and Trump in the White House it seemed to be a double whammy for the world economy according to the Guardian on the 2nd August 2019, where 'Brexit and global trade fears deal a blow to factory output'…….'British factory output has fallen at its fastest rate in seven years as the economic risks posed by a no-deal Brexit rise and as global demands falters. According to the monthly snapshot from IHS Markit and the Chartered Institute of Procurement and Supply, manufacturers cut production due to fading demand at home and abroad. Output and new orders shrank as factories came under pressure from uncertainty over Britain's future trading relationship with the EU and from the US-China trade war'. This was hyped up again by Donald trump with 10% further tariffs on 300 billion with of Chinese exports, from September 1st, 2009, which the USA imports. The result was the hurting USA consumers, which Trump denies as the Sunday Observer noted on the 4th of August 2019, 'when Trump turns up the heat in the trade war, Americans will feel it too'. As they note, 'From next month, almost everything China sends to the US will be affected.' In bald terms, that means Americans are going to be paying more for their smart-phones, laptops and clothes. Trump boasts that the US going to be "taxing the hell out of China" but he has got the economics completely wrong. The taxes will be paid by Americans faced with paying more for imports. Therefore, in essence he seems to have very little understanding of how modern capitalistic economics work, or anything else for that matter? However, on reading 'Trump's *The Art of the Deal,* the 2016 version of the 1987 original, you would think that he is a philosopher king, which I am reading after writing over 30, 000 words of this project which I think, is the correct way around to approach it? As I am of similar age to Trump and at one time worked in the building industry, albeit only as a tradesman, I have a little knowledge of how it works and the narcissistic nature of some builders. Trump certainly fits this profile and as I perceive the book, he seems to be a bit like a Julius Caesar character/personality, this time... (Have been reading him at the same time as the book about Trump and others) for example, kill or be killed, for a gain. The book I have in front of me about Caesar is called *The Conquest of Gaul,* which was probably called Gaius Julius Caesar's Notes on his Achievements when Caesar was dictating it to his scribes, which was 'personal propaganda intended to impress his contemporaries'. We could say a similar thing about Trump's book about the *Art of the Deal* written mainly by Tony Schwartz...or at-least ghost written by him? Chapter 9 of Trump's book sums up neatly what I mean, called 'Wynn-Fall; The battle for Hilton'. Conrad Hilton had started a hotel business in 1921 and built it into a huge empire and by about 1966 his son Baron had taken hold of the organization, after joining it in the early 1950s. According to Trump he was not too successful in a couple of his projects but very successful in buying two Nevada casinos in Las Vegas for about 12 million dollars, which were making millions for the family. Based on these assumptions Baron Hilton decided to try his luck in Atlantic City, by buying a site 'at the Marina around the time gambling was legalized'. However, he did not have a licence to operate a casino/hotel complex in Atlantic City, albeit he had started to build one on the land he had bought. A big mistake, so it seems, and as soon as Trump found out about the problem, he offered to buy it from him for a good price. But 'very shortly after that, Steve Wynn of the Golden Nugget decided to make a full-scale assault on Hilton, seeking control of the company'. Another underlying problem in this whole saga according to Trump was that Baron's father, when he died, hardly left him anything in his will.... 'disenfranchised his children and grandchildren'...hence leaving his son 'just another high-level manager who lacked the power of a major stockholder'. Which meant that he had very little control over events as an individual. Trump likes to brag about his image as a buccaneering businessman, meaning he has loads of power and control over his own actions, a constant theme of the book as was the movie: *American Gangster* starring Denzel Washington and in theory based on a real story. Perhaps, ironically, he seems to be putting Steve Wynn down for being a class act and very smooth character in his 2000-dollar suits and 200-dollar shirts, which may have got up Baron Hilton's nose, according to Trump. Where Baron Hilton 'was born wealthy and bred to be an aristocrat, and he is one of those guys who never had to prove anything to anyone'. Or what Trump notes is 'a member of what I call the Lucky Sperm Club'.... having read dozens of sociology books over decades; I have never noticed class described in such away. I presume therefore Trump seems to look up-to British Royalty like his mother (p,80 - his father did not) did, albeit Frank Sinatra may have seen class in a similar way, as he was also impressed by British royalty. This little saga in chapter 9 ends up with Baron Hilton selling the nearly built complex to Trump for 320 million dollars. According to Trump himself, the money was borrowed from the Manufacturers Hanover Trust after a two-minute talk on the phone to John Torell, who said; '"We have a deal", just like that? It goes to show you the value of credibility. 'In return, I did something I'd never done before: I personally guaranteed the loan'. He then goes on to brag what a fantastic load of money he made straight away with the hotel casino complex, which he called Trump's Castle and put his wife at that time, Ivana, in charge, who is now sadly dead. He held back 5 million dollars for any problems that may have arisen from the completion, which he says really cost 30 million dollars, which is still in dispute with Baron Hilton, at least in 1987, I think? After the major deal had been done with Baron Hilton, he pursued Bear Stearns to issue bonds on his investment and according to Trump 'anyone who bought the bonds are now selling at a premium'…. this was at the time of writing again in 1987, I presume.

Throughout writing this book my emphasis, and several journalists at the BBC at long last seems to think that it is more likely than not, is that the USA will pick a fight with China this century. Iran was also a bad boy in Trump's playground, as proved on the 3rd of January 2020 when he targeted and killed General Qassem Soleimani, on his arrival at Baghdad airport, with American MQ-9 Reaper drones, and several other people, including the General's son-in-law, died. Soleimani was one of the most important people in Iran, second only in senior rank and importance-to the President. He may have been tricked by other states in the Gulf into setting up a meeting with the prime minister of Iraq on the Friday he was killed. Was this leaked to the CIA and Washington so they could kill him? 'America and its allies have had previous opportunities to assassinate Soleimani. They chose not to, fearing a backlash. Donald Trump said Soleimani was planning attacks on US personnel in Iraq. This would have been true at any point in the past 16 years' (14). I would suggest that further attacks on US personnel were probably a load of tosh as are most things Trump asserts? 'Economical with the truth' (Mark Twain et al) is the mantra of Trump's being 24/7, as was Boris Johnson's in Number 10 Downing Street, who ostensibly tried to 'close the BBC' (for good) for so-called pumping out propaganda? Which some of it is, especially where not being objective and impartial about labour policies at our general elections, a constant theme of their out-put? However, GB News is allowed to pump out Right-Wing Propaganda 24/7 and criticize the BBC on a regular basis.

Saddam Hussein was a leading member of the revolutionary Arab Socialist Ba'ath Party in Iraq, which was a mix of Arab naturalism and socialism, He nationalized the oil industry and the banks. He was a Sunni, the minority that made up only a fifth of the population, the majority are Shia. Thence when the USA smashed up the State and hanged Saddam Hussein and created a western liberal democracy form of government (in theory), the Shia now have the upper hand and some of the Sunni group have turned into Isis. This was the new enemy that even Iran in cahoots with the USA coalition was trying to defeat. The same group in Syria was trying to overthrow the Bashar al-Assad regime. To date this has not happened because of the late Soleimani's help (he was a Shia, like most people in Iran), and the help of the Russian government. In fact, it is not too far a 'stretch' of modernity that the sanctions the USA and others impose on countries they disagree with is very similar to medieval sieges, and nothing more. So, making 'America great again' boils down to making everyone else poorer, something Boris Johnson does not seem to understand, does he...or maybe he did?

This also applies to the coronavirus crisis, where Trump denied the 3.4% fatality rate that the World Health Organization ascribed this disease, when talking to Sean Hannity on Fox News in a phone interview broadcast live during February 2020. He seemed to think the true figure was maybe under 1% and blamed fake news channels and the Democratic Party for whipping up a scare, so that markets would react to the crisis, which they had already. This whole problem could have contributed to Trump's nemesis at the Presidential election. Another reason Trump may have been very concerned about all this was that tens of millions of Americans t have no medical insurance whatsoever, so would not be able even to be tested for the coronavirus, or have any help if needed. The whole American medical system is based on extreme profits of the most outrageous kind, where in many cases operations are carried out that are not always needed because it's based on monetary gain, the more you do 'the more you get paid' model...source - BBC Radio 4 1st May 2020. Apart from Trump, this new situation could be very embarrassing for the whole USA ruling class. Now it seems that more Americans have died of the coronavirus than died in Vietnam, about 100,000 as of end of May 2020 (over 1 million now July 2022) - quite an indictment for a President who when first hearing of the virus said it was a hoax and nothing to worry about. Also, over 33, million Americans have now signed on the dole, so if we are not very careful this could turn out to be the worst recession of all time since the start of the Industrial revolution and certainly worse than the 1930s. In fact, it may be the worse one in the UK for over 300 years when Queen Anne was on the throne, according to the Guardian (8th May 2020). The real danger was that Trump in the USA and Boris Johnson in the UK with the help of the extreme Right-Wing press might have looked around for scapegoats (see also below and above). China now seems to be at the top of the list (1st May 2020) according to Trump; he knows from secret sources, probably the CIA or other government agencies that the virus was 'engineered' from Wuhan?

I should also note that Covid-19 is class based, apparently like all aspects of the capitalistic epoch in the UK. According to the Daily Mirror (2nd May 2020+the Guardian June 2021) 'people in the poorest areas are twice as likely to die from Covid-19 as those in the richest places, figures show'. The statistics show clearly that Brent in London, for example has 141.5 deaths per 100,000, Liverpool 81.8 per 100,000 and so on. I would have thought this would also apply to the USA where it seems that poor black people have been dying more than a small percentage of rich whites. I should also note that Boris Johnson's current wife Carrie Symonds has given birth to a little boy and a little girl. This makes 7 children by 3 different women, though a question mark hangs over how many, if any, other children he may have fathered. All rather 'rich' when one considers he once said that single mothers were 'ill-raised, ignorant, aggressive and illegitimate'. Only in a ruthless 'One Party State' like the UK or as I call it now North Korea on Thames, with deep apologies to North Korea - could you get away with such crass remarks, when millions now do not always get married and have children out of wedlock. As an ex-Bullingdon boy Boris Johnson probably hates the working class, while pretending the Tories love them, as we know from The Riot Club (sic) the Bullingdon boys do hate the working class! Plus, we do have inside knowledge of this exclusive club as a woman who allegedly acted as a scout for potential members of the Bullingdon Club in the mid-1980s has said, according to her, that female prostitutes performed sex acts at its lavish dinners, women were routinely belittled, and intimidation and vandalism were its hallmarks. This would have been when Boris Johnson and David Cameron were at Oxford. Johnson also wrote in 2007 in the Daily Telegraph, that the population at the time was 6.7 billion and if he lived to be 80 it would have trebled in his lifetime, but constantly kept off the political agenda (apart from China), perhaps we now know why if Private Eye is correct (No 1521).

According to George Galloway (RT TV -14 May 2020) China is already now the new superpower, and it would be very unwise for the USA to pick on China economically or with a nasty fist fight, because it is very unlikely that Europe as a block or any Nation State would want to join in. This is partly to do with the so-called new Silk Road that China is building all around the globe and gaining many new friends. Albeit RT (same evening in a news programme) had noted that there is now a new cold war starting between China and the USA as I have kept saying from day one of this project. Which if we are not very careful could end in disaster for the whole globe and the whole of mankind. All of history is on our shoulders and that is why we must so be aware of a maverick like Trump! Patrick Cockburn in the 'I 'newspaper in the UK (16-17 May 2020) notes that 'demagogues are proving dangerous for their people in a time of crises'. Basically, saying that Trump and Johnson were one of a kind, nothing more than charlatans and con-men that are good at winning elections by some very dubious methods, like whipping up the hatred of foreigners and crude crass nationalism, but when it comes to crisis like covid-19 they are somewhat lacking and misleading, which has been a disaster for the whole populations of both countries. As Cockburn asserts, out of the '300,000' who have died so far world wide a 'third' of this figure is from the USA and the UK. In other words, 'they have paid the ultimate price for their governments' slow and incompetent response to the spread of the disease'. In the UK at-least '15,000' old people from hospitals were moved out and put onto old people homes, a sector in which my eldest son works as a senior nurse. They were not tested, and a lot of them had the Covid-19 virus, which led to thousands dying of the virus, maybe over 60, 000 in the UK. In the USA Trump's approach might be said to have inflicted a far worse epidemic on Americans than would have happened otherwise, now that over 132,000 have died as at the end of July 2020. Trump has always blamed China for the outbreak of this virus, albeit no one knows for sure, saying that it worse than the attack on Pearl harbour and the World Trade Centre. In the past the Americans have dropped all sorts of biological weapons on the Far East. Iraq, Cuba, Panama et al and have carried out experiments on its own citizens according to William Blum in Rogue State...2014 paperback edition. This is the main reason that I think we should be very careful about putting blame on China, about where this specific virus came from in the first place? Albeit on the 5th of July 2020 the Sunday Times (UK version) had a huge spread on a virus called 'Seven-year Covid trail revealed' from their

'Insight' team of 3 men which is normally quite objective, but in these nefarious times I would be very careful that it is? According to this very long article in 2012 six scientists all dressed up in white hazmat suits and respirator masks were taking bat samples from a disused copper mine, (where 6 men had become ill from and 3 died) - which was a breeding ground for mutated micro-organisms and pathogens deadly to humans. The samples were frozen and sent back to the laboratories in Wuhan who were looking out for the causes of the Sar's outbreak in 2002/3. The analysis proved that part of a faecal sample that was frozen 'is the closet known match to the virus that caused Covid-19'. This is where this specific story becomes, I would say, slightly squalid in that they are questioning what happened to these samples in the years between its discovery and 'the eruption of Covid-19'? And later in the article it is suggested that even the Chinese expert called Shi Zhengli thought the virus from the cave was not an exact match to the new virus, but probably originated in bats. Wuhan, where she works and her laboratory is stationed, was made famous in 1966 because this is where Mao Tse-tung took a symbolic swim at 72 in the Yangtze River before launching the Cultural Revolution which even the wonderful Michael Woods (DVD on China) said was a mistake, like tearing down a statue of one of the most famous and wises men that has ever existed called Confucius. I am Glad to say he is back in vogue under President Xi, with schools teaching the virtue of education and the statue has been reconstructed, with millions of tourists visiting it yearly. No one knows for sure who patient zero was who caught Covid-19 but more than likely it was a 70-year-old man with Alzheimer, who's symptoms started on the 1st of December 2019 according to his family and within three weeks 60 other cases had occurred and a week later it was reported to the provincial government, by which time it had already spread to Europe. However, it was only when Shi returned to her laboratory on the 31st of December to identify the new coronavirus that China reported the problem to the WHO.

Now Hong Kong has a special relationship on trade with the USA but because of the New Security Law that China is bringing in this year 2020 'Mike Pompeo said the US would no longer maintain special trade relations with Hong Kong or consider it an autonomous region, as it has done since the 1997 handover by the UK to China'…. quoted in the Guardian on the 28th of May 2020. In this specific article it also notes that China is standing up for itself against USA aggression in the South China Sea and India putting extra troops on its border with China. The decisions of Trump and Pompeo (two of the most dangerous men in the world) could have had a serious impact on the Hong Kong economy and the reason they did it was that China uses the ex-British colony as a portal for dealings with the outside world. Apparently, Trump wanted to negotiate between China and India over the disputes on their borders, you could not make it up, could you! Some say that Trump would have liked a Nobel prize for blowing up the world; sorry, that should be for saving the world.

Donald Trump cancelled the G7 meeting at Camp David USA scheduled for June 2020 (ostensibly because of Covid 19), and transformed it into a video conference of world leaders. He seemed to think the format is out of date and so perhaps wanted a new one including Russia, Australia, South Korea and India, the idea maybe being to counter the rising power of China. Also, Angela Merkel on the phone had told him that a conference in Washington would be a 'health risk'. It was a stormy affair over issues like the Nord Stream 2 gas pipeline and his belligerence towards Hong Kong. His new plan was perceived as very controversial because the West has tried to side-line Putin since the annexation of Crimea in 2014 and Merkel & Macron did not want to be seen as giving a platform to Trump on his Chinese strategy so close to the November election. 'The Republicans see a tough approach towards China as an election-winning formula', albeit that

Joe Biden's view on China is not much different to the president (The Guardian - 1st June 2020). Trump also withdrew all funding and membership from the World Health Organization (WHO), which move Europe opposed. China may have not been as upfront as they should have been in December/January over the Coronavirus, if the Associated Press were correct in their assessment. It was not until the 20th of January that China confirmed Coronavirus, (later to be called Covid-19) was contagious and it was 30th January before the WHO declared a global emergency (same source 3rd June 2020). So far from this aforementioned date, and at the time of writing, this disease has affected 6 million people and killed 375,000 worldwide, in a world where the population has now 8 billion, according to the UN announcement of November 15 2022. The WHO praised China for its swift action in this whole affair and that was the reason that Trump claimed this organisation was biased toward China. Warnings started in Wuhan city in December that the virus was a SARS-like phenomenon and sadly one of the doctors who first spotted it died. Wuhan was not locked down until the 23rd of January 2020, by which time 5 million residents had left, travelling within China and overseas. It was only because of the nature of globalization in the 20/21st century, with air travel, that this virus travelled so fast. In the past it would have taken months or even years to travel around the globe. Over centuries Europe and the world have suffered numerous pandemics which have often helped to change society dynamically, like they did in the Middle Ages. Therefore, the ruling classes around the world are becoming increasingly paranoid, especially in the UK and the USA, where neo-liberalism has been the most successful at making the rich very rich while the majority are getting relatively poorer. Of course, all this has been a worldwide trend for the last 40 years. Basically, what we call democracies, like the USA & the UK, are just plutocracies masquerading as democracies. An example of this is the election of Donald J. Trump, who, according to a letter in Private Eye (1583), managed to get elected in 2016 with only 26% of the population turning out to vote for him.

The impression given in the West is that North Korea is a paranoid nation run as a 'One-Party State' with Kim Jong-Un having all the powers. Japan annexed the country in 1910 and ruled it until it's defeat in 1945, and treated the population like dirt. Kim 11-Sung, the founding father of North Korea in 1948 was one of the few freedom fighters against the Japanese over decades, and who has now completely written out of the narrative by Western elites. Like all history it is not black and white, wherever it takes place, so human rights abuses like hunger for millions may have taken place, as happens in the UK. However, there is always an underlying reason for sanctions applied by the USA. In a very strange documentary shown on BBC4 (British TV - 13th October 2020) a Danish film maker got a friend to pretend that he was an admirer of North Korea, but in fact was just acting the role and fooling everyone, including the North Korean government. The whole thing to me was so surreal; it was like explaining the British Royal Family to an alien, now in power for a thousand years and maybe for another thousand years. But what became clear to me was that the West may try to pretend that North Korea is a third world country but when it comes to modern technologies it is not. Hence, the education system must be quite good like it is all over Asia, the love of learning seems to be in the DNA of everyone, wherein the UK, for example it is not, with millions semi-illiterate and brainwashed by the BBC (?) and the right-wing press. The corruption in Africa, especially in ex-British colonies were also very relevant in this documentary and a bloody disgrace, if true? Also, the State seemed to be quite clever at getting around USA sanctions, by using a system of triangulation.

The road to hell is paved with good intentions so we are told, which is a good metaphor for the insanity of Brexit in the UK, and with the fallout of Covid-19 which has already made tens of millions unemployed in the USA and millions in the UK, in one of the worst economic downturns in history ensued (August 2020). The Boris Johnson administration ran scared, because as I see it if we are not very careful in the USA and the UK, there could be mass starvation on a huge scale, especially in the UK where pensions are too low, unemployment payments are too low and wages in comparison with the cost of living are too low. This is a problem which seems intractable and could be triggered at any time in the future unless mass social policy change is set in train. Hence, the reason I would have thought why Boris Johnson said that we cannot have anything to do with Huawei after 2023, going back on his word previously, thus sucking up to Donald J. Trump, who would have liked to see this company go bankrupt, which is very unlikely as they are a worldwide organization and very successful. I would also suggest, as do many social scientists in the UK (BBC Radio 4 May 2020) that Johnson did not want an agreement with the EU and wanted to crash out of the whole trade/tariff system, potentially putting a huge strain on the food supply (food security is not now that important any more according to this Tory government…May 2020). Only France is self-sufficient in most commodities according to Max Keiser on the RT TV channel…. May 2020. The contradiction here is very simple, albeit that we may get very cheap food like chicken from the USA, and export lamb to the USA if the tariffs are too high in the EU, but this will also put many farmers out of business in the UK. So, I would have thought that there may be real food shortages down the line in the UK, where food riots may become the norm with troops and tanks on the streets to guard supermarkets. We can only hope that along with other tsunamis coming down the road in the UK, where most working-class people will not be able to afford an electric car after a Tory government enforcing the banning of all diesel and petrol cars in the next 12 years, that once and for all we will see the end of one of the most ruthless ruling class in the world, with it going the way of the French revolution, we can only hope?

Mass unemployment and hunger may come to pass in the USA as-well, perhaps there will be a repeat of the French revolution in both the UK and US, we can only hope folks. As the evidence mounts up against Boris Johnston in the UK and Trump in the USA from many sources, like John Bolton's book that Trump is tried to get banned, called *The Room Where It Happened*, we can see and understand how uneducated and dangerous Trump really is in the big scheme of things. In the book Bolton notes how apparently Trump wanted president Xi to help him the next election by buying grain from the states that produce it, also he did not know the UK is a nuclear power, and he offered to halt US criminal investigations of Chinese and Turkish companies. He thought Finland was in Russia, and opined that to invade Venezuela would be cool. Trump called the book a work of fiction but as the Guardian (19th June 2020) pointed out if this was the case why did he try to prevent it being published? What is so ironic about the Bolton book is that he himself has been a Right-Wing 'luminary' for decades, which speaks volumes about USA political discourse in the 21st century. The reason is obvious, because Bolton asserted that Trump was not fit for office, lacking in competence to carry out the job, stunningly uninformed and easy to be manipulated by foreign adversaries. 'As Trump's longest serving national security adviser, Bolton attended the president's meetings with Russia's Vladimir Putin, China's Xi Jinping and summits with North Korea Kim Jong-Un before resigning from the White House last September'. Apart from what I have already written about in this book, it seems that Trump did not mind the Chinese government carrying out mass incarceration of Muslim Uighurs and said it was the right thing to do. The British did this in South Africa and Kenya (see above), however it does not make it right – but then it is very unlikely that Trump would have known about these disgraceful processes, maybe? According to Trump it was Bolton's fault that the North Korea discussions failed because the idea was to follow the Libya model, which Muammar Gaddafi went along with to appease the West, a process which, of course, culminated in his demise. The West had been trying to achieve this objective for decades, see for example Richard Tomlinson's *The Big Breach*. Some have suggested (the so-called experts) that Bolton went along with this idea to sabotage the talks. This in fact may be true, or false, depending on how we perceive the issue. It seems that when Trump heard about this book, he tweeted that 'Wacko John Bolton's exceedingly tedious (New York Times) book is made up of lies & fake stories. Said all well about me, in print, until the day I fired him. A disgruntled boring fool who only wanted to go to war. Never had a clue was ostracized & happily dumped. What a dope'! Love and hate at the top of politics is quite revealing don't you think?

Ben Chacko in the Morning Star (23 June 2020) in an excellent article called 'What's behind the new cold war between Washington and Beijing' provided an analysis about the recent dispute between India and China which actually goes back to when the British ruled India in the 19th century, especially between the 1860s and 1890s. Secretary of State Mike Pompeo blamed China for this dispute, probably without any ontological knowledge whatsoever? Modi, the Indian prime minster, acted very much like Trump, Boris Johnson and Bolsonaro of Brazil, in a macho nationalistic 1930s manner. Chacko sees this new cold war as a containment project directed by the USA, but against the interests of most Nation States in the world, especially India. As he goes on to explain, the USA is becoming hysterical over the rise of China. Pompeo actual called China a 'rogue actor' over the latest dispute, ironic when one considers that according to the great

William Blum the USA is a 'Rogue State' and the most dangerous country in the world. Therefore, is it not a bit of a cheek for Pompeo to effectively call the kettle black? Trump is also blamed China for the Covid-19 virus crisis, saying its behaviour was worse than Pearl Harbour and 9/11 attack on the World Trade Centre and describing it as a Chinese bio- weapon. In doing so he gave credence to the theory it may have been engineered in a Chinese laboratory, which is very unlikely because a lot of viruses comes from animals, especially bats, as in this case. A constant theme of Trump's time in office was that if he did not get his own way, he took the USA out of all sorts of organizations, as I have noted in this project. Over this virus he has took the USA out of the World Health Organization (WHO) because, according to him, it was not impartial towards China. It could be argued that Trump in the USA and Boris Johnson in the UK did very badly with regard to this whole Covid-19 crisis, and thus are constantly trying to divert attention away from their respective country's drastic death tolls, two of the highest in the world. Whatever the outcome of a commission into this whole saga in the future, the UK and the USA were late at trying to close society down to prevent the spread of the virus and the USA was playing like a selfish school kid who did not want to share the ball with other players. The US even wanted to buy a German pharmaceutical company working on a vaccine in order to move its production to the USA, and provide its treatment for the population of America and nowhere else. What is so concerning, as Chacko notes, is that the UK could be dragged into this new cold war whether we like it or not. This will be inevitable as we have left the EU, which as far as I and many on the left are concerned counts as one of the craziest things the UK has ever done in the last 1000 years of history, albeit that many on the Left of the political spectrum disagree with these thoughts. But as I noted in my book about Thatcher, this insanity may have caused more damage to the UK economy than Thatcher herself did, this idea having been repeated by people like Michael

Heseltine and many others, even Dominic Cummings, the person responsible for the simplistic messages put on buses etc, but who did not seem to understand what the final conclusions of his actions, would be on British society?

The narrative being pushed, or as I like to call it 'upside down' logic is that it is China who is the bad guy in the new cold war saga when in fact it has been Trump's America who picked fights to destabilize the economies of Iran, Venezuela and China, while also trying to rig deals in the middle east that would benefit only Israel etc. Of course, what really lies behind all this baloney is the rise of China as an economic powerhouse. This is the root of the global campaign to sabotage the Huawei Corporation and punish countries which continue to work with it. The Bolton book of course upset the apple cart here a little, when Trump wanted president Xi to help him win the 2020 election. It should be noted that Biden's Democratic Party is nearly as bonkers about China as Trump is! In time I presume historians will make up a new narrative for this sort of madness. And in the past President Joe Biden as a democratic politician has hardly been any different in voting behaviour from the Republicans, especially on law and order in the time when Clinton was president and the prison population soared, according to Thomas Frank writing in the Guardian (23rd June 2020). Of course, like most politician in the USA and UK they are all caught in the web of the epoch, trying to do a balancing act between pretending to support the majority, while at the same time supporting the capitalist class. Thomas Cook seems to think that for most of the time Biden was on the side of the capitalist class, so now he is trying to row back and present himself as basically a decent man in troubled times.

Boris Johnson became Trump's poodle (July 2020), especially over his about turn regarding Huawei, where only a few months previously he said we could operate with about 35% of their equipment in the UK. Now with pressure from Trump and his nationalist thugs he said that everything already installed by Huawei must be taken out by 2027. Boris Johnson, who went to Eton and Oxford and thinks of himself as another Pericles, Caesar Augustus and Winston Churchill, has in fact turned out to be a somewhat incompetent politician with a hazy grasp of policy. He was thrown out of office by his own party…. July 2022, followed swiftly by his successor Liz Truss on 20th October 2022. According to Sonia Purnell (BBC Radio4 23rd July 2022), who worked with Johnson in Brussels for the Daily Telegraph before he wrote his weekly column of questionable content for that paper, he shouted and bawled out nonsense for about ten minutes to a real PLANT in their office?

Johnson taking us out of the EU when there was no need for it, having one of the highest death rates in the world with Covid-19 under his premiership, and the economy crashing while wanting new partners and all the world to trade with 'Global Britain' is not making life a pretty picture for the working class for decades to come. Also, the harm to industry and society could be devastating. Even the Sunday Times (19th July 2020) suggests that if all the University students decided to stay away from the UK, or were told to by the Chinese Government, it could 'wipe out' that sector of society, and its wider impact could spread to most cities where they come to study. In this context, 'the government last week stressed that it wanted a "modern and mature" relationship with China. But No 10 is under growing pressure from Tory MPs and the Trump administration to reduce its reliance on firms linked to the Chinese state, increasing the risks of retaliation'. I must admit I am not too sure what this means, are you? Even Lord Browne (UK Chairman), of BP fame and nicknamed the 'sun King', left the board of Huawei and his £100,000 salary, which other associates were not too happy about according to the Sunday Times business section, reporting on the same day (19 July 2020). The reason seemed to be because the Americans would not let the company use its own chips and software, hence making its supply chain 'less transparent'. However, what was transparent to me was the wholesale attack on China by the British Establishment as an 'addendum' to Trump's behaviour - as I note above this does not really make sense if you think about it logically. On the same Sunday as the Times wrote what I have written above the Andrew Marr show on British TV interviewed the Chinese Ambassador to the UK, who is Liu Xiaming. While writing this book it seems to me, he comes across as a basically decent, well-educated man standing up for China, which is his role, naturally. But what I noticed was that Marr attacked him voraciously for all sorts of misdemeanours that the CPC is up to in China, according to the USA and the UK. Accusing China of becoming aggressive, spying by the backdoor, fermenting unrest in Hong Kong, treating China's Uighur Muslims very badly and so on. Mr Li stood up for himself - noting it was the USA and its allies who were causing problems by acting aggressively and starting a 'new cold war', and statin in his opinion that the UK was 'dancing to the Americans tune'. Marr also interviewed the Russian Ambassador, accusing Russia of hacking and other activities, but not mentioning whether Russia did help Trump and Johnson with their objectives, like the UK leaving the EU and Trump beating Hilary Clinton. Rich Russians have poured money into the Tory party coffers. The Tories, being the nasty party of lies and disinformation, like the Brexit party, even tried to tie the Labour Party into possible leaks from Russia hacking, which was probably pure tosh as the Tories tried for over 6 months not to publish a report from the intelligence committee, which might show up crimes of the Tory party.... published on the 21st of July 2020. What was never mentioned on the Andrew Marr show was that the Chinese have invested about £50 billion in the UK economy and Huawei investment in the UK is small beer compared with the world. Only 1600 employees work here out of 194,000 globally, and 20,000 5G base stations have been installed here out of a total of 500, 000 they hope to install worldwide. Ironically, BT and Vodafone who have been in business with Huawei since at least 2005, have warned the British Government that their insane action may cause 'mobile blackouts if they were forced to remove Huawei hardware too quickly'. This shambolic prime minster went to Eton and Oxford; you could hardly make it up, could you?

When you are in trouble 'Bring on the Empty Horses' is the title to a very funny book by the late great David Niven. It is all about his adventures in Hollywood and constitutes his second autobiography. However, this whole saga about Trump was not funny but very serious when such a dangerous man was president of the USA with his finger trigger on nuclear weapons. Part of his 'tool box' was to take a leaf out of Mrs Thatcher's playbook and accuse anyone who opposed him of being a 'far-Left fascist' He was doing this at Mount Rushmore on the eve of Independence Day 2020. In essence this was mainly an attack on a great new pressure group called 'Black Lives Matter', a radical black representation group for the 21st century, which follows on from the 1960s and 1970s groups that opposed racism and campaigned in the USA on all sorts of issues such as racial equality. Considering that racism has been endemic in both the USA and UK for 400 years since the birth of the slave trade, it should never be forgotten that it made a few people very rich in both countries, and some of their families retain that wealth to this day. This is how the English Sunday Times (5th July 2020) reported this attack on the so-called American Left, 'On Friday night, in the shadow of South Dakota's Mount Rushmore, with the granite visages of these four men towering 60ft above him, President Donald Trump declared his own grand civilization struggle: a culture war against the American left. "In our schools, our newsrooms, even our corporate boardrooms, there is new far-left fascism that demands absolute allegiance", said Trump in a defiant and jingoistic Independence Day oration. "If you do not speak its language, perform its rituals, recite its mantras and follow its commandments, then you will be censored, banished, blacklisted, persecuted and punished". He warned, make no mistake, that this left-wing culture revolution is designed to overthrow the American Revolution. "Our nation is witnessing a merciless campaign to wipe out our history, defame our heroes, erase our values, and indoctrinate our children", said Trump, taking direct aim at the 'Black Lives Matter' protest movement, promising to "preserve the American way of life and insisting that real Americans kneel only to God" (15). He went on to say that angry mobs are trying to tear down the founding fathers' statues, saying he would not be intimidated by evil people. From a neo-brute this takes some believing, but he was only really using this sort of rhetoric to stir up patriotic fever in his uneducated working-class base of support, trying to win the election in November 2020, which he lost. With a resurgence in the coronavirus pandemic in important states (July 2020) that he had to win, and his poll rating dropping through the floor, he was maybe in the same situation President Johnson was in the 1960s. Unfortunately, some say that when Trump is trapped like a wild dog in a corner, it is when he is at his most dangerous. The only hope on his horizon may be a V shaped recover in the economy, which if it does happen, he will try and take credit for it. But it seems he will never be able to paint Joe Biden as a dangerous left-winger, because to most people in America, he is just good old uncle Joe, coupled with is ethnically diverse Vice President Kamala Harris. Trump has also been trying to court the religions vote again, which is huge in America, because as we all know when he walked over to a church near the White house (midyear 2020) and held up a bible after tear gassing protesters - God is on the side of the USA at home and its outrageous foreign policies adventures abroad? Apparently, the bible is Trump's favourite book, and he and seeks solace in the best-selling Catholic writer Dr Taylor Marshall and Archbishop Carlo Maria Vigano, who's words of wisdom are the same as his, even suggesting that the USA 'deep state' operatives may have caused/been behind the protests of the 'Black Lives Matter' rebellion on the streets. According to an article in the Guardian 0n the 8th of July 2020, 'Mr Trump's world view is quintessentially Manichean, devoted to sowing division and mobilizing discord for his own political ends: he also has a taste for the apocalyptic, as demonstrated in his American carnage inauguration speech'.

You do not have to be mystic Meg (British Astrologer- born 1942 and now sadly dead) or a soothsayer like Rasputin to understand 'sowing division and mobilizing discord' is the essence of being Trump that even the Sunday Times (19th July) seemed to get concerned about, illumined by the bellicose behaviour of Trump and then his poodle Boris Johnson in the middle of 2020. In the 'World News' section they had an article called 'Wargames come with high stakes as US and China risk conflict'. This is about war games in the south China sea over the Island of Taiwan that China claims as its own. This is something like the Isle of Wight in the UK being claimed by China, a joke of course. However, it obvious to a blind man that this territory does not belong to the UK or the USA, albeit that the USA are supplying arms galore to them and are the protector of last resort to Taiwan in an emergency. 'The region's waters have been churned into a cauldron of superpower confrontation by the breakdown in relations between America and China - a new cold war driven by the ambitions of President Xi Jinping and the increasingly desperate electoral calculus of Donald Trump'. The Americans periodically send military vessels into the waters of the South China Sea according to the Sunday Times, this sea being home to the world's most lucrative shipping lanes. Reports of armed Chinese fishing boats sinking and threatening other countries in the region would, I think have been open to conjecture, especially as these reports were in the Sunday Times, a paper owned by Rupert Murdoch, who is worth billions and who once told John Le Carrie in a restaurant in London that Brits are 'wood' from the neck up, meaning brain dead, I presume? The Chinese may have been in a brawl with, or near to ramming of a US warship in 2018. At least this incident, I presume, had hard factual empirical evidence beyond reproof. 'Given the militarization of the South China Sea, the prospect of an accidental collision and the potential for unmanaged escalation of hostilities are strong and they are mounting'; according to Alexander Neill an Asian Pacific security consultant in Singapore.

The 6th of August 2020 was the 75th anniversary of Hiroshima being destroyed with an atomic bomb, killing at least 75,000 on the day with 150,000 dead by December 1945. A few days later Nagasaki was subjected to the same treatment with another atomic bomb. At the same time, the Soviet Union forces were over coming Japanese forces in Manchuria, which was the catalyst for Japan to surrender. The invasion in Manchuria had been agreed at Yalta, which it seems was the final straw in the wind for Japan to surrender, and not the dropping of the bombs on Hiroshima and Nagasaki, albeit the USA Air-force likes to pretend it was whereas the USA navy said it was not necessary as Japan had already been defeated. In the National Museum of the US Navy in Washington DC on a plaque, it says this: '" The use of this barbarous weapon at Hiroshima and Nagasaki was of no material assistance in our war against Japan. The Japanese were already defeated and ready to surrender" wrote the Admiral Leahy, who presided over the combined US-UK chiefs of staff…. The Guardian 6th August 2020. Even Dwight Eisenhower, the General who helped win the war in Europe also thought the bombings were unnecessary, apparently telling his biographer Stephen Ambrose, but some historians like Rev Wilson Miscamble a history professor at the University of Notre Dame seems to think it did help to end the war early and save hundreds of thousands of lives. Kate Hudson of CND wrote an excellent article in the English Morning Star about 'another Hiroshima is becoming increasingly likely' which I also believe is more than likely if we are not careful, with warmongers like Trump having been in the White House and his poodle Boris Johnson having been in No 10 in the UK. When the bomb called 'Little Boy' was dropped on Hiroshima it destroyed '13 square kilometres of the city'. 'The heart of the explosion reached a temperature of several million degrees centigrade, resulting in a heat flash over a wide area that vaporized all human tissue. Within a radius of half a mile of the centre of the blast, every person was killed'. The destruction was beyond belief throughout Hiroshima, in the immediate area 90% of the population died and 63% of all buildings were destroyed with a further 92% of more peripheral buildings having some sort of damage from the fire storm. Kate Hudson goes on to explain the reason she feels that the route to further disasters seems overwhelming, through several interlocking crises. The degradation and destruction of the planet, in its many forms because of how society is structured, in late capitalism. The coronavirus pandemic which turned into a global health problem, which exacerbates the economic and social crises which follow from almost 40 years of neoliberal globalization. The onslaught and attack on democracy, fake news, the brutalization of communities, attacks on human rights, the rise of the far right, especially in the USA and the UK. Some of us would suggest this process is already in process in the institutions of No 10 (David Lammy) and formerly the White House, leading the charge against all progressive movements, like 'Black Lives Matter' which is at least a shining light showing that people power is a force to be reckoned with. The only way the ruling classes know how to deal with these disputes, at home and at world level is through violence. In the USA Trump even sent federal troops into Portland and several other cities, pretending he was tough on crime, and postulating that democratic representatives did not know how to handle the situations. At the state level only a small number of people get hurt when troops and police attack protesters, in their many forms, but when armies attack other countries, many get hurt and die. Which is a theme-of history for thousands of years, Britain trying to pretend it is still great, when it is sliding very fast down the scale of historic empires, yet still has nuclear weapons costing hundreds of billions, the cost of which was set to expand further when Boris Johnson was in power. All this utter nonsense so we can still be at the 'top table' of modern nations, albeit we were not ready for the covid-19 crisis, with one of the worse death rates throughout the world, along with Brazil and the USA, all led by maybe 'reckless leaders'. In the UK successive Tory governments have not only run down the NHS and local authorities, but have also sent millions into poverty again, through the insanity of austerity. However, Kate Hudson, (like this author), was very concerned, and indeed many intelligent people around the globe, at the policies carried out by Donald J. Trump. As she notes: 'his withdrawal from key treaties and the possibility of the resumption of nuclear tests all increase the risk of nuclear war'. She seemed to think that the USA is a declining power, which is true now that China is in the ascendancy, and in essence this is what this book is all about. Again, according to Hudson 'the US National Security Strategy focuses on what it describes as strategic rivals or competitors, notably China and Russia; its goal is to be able to defeat them militarily, so it seems preparing for war on a massive scale'. These ideas and policies are driving us toward the insanity of another world war, so must be stopped by worldwide action before Dr Strangelove Armageddon becomes a reality. (16)

Should Donald J. Trump gets elected again by some strange chance in November 2024 I would say we never can be too sure if he will be more dangerous than he was previously. To be the president of law and order you must have disorder. I would postulate that Trump, if he became

President again, would stir up more trouble with the Left, with lots more black people killed by the police.

On the 29th of August 2020 Jacob Blake was shot at least 7 times in the back in Kenosha, Wisconsin, with the reasons for this being somewhat hazy, albeit some claimed he was carrying a knife? Riots spread after this event, as in other cites when this sort of action has taken place, like the 'Black Lives Matter' protests after the death of George Floyd. The Republican national convention was up and running at the time, from the White House and other venues. Was there a connection I ask myself, to Blake's tragic shooting? According to the Guardian (26th August 2020) in 2004 in the same town as Jacob Blake lived a man called Michael Bell who was only 21 when shot in the head by their police force, because he may have been drinking. In Kenosha police do not have cameras on their being so the only evidence for what happened to Bell was from the camera on his dashboard, which showed he was not armed, a terrible indictment of police behaviour in the USA. At the convention from the White House and other places (which may have been illegal) Trump portrayed the Democrats as a danger to society, which is very ironic as I would argue it was Trump's presidency that posed a threat to the USA and the world, a view I think reinforced by the action President Biden has taken to tackle 'domestic terrrorism'. Trump and his team of conmen tried to suggest that Joe Biden is left of Lenin, which is of course rubbish of the highest order. In fact, a 'movie' of impressions and perception was constructed according to Daniel Strauss in the Guardian (26th August 2020) by Trump's team, a form of 'Apocalypse Now' vision where if Biden got elected the prisons would be emptied, gun owners would be disarmed and MS-13 would be invited to become Americans neighbours to live next door, and a terrible socialist state would be set up. I am pleased to note that as far as I know none of this happened so far. This was the same trick played on the uneducated majority in the UK in 2019 by the ruling class party (the Tories), and it worked, with a powerful right-wing press spewing lies and propaganda 24/7. The trouble Trump had was that 63% of the population did not believe he handled the Covid-19 crisis very well. Only 36% did. Now we know that to date hundreds of thousands of Americans have died from the virus. A constant theme of Republican Conventions has been the debate around what is labelled 'cancel culture' ideas, 'the blanket censorship of public figures' which is being portrayed by the extreme 'Right' as a form of political correctness gone mad. Usually, public figures are said to be cancelled after it has been discovered that they have done or said or written something offensive, which may have started on twitter. Freedom of speech, enshrined in the first amendment to the constitution of the USA, like the second amendment rights enabling the ownership of guns, are all part of being an all-American citizen, so anyone who challenges the narrative of the 'Right' is a bad guy/girl. The right to critique governments is all part of the American democratic process, so it is slightly strange that US politicians on both sides seek to 'shut down' debate. It seems to me like in, the UK where no one is supposed to critique the Monarchy, and ridiculous rich aristocrats, which I have done in previous books because they are all anachronistic. So, in the USA it's mostly the extreme 'Right' who try to control the narrative of how society should be organized only on capitalist lines. Any form of socialised health care, when discussed is thought of as a very dangerous idea (see below) and if a black man is called the 'N' word it is of course a disgrace, but probably not to the conservative thinkers in the USA, who would like slavery brought back, albeit wage slavery is the new embodiment of this whole economic model. *Democracy in America was* written by Alexis de Tocqueville in 1835 He was a French aristocrat, diplomat and political scientist who understood society in its form at that time was good for most as it was being formed, but he also conjectured black people had a rotten deal and might well become dangerous in the future. I think it very unlikely that Trump has ever heard of his books?

A case could be made for saying Trump has become paranoid about everything, including the narrative and anything else he cannot control. In essence he sees a bogeyman around every corner, where even Tik Tok is a threat to the whole of the USA, because it is a Chinese company. Strange considering this company was one of the sponsors of the Euro Cup (July 2021) that took place in Europe. As a 75-year-old intellectual (well maybe) I am not savvy about the social media phenomena but can email, am on WhatsApp and so on. However according to Trump, he was going to ban Tik Tok from the USA because of the data that China may be collecting about young people around the globe? Considering that this platform seems to-be about young people wanting to be famous and get rich at the same time, I would have thought that this is very unlikely. 'Trump has claimed Tik Tok could be used by China to track the locations of federal employees, build dossiers on people for blackmail and conduct corporate espionage. The company has said it has never provided any US user data to the Chinese government, and Beijing has attacked Trump's crackdown as political. (17) Oracle, which is owned by a Trump supporter and primarily makes database software and competes with Amazon and Microsoft, wanted a stake in Tik Tok. It seems Microsoft had wanted to buy the company with Walmart but may have been pipped at the post by Oracle albeit it needed approval from the neo-brute Trump, (after Aristotle) according to the British Guardian. One reason that Trump seems to be so paranoid about everything, including the rise of China, is that Vladimir Putin has some sort of leverage over him, concerning a possible sex scandal. No one knows for sure if this is true. Even Kim Darroch, the ex-British ambassador in Washington between January 2016 - December 2020, is 'sceptical' about this hypothesis. As all Putin wanted to do in 2016 was to get anyone elected as the President of the USA that was not Hilary Clinton, which happened and Darroch was forced to resign because of leaked emails that gave a dim view of Trump and his chaotic and tumultuously organization in the White House. Darroch, a career diplomat is now in the House of Lords as 'Lord Darroch of Kew' and is the author of a book called *'Collateral Damage'.* He was also very concerned about the level of violence that could erupt in the aftermath of a close-run US election in November, which happened.

While chaos was all around Trump at home and diverting attention elsewhere, he pretended he was a world statesman on the world stage, as I have shown in this book from many different sources. Especially for instance, boasting of a close relationship with Kim Jong-un, whom he casually forgot was prepared to go to war with the USA in 2018. Also, he fostered close relationships with Putin, Benjamin Netanyahu and anyone else who seems to be a strong leader, like he pretends to-be. I presume something like the 1930s all over again, hence very dangerous for all of mankind.

The Middle East is a fetish of his behaviour, perhaps because his eldest daughter Ivanka, adviser to the President, converted to the Jewish faith to marry Jared Kushner. 'UAE, Bahrain and Israel sign historic accords at White House' a heading in the British Guardian 16th September 2020 read, about the latest agreement between Israel and these two states, forged out of the old Ottoman empire mainly by the British and France many decades ago. 'Today's signing sets history on a new course Donald Trump told a crowd outside the White House where the deal was signed, this is an incredible day for the world, he said'. We have heard this tosh before many times, especially in 1993 when Yitzhak Rabin and the PLO leader Yasser Arafat shook hands on the same spot with Bill Clinton. The underlying problem has always been that Israel has been a 'pariah' in the middle east since its founding in 1948 when tens of thousands of Palestinians became refugees, between 1947 to 1949., but after the 1967 six-day war, 'the Palestinian residents chose to stay rather than flee their homes'. Now, through shifting sands and many Middle East countries becoming 'apathetic' about the Palestinian cause, Iran is becoming the new enemy that must be destroyed. In fact, there is a short add on to this article that should shock us all to the bone because according to Politico, who started as a web site in 2007 and is now a huge media organization (some of us are just news junkies), the suggestion from intelligence sources was that the Iranians were going to kill the US ambassador to South Africa to avenge the killing of Qassem Suleimani. Had they done so the threat was that Trump would crush Iran by a '1000 times harder than they hit us'……. this illustrates the level of threat this man imposed on the whole world. Anyone who has a broader perspective and may have read Noam Chomsky and others of a similar ilk, along with the Morning Star in the UK who are very good on foreign reportage, will be very aware that Israel has been stealing land from the Palestinians from day ONE (see above), and are still doing so, always trying by hook or by crook to stop intelligent people 'exposing lies and telling the truth' …about its actions. The history of the Middle East for thousands of years has been extremely dynamic, with different power structures and individual kings and Queens fighting for control of land and cities, including the British in 1917…. the record preserved for ever in movies like *Lawrence of Arabia*. However, like everywhere else in the world the Middle East originally did not have a fixed static society but was only occupied by hunter gatherers or nomads. Now the Jewish people claim that they are the rightful owners of the holy land or Palestine. To legitimize this belief, according to Hugh Humphries in the Morning Star (23rd September

2020), they are constructing tunnels in East Jerusalem, often underneath homes occupied by Arab people (and undermining their foundations) to create a tourist attraction, called the 'City of David'. Ironically, even David Gavron seems perplexed and not certain that King David (if he existed) did take the city of Jerusalem 3000 years ago. Most Jewish people seem to think that this is an axiom. 'Corroborating evidence is required and some indeed exists, but it is not conclusive'. Certainly, up until 1993 there was no hard-scientific empirical evidence about these events until a triangular piece of basalt rock, measuring 23 x 36 cm and inscribed in Aramaic, was found. Identified as part of a pillar erected by the King of Syria and later smashed by an Israelite ruler who may have been David, who knows? In any case, the dates do not add up according to other dubious sources.

We shall return to a pretend King who we do know exists in the 21st century, namely Donald J. Trump. According to Carlos Martinez in the Morning Star (24th September 2020) Trump must not be allowed to construct a 'potentially disastrous new cold war'. In this well thought out article he asserted strongly that this is now 'an increasingly connected world' and that going down the road of isolation is bonkers. The reason that I am a Remainer in the EU debate in the UK is that the whole idea of setting up the European Union in the first place in the 1950's was to stop another slaughter of millions in this century. Martinez starts his analysis with the visit of Richard Nixon who met Mao in China in February 1972. Nixon probably only went there to attempt to gain some sort of leverage against the Soviet Union. Also, maybe to tap into a potential market of hundreds of millions, to sell stuff and pretend that China did not exist as a State, as he hated any form of communism, but at the same time to buttress Taiwan's existence. This was a new strategy at the time, (see also above) - but under Barack Obama in 2011 the administration announced something called 'pivot to Asia' which was nothing more than the cessation bombing the Middle East (in theory) and the advancement of American interests in the Pacific. These ideas were not completely new, but setting up the Trans-Pacific Partnership was 'to join in the efforts to prevent China's emergence as the pre-eminent regional power in Asia'. Trump, a confirmed climate change denier, would have taken the USA out of the Paris Climate Agreement from November 2020, had he won the election. This agreement, signed by most nations of the world, was opposed by Trump simply, I believe, because Obama was for it. Incredible, but it seems to hold some truth, as I have described in this book from many sources.

However, the biggest long-term problem that Trump winning the White House has been for society as a whole, in the USA, is that the Supreme court of the United States ended up stacked with conservative minded people. Because it the highest court in the land no one gets fired and judges stay there until they die, like the amazing and wonderful Ruth Bader Ginsburg has just died at the ripe old age of 87. She was nominated by Jimmy Carter to the U.S. Court of Appeals for the District of Columbia Circuit where she served until her appointment to the Supreme Court in 1993. Trump nominated Amy Coney Barrett, a catholic with extreme right-wing views, to replace Ginsburg. According to the Sunday Observer (27th September 2020) she belongs to a covenant secretive community called 'People of Praise', a highly authoritarian structure. This group emerged from blending Catholicism and Protestant Pentecostalism in the 1960's which apparently adopted practices such as speaking in tongues. Massimo Faggioli, a theology professor, noted that 'there were tensions between serving as a supreme court justice, one of the final interpreters of the US constitution, and swearing an oath to an organisation that lacks transparency and visible structures of authority that are accountable to their members, to the Roman Catholic church, and to the wider public'.

People of Praise is headed by an all-male board of governors, albeit they may not be any different than what goes on in any conservative Catholic circles, which may be nothing more than a cult per se. Barrett, who has 7 children, also has very disturbing views and ideas, according to the democrats who oppose Trump's nominee to the Supreme Court. As a professor at Notre Dame Law School, she opposed Obama's Affordable Care Act because of the nature of the Act to offer coverage for contraception in its many different forms to the millions who may have wanted it. She has been instrumental in the overturning of the 1973 Roe v Wade decision that legalised abortion nationwide. This happened in June 2022. She is also hostile to environment regulations, which would be very good for big polluters. The Roe v Wade decision of 1973 being overturned seems to be the main reason that all liberals in the USA were so concerned about the possible idea of Amy Coney Barret being elected to the Supreme Court. In 2006 she called act of termination barbaric in an advert she and her husband Jesse signed in Indiana, claiming that most people in the USA are opposed to abortion as a method of birth control. Even the White House might have been concerned that her extreme views may have prevented her having an easy ride in the Senate, according to the Guardian (2nd October 2020). Supreme court judges do not make the law as written but only interpret it. With other groups like St Joseph Country Right to Life being just as big a threat to the pro-choice activists as supporters of Barrett, suggesting that doctors who perform abortions are criminals. However, the new tack seemed to be more culture wars by the Trump administration, when it came to the confirmation hearings procedure regarding the Supreme Court appointment of Barrett. Here he was trying to trick the Democrats to be anti-Roman Catholic throughout the procedure, which could have harmed them in the upcoming election, with 70, 412,021 registered Catholics in the USA, which constitutes 22% of the population. That is a huge part of American citizens to upset. After a four-day confirmation hearing in the senate Amy Coney Barrett was confirmed as a member of the Supreme Court, and this institution is now rigged in the conservative favour by a margin of 6 to 3. This seemed to be the only big issue Trump was able to succeed at, apart from giving his rich friends more dosh. As to my knowledge Hilary Clinton never went to prison, and the Great Wall of Trump between Mexico and the USA was never completed and was never paid for by the Mexican government.

While researching and writing this book also sorts of events have happened as I have documented throughout, but one which occurred was nearly beyond believe in that President Trump and his wife tested positive for Covid-19 and 'The Donald' was been sent to the Walter Reed Medical Centre (WRMC) 10 miles north of Washington DC for treatment (week ending 3rd October 2020), a bit like what happened to Boris Johnson the prime minister of the UK previously. Considering that Trump dismissed the virus as nothing to worry about originally, this seems to have been an act of God. The timing was just a few days after his first pre-election debate with Joe Biden in Cleveland chaired by Chris Wallace of Fox news. That all went wrong for Trump according to most pundits, apart from the Right-wing media like Fox news, who said he acted like a Lion King and a Shark, not at the same time I presume? However, most commentators said it was a chaotic night for Trump, who interrupted Biden at-least '73 times', some saying that it was a 'dumpster fire' a 'train wreck' and a 'shit show'. The Sunday Times (4th October 2020) promulgated the idea that the latest nightmare for Trump was due to his own behaviour, others in his staff and many people in the Republican Party. Especially when he threw a party in the Rose Garden for Amy Coney Barrett and 150 guests to celebrate his recommendation for her nomination to the Supreme court. After that event at least 6 people or more tested positive for the virus and no one seems to know for sure when Trump may have caught it. A few days later he was back in the White House, after first leaving the medical centre to visit well-wishers outside of the WRMC, which the doctors said was an insane act, but who cares if Trump is on stage? He did not seem to care a hoot about the Secret Service men who guarded him and drove him around in his bullet proof car, according to the Washington post. Losers, I presume? In theory Trump recovered from Covid-19 as of the 10th of October 2020 and said it was a 'blessing from God' that he got it and that he would go on campaigning for the top position in USA society, adding that the drug given to him should be free to all Americans. Well, I never, Donald J. Trump discovering the wonders of the NHS in the UK when all Tories government since 1948 has been trying to destroy the big socialist idea...especially since 1979. Lucky for some on the 7th of October 2020 there was a rational debate between Mike Pence, the Vice president who is a born-again Christian but born a Roman Catholic, and the wonderful and amazing Kamala Harris, Joe Biden's running mate, who stood up to Pence and who Trump called a 'monster' in the aftermath of her performance. So, I presume he was very afraid of her for being mixed race and very intelligent. Her Mother is from India, her dad was born in Jamaica, and both are highly intelligent. She was District Attorney of San Francisco from 2004 to 2011 and Attorney of California from 2011 to 2017 and then a Senator for the State of California. Now, of course, she is Vice President in the Biden administration, and is continuing her life long fight for social justice. She seems to be the diametric opposite of Donald J. Trump, whose whole life on earth has just been about him and no one else, increasing his enormous wealth, which maybe or not be true, because he has gone through several bankruptcies. According to the New York Times for many years he never paid any taxes, had a huge rebate from the IRS and last year only paid a few hundred dollars in federal taxes. No wonder according to F. A. Hayek (Mrs Thatcher's guru) 'social justice' does not exist!

Trump also seems to think that most people are losers. Even dead soldiers in their own graves are losers apparently, for being stupid enough to sign up, which I presume includes Joe Kennedy junior who died in a bombing raid on France in the Second World War. Jack Kennedy was lucky in that in August 1942 PT-109, a Motor Torpedo boat which he commanded, was sunk when it got rammed and sliced in two by a Japanese ship called Amqiri at night. Amazing only two of the 13 crew were killed, the 11 survivors making it to a small island nearby, from where they were rescued sometime later after Kennedy wrote a message on a coconut. According to a digital channel in the UK called More4 (14th October 2020), this whole slice of history which was glorified in a Hollywood movie released in 1963, 5 months before Kennedy was killed, was not completely honest in that Kennedy should have been court martialled and not made into a hero at all, but because his father was such a big wig in USA society, he managed to twist the story of his second son into that of an all-American action hero. Very unlikely that Hollywood would be able to do a similar job on Trump, I would have thought? Apparently, he has now had 14 books ghost written about him…….*The Art of the Deal,* his first book that I have read and used in this project, he wanted to use instead of the bible to swear him in as President of the USA…an aide said it was not a good idea, in January 2016.

I should note that not everyone agrees that Kamala Harris is wonderful. For example, Caleb Maupin who has just written a book about her and other issues in the USA. Maupin's day job is working for RT, and I like him when I see him on news reports. The Morning Star got a hold of a copy of his latest book and did a review. If Helen Mercer's analysis is correct it is a book that I will buy, though Maupin may not have everything correct about Harris. Harris was born on the Left. Her dad was a Marxist economist, but now seems to have moved toward the Right with the help of Hilary Clinton's faction in the Democratic Party. While as an attorney general in California between 2010 to 2017 it seemed that she did nothing for the poor, but some say she was the 'Queen of mass incarceration', and on foreign policy she is close to Israeli lobbyists and bellicose about Russia and North Korea. Like everywhere under capitalism in the world, different companies support different factions within political parties, so it seems that the biggest banks, major oil companies and silicon-valley tech giants are supporting Biden and Harris, while other corporates support Trump. The book also examines the complexity of the Left in a fairly detailed analysis from a USA perspective, starting in 1945. I think of myself as well read, but I am no expert on this issue as it is so complex, especially in America because of the influence of agencies of the Government in trying to stop the Left becoming successful. This is the case not only in the USA but also in Europe and, let's face it, everywhere, as maybe stated by Chomsky et al. Maupin thinks the new Left is a fake, especially in the USA, and a child of the CIA, which if true it is very sad indeed! He further thinks the class war was watered down by the Frankfurt school of critical social theory. Personally, I am not convinced of this argument, because I have read Herbert Marcuse and others from this school years ago and was very influenced by their arguments. They were often featured in good sociological textbooks that I have read as a major source on subjects like the brainwashing of the majority that goes on, especially in the West according to Marcuse et al. I should just add a foot note to this section, about the wonderful and beautiful Kamala Harris, the Vice President. In an RT UK programme shown on 7th July 2021, titled Going Underground, Afshin Rattansi interviewed Professor David Nutt, an expert on drug policies, who noted about what I have written above, but apparently thought she has now recanted on at least some of her ideas and sentencing policies which she enacted when she was attorney general of California, with regard to the insanity of drug policies.

Trump lost the Presidential election in November 2020, but be warned he may try again in four years' time, if he has not been committed to prison by then. Some say that his outrageous behaviour regarding election fraud etc is directly related to reasons that he may end up in prison subsequent to his leaving the White House. From dozens of defamation lawsuits sparked by his denials of sexual assaults on women, to possible falsifying company records and tax avoidance, the list, if the Daily Mirror is correct in the UK (7th November 2020), seems endless. Trump might have to flee to another country, but surely not North Korea, or North Korea on Thames (sic), could it be…… or maybe a bunker with Edward Snowden in Russia could be option 3? Even Mary Trump, his niece, sued her uncle, albeit unsuccessfully, in matters related to tax affairs. The judge threw the case out, saying it was inadmissible as matters were settled a judgement given 20 years earlier. A further complication is that Trump in turn sued Mary over the same matter. Thus are the joys of mega-rich families! One thing is for sure. Now he is out of the White House, Trump seems to face an unending stream of controversies regarding his financial and political affairs.

This book will, I hope, not be only an unauthorised biography about a mad man and 'lunatic' (Obama's words), but also a **WARNING FROM HISTORY**…this I believe also applies to class driven neo-brutes, like: Boris Johnson and Mrs Thatcher and Liz Truss et al who helped to crush the working class in the UK. Boris Johnson, of course, metamorphosed into a 'man of the people', an impressive feat considering he went to Eton, Oxford and was also a member of the notorious Bullingdon club, along with David

Cameron and George Osbourne. Apparently, according to those who 'know', the modus operandi of this 'select' club was to use prostitutes at dinner parties for oral sex, shout and scream that plebs were an obscene form of life, often doing so on top of dinner tables while said plebs waited hand and foot on them, doing all the crap jobs in society including being servants to the rich and powerful. They also smashed up the bedrooms of new club members, and trashed restaurants they visited. However, when Jo public does similar acts of destruction they are normally locked up. Here we see clear evidence that there is **ONE** rule for the rich and one for the poor, the damage to restaurants paid for by rich parents. As an America author said decades ago, (which I read) in our sort of society structured in this way: *the Rich get Richer while the Poor go to Prison.*

One of the most important books ever written about this sort of narcissistic behaviour of people like Trump and Johnson was written by Oliver James called *Affluenza* and published in 2007. Basically, it is about the damaging psychological effects of selfish capitalism on everyone who is trapped in such a society, especially the English-speaking parts of the world like America, the UK and Australia. The wider the gap between the have and have-nots, the worse will be the effect on the population, hence the reason why the USA and the UK are so badly affected by this societal model, according to Oliver James. I first noticed this concept myself years before Oliver James ever came up the idea whilst living in the West Midlands, after leaving the Royal Air Force in 1975, having moved there with my wife of the time and two small children. In fact, I was so shocked, especially by the behaviour of uneducated owners of small businesses that I did suggest in my first book that what I detected was misanthropic behaviour of the worse kind, which included ghastly racism, of the worse kind. The English ruling class are past masters of whipping up the hatred of anyone that is not white at every election for generations, the same tactics that Trump uses in the USA.

I was informed by a wonderful friend in the USA, who originates from Nigeria, that Joe Biden had won the Presidential election, a great day for the world and even for an old man like me at the age of 72…. now 75. Hence, why I have had to re-jig the title of this book to include Trump's offspring in the same position as he is now, for who knows what will happen sometime in the future(?).... because the Trump brand is now quite strong, unless he ends up in prison that is. Like Boris Johnson, his whole life has been based on fabrications and conspiracy theories, which Sarah Baxter in the Sunday Times (8th November 2020) thought he would seek to continue with, especially digging dirt up on Joe Biden's son, and anything else that most people would think a little unhinged. He is also very influenced by Roy Cohn, the McCarthyite lawyer, now deceased, who used to tell him attack, attack, attack and never ever admit defeat……an old John Wayne line from at least one of his movies, made when Trump was a very young boy; especially never ever apologize to anyone. This is what he was up to inside the White House while I writing and researching this book. The Guardian (9th November 2020) has done a wonderful job of making a list of things that others have noted over the last 4 years, that has happened while he was in the White House, like the 30,000 (on leaving the White House) lies that the Washington Post fact checked, finalising their check on the 9th of July 2020. Including the 5 miles of the new WALL that was built albeit 307 miles of replacement and improvement of the existing wall. The 350, 0000 Americans that have died of Covid-19 as of the day I wrote this, also the 285 days he had spent on the golf course at the time of writing, while he decried Barack Obama for doing the same while he was in office. Ninety-nine was the number of environmental regulations Trump reversed, like clean water and clean air protection, also the protection of wildlife. In addition, the regulation of prevention of toxic chemicals getting into the environment was abandoned. Twenty-six women have accused Trump of sexual misconduct, he only paid $750 in federal taxes for both fiscal years 2016 and 2017. An 87% proportion of his cabinet were millionaires, with two centimillionaires, (worth one hundred million) and one billionaire, as of course is Trump himself, in theory.

The Covid-19 crisis was arguably his most dangerous mishandling of events (similar to Boris Johnson in the UK). At least 22 million people lost their jobs in America, 900 abortion clinics lost their federal funding. At the time of writing 552 tweets had been put out by Trump since he first walked into the White House. As course, as we all know, Trump was subsequently banned from Twitter. This must have been frustrating for him because it was his favourite medium for labelling as 'fake news' any form of expression used by anyone or any institution that disagreed with him. The irony is that with Elon Musk having now taken over Twitter, Trump has been reinstated on the platform, but at a time when he lacks the kudos of the Presidency. In the UK, the extreme Right-Wing press spew out lies and propaganda daily, which some of us who are better educated would call 'fake news', and 'alternative facts'. I know people who read the Daily Mail every day and are so brainwashed by this nonsense, that I fear for their sanity? The Guardian once called Paul Dacre (who was the editor of the Daily Mail for years) the most dangerous man in the UK, which I believe was and is still true to this day, as he still has some sort of management role at the parent company.

On the day it was reported by Pfizer had announced that they have invented a vaccine for covid-19 Trump tweeted it was all down to him, apparently another lie as it has all been researched with private money, with nothing contributed from USA government funding whatsoever.... Russia and China also have a vaccine for this virus but this fact is all but written out of history by Western news agencies. The trouble Joe Biden had to take on when in power from the 21st of January 2021 was beyond belief because of the chaos that Trump caused. For instance, getting back into the Paris climate agreement, improving relationships with Iran, re-joining the WHO, the terrible death toll in the USA from covid-19, now getting on for 240,000 (10th November 2020), the crashing of the economy, etc. However, as I noted above, even in October 2022 Biden's government is taking a hard line against China, like Trump, asserting that US companies must not export semiconductors and electronic chip making equipment to China, according to the UK Guardian on the 19th October 2022.

No doubt Trump will be sniping from the side-lines, either to try and return in 2024, or get one of his children into the White House. In fact, Joe Biden must improve the lot of the majority of the population by improving the minimum wage and other issues, like health care for everyone, albeit within four more years' time many more old people will have died, maybe more Trump supporters than Biden ones, and a younger generation will be able to vote.

According to RT TV - *Watching the Hawks* shown between 9th and 13th of November 2020 (in the UK) the election in the USA cost '14billion dollars', the most expensive in history and double the 2016 event. If this is true it is nearly beyond belief that so much money can be spent on such an event when the basic underlying structure of society will have not changed one little bit. The problem in the USA is that the whole system was designed from day ONE in 1776 so it should not resemble the British Monarchy, but that the new/old ruling elite should keep control of society. As of 12th of November 2020 Donald J. Trump had not conceded to Joe

Biden, who won by over 5 million votes, and 'The Donald' was trying to impose his own friends into the bureaucracy of the State. A very worrying trend that also happens in the UK, where Tory governments always try to control every aspect of life in the UK. In fact sometimes I do wonder if Britain is now where Germany was in 1933, as it is very unlikely that this brutal ruling class will ever let Labour come to power again this century (even though at this moment in 2023 Labour has a substantial lead in the opinion polls and will only be Tory lite again), with the help of the extreme Right-Wing press spewing out lies and propaganda, and the new tools deployed in No. 10 to resemble those utilised by the White House. There is no doubt about it that the British Aristocracy, or at least a strand of it, was sympathetic towards the Nazis in the 1930's. Himmler built the SS and their derivatives on the norms and values of the British ruling class, I presume because of the brutality they imposed on everywhere they conquered and took over, causing absolute misery in places like India. 'The ideology of British rule was that of the 'Herrenvolk' and the master race an idea inherent in imperialism' which was very plain to see India and elsewhere (18).

According to the great John Crace in the Guardian (5th January 2020) the ex- British prime minister Boris Johnson is a 'narcissistic charlatan' and in essence a miniature Donald J. Trump, who according to the Washington Post has told at least 30,000 lies while in the White House. Similarly, Boris Johnson might be said to live in a world of make believe, as according to Dominic Cummings he does not know what is a lie or what is the truth. Some might contend he has never done a real job in his whole life and has not got a clue how the majority live their lives, often struggling just to feed themselves. This situation got a lot worse in 2022, even as Johnston opined that earning £5000 a week was 'chicken feed' when he worked as a journalist on the Daily Telegraph, a few years ago...? Owned by the billionaire Barclay brothers, who Boris Johnson still called the 'bosses' when prime minister and since being kicked out of No 10 has earned over £5 million in speeches etc.

The Washington Post at the beginning of January 2021 got hold of a tape recording of Donald J. Trump on the phone trying to persuade Brad Raffensperger, a Georgia state official 'to overturn the presidential election in his favour'. The debate revolved around that Trump would not admit he lost the November election and that Jo Biden won by fraud. The problem Trump had here (is) that he never wanted to be called a loser or perceived as ONE. In the recording to Raffensperger he wants him to find 11780 votes and pretend he won Georgia by hundreds of thousands of votes. He even threatened Raffensperger by saying that he was committing criminal offences with other State officials by not overturning the truth. The ironic fact about the call is that Brad Raffensperger is a republican official, and it looked if that it was Trump that may have committed an offence against the whole electoral American system. The FBI was urged to open a criminal inquiry into Trump's behaviour over this issue.

Every time I sit down to work on this project, I think to myself can the world in the **West** get any crazier in this epoch – but on the 6th January 2020 all the news TV channels I saw showed what you could only describe as a 'Banana Republic' in action. No, not a Latin America country but the USA in all its glory.... and also asserted as such by George W. Bush, the ex-president. As the British Guardian (7th January 2020) reported it the next morning 'Chaos as pro-Trump mob storms the US Capital'. Rioters broke down barriers and surged into the Congress building, one person was shot, and four others died through underlying health issues. You could hardly make this up in this epoch because the theory of a liberal capitalist democracy is that it is a stable phenomenon, which of course it is not because it is basically a rigged political system run by the ruling plutocracies, especially in the USA and the UK. However, this was the hard-line Trump supporters trying to stop the final count of what had already happened but in normal times no one ever gets excited about it. The Guardian and other news outlets even suggested that it was the most dramatic event to challenge the US democratic system itself 'since the civil war', others said since the British burnt down the White House on the 24th of August in 1814, which was a retaliation against the American attack on the city of York in Ontario in Canada during June 1813. This action was directly related to Donald J. Trump's rhetoric, by his telling his supporters: 'to converge on Congress', which they did because he had won the election in November outright by hundreds of thousands of votes, in a 'landslide election'...not. Ironically, the national guard that had driven the 'Black Lives Matter' off the streets were absent, looked bloody suspicious too me. Trump was probably also riled up because the Republicans had also lost two senate seats in Georgia, or by this time it was becoming clear that this was the case. The Mayor of Washington got so concerned that for the next fortnight Washington was under a curfew from 6pm on the 6th of January 2021. The Republican Party is also the party of 'Law and Order', which made this more of a farce then it really was. The Tory party view themselves in a similar light in the UK. Jo Biden called this whole disaster for the USA an 'assault on the rule of law' and said it 'borders on sedition'.

Rebecca Solnit noted in the Guardian (8th January 2020) that 'Trump built an army to enforce his reality. This was inevitable'. She called the whole thing a 'coup attempt,' which it was. In some ways Trump can be compared to fascist leaders of the past, in that he might be said to construct his own social reality, which is very similar to Boris Johnson in the UK, to whom David Lammy said Johnson was 'an extreme hard-right fascist'. The chaos that has been created in the USA by Trump (very similar to the Brexit insanity in the UK) is mostly whipped up against foreigners and takes the form of white male rage against everything they perceive as 'liberal values' in their world. The sad truth in America and the UK is that most working-class people's standard of living has hardly gone up in decades. The Republican Party's far-right groups, like the Proud Boys etc., have all helped to legitimize Trump's insane narrative. On Channel 4 news in the UK (7th January 2020 18:40) Krishnan Guru-Murthy interviewed a professional gentleman from Vienna, in Austria, who was extremely angry about this whole saga as he saw it and said, 'fascism is a force in the USA', which is not far from the truth. (Fiona Hill also noted on USA TV that if Trump was to get re-elected, that society would be ripped apart). Rebecca Solnit went on in her article to assert how Trump had got away with this during his Presidency by saying that: 'Trump is the most prolific liar America has ever seen, and his lies were an essential part of his authoritarianism: a refusal to be bound by facts, even the facts of what he had said or done the day before. He demanded a parallel narrative in which he had won the election; and he laid the groundwork long before to claim, if he lost, that it was illegitimate, as he did in 2016'. In a video after the mob had broken into the Capital, Trump said "We love you", as he told them to go home'. But he also reasserted that the election had been stolen, which is why they were there in the first place. His daughter Ivanka apparently deleted a tweet in which she called them "American patriots". Like all forms of might be termed 'pseudo fascism', wherever it hatches out into day's world - Trump supporters regard their leader and themselves as above the law. Frightened that he may be impeached again, or the 25th amendment be invoked, he did a volt-face, calling for 'unity' and 'outrage' of the violence he had created in the first place by suggesting that there should be a 'orderly transition of power'. Apparently, Congress was so appalled by this whole saga that on Monday the 11th of January 2021 the Democratic Party went ahead with an impeachment process in Congress to try and stop Trump from getting anywhere near the White House again, ever. As a side note he also informed the world he would not be at Jo Biden's swearing in ceremony on the 20th of January 2021, although Mike Pence was.

Twitter and Facebook banned Trump completely from these platforms once he lost the Presidency. The RIGHT, including Roger Stone, was up in arms about this as such actions were against, at least in theory, free speech. Even Tom Slater, writing in the British Sunday Times (10th January 2021), pointed out that because Trump had 89 million social media followers, the case might be made that Facebook and Twitter have been waiting for an appropriate excuse to ban him from their platforms, which they duly did. Of course, with Twitter now being owned by Elon Musk, Trump has been restored to this platform. What is so strange about this critique of Slater is that Rupert Murdoch who owns this paper is one of the richest people on the planet, so no different than Big Tech billionaires. Whose propaganda controls millions of minds all around the world; who prey on the uneducated like my old mother who believed in every word the Murdoch papers said? This story has been a gold mine for Russia, China and the world who are sick and tired of being lectured to by the USA, (and its lapdog the UK etc) whenever they in theory do something out of the zeitgeist of the West, within their own parameters. Amazingly, Trump is still calling out the lie that the people who stormed the Congress were 'Antifa' left-wing activists and not his supporters, who were responsible for death and destruction inside the Capital. Chuck Schumer (sic) even noted that 'what Trump did today, (12th January 2021) blaming others for what he caused is a pathological technique used by the worst of dictators'. All the hard scientific empirical evidence might be said to show that Donald J.

Trump has lied virtually all his life, throughout his business life, pretending that he was richer than he was, and promulgating tens of thousands of lies and disinformation throughout his Presidency…. (Main sources here the Washington Post) …probably over 30,000 lies. In essence, very much like Boris Johnson in the UK, who seems to live in a parallel universe to most of us, who according to Dominic Cummings (ex-special adviser), does not appear to know the truth from a pack of lies. An excellent BBC2 TV documentary called *The Trump Show: The Downfall*, was screened on 24th January 2021, maybe called after the brilliant movie about Hitler in his bunker in Berlin in 1945? Called the *Downfall.* The most revealing part of this hour-long programme to me was when the producers interviewed Anthony Scaramucci who was Trump's communications director. He only lasted 10 days in the post but noted that Trump was 'a nutter and a sociopath' and a fan of the movie 'Citizen Kane' and seemed to have identified with the character in the movie and was obsessed by the film. The lead was played by the great Orson Welles and the film was partly based on William Randolph Hearst's life and times and Chicago tycoons Samuel Insull and Robert McCormick. In my notes I was taking at the time I wrote that any well-read person would see Trump's close connection/persona to Caligula or a mafia don. However, worshipped like a pop star or a god by his millions of fans, with thousands turning out for his rallies, as he bragged about his 'tax cuts' and 'stronger boarders' and so on, even getting Nigel Farage to support him, calling him the 'King of Europe', at one of his rallies. Farage said such tosh as Trump was the 'bravest person he had ever met' and decrying most of the mass media and the state bureaucracy for being against him over the last four years. Trump also understood more than likely that the postal votes would go against him, hence the attack on the postal service once he was made aware that millions were voting this way. This was proved correct on the 4th of November and a few days later as the counting continued, at the start of the count Trump thought he had won, but once the postal votes were counted, he was losing the election. At the press conference just after these events he said that he had won and the result was 'a fraud on the American public'. This sort of behaviour, trying to control the narrative, is well known from the days of Hitler and Goebbels to Margaret Thatcher, Trump and Boris Johnson in the UK to this day. In Trump's case he also tried to use the American court system, with Rudy Giuliani's help, to overthrow the result that Biden had won with 81,268,757 against Trump's 74,216,722 votes and using his children as outriders, telling everyone who would listen saying that 'mail ballots are a fraud'. This led Trump's supporters to believe the lie that Trump had won and shouting the slogan 'stop the steal' on nearly every street corner in the USA, which finally led to the attack on Congress on the 6th of January 2021. The final effort to stop the results of the election. Joe Biden's view about the election was that it had very little to do with representing the people of the USA as far as Trump was concerned, but was, in fact, all 'about him' (Trump) as a sort of 'virus' that I presumed had contaminated society over the last four years....and not far from the truth.

James Comey, who may have been partly responsible for Hillary Clinton's defeat in 2016 when he was head of the FBI (director) at the time, seems to deeply regret what he did at the time in his latest book called *Saving Justice: Truth, Transparency and Trust,* breaking protocol about the reviewing of 'classified information' in emails sent by Clinton from her private email server just 11 days before the election. Trump exploited this to the full claiming he would 'lock her up' for the careless use of her email system. Comey was in deep water with his wife Patrice who said he would 'get slaughtered for this' whole sorry saga, which made into a TV drama in the USA. Comey also saw through Trump while having dinner with him, when apparently never stopped talking in front of his guests, and the menace and pure meanness of his persona shone through, a side of him not normally seen in public. While at dinner Comey noted how he tried to concentrate to the full so he could write it all down afterwards, throughout the 90-minute meal. Like all conmen he wants to draw everybody into his world and as he was the President, he tried to make people believe he was telling the truth? Comey was fired on May 2017 by Trump who is now completely shocked and sickened by what happened in January 2021 on Capitol hill and questions why it was not defended at the time, calling it 'our Chernobyl' (Source: The Guardian 19th January 2021 - Steve Bannon's favourite paper). Donald Trump's delusion may have hit new heights according to Sarah Baxter, who lives in the USA, writing in the Sunday Times (6th June 2021) where she stated they were having another recount in several States in the USA, or such counts were being demanded by Trump and QAnon supporters. When completed they thought he would be back in the White House by August 2021, which it seems Trump believed also. Albeit some are suggesting that the stimulus Joe Biden's team gave the economy, basically trillions, made the workers lazy and not wanting to return to low paid crap jobs. Who can blame them?

Every four years on the 20th of January the new president elected the previous November is sworn in as the new or re-elected president, all men since 1789. The first was George Washington, the 46th Joseph R Biden Jr. The ceremony itself has been very similar for decades and I must admit I was touched watching Joe Biden being sworn in after all the terrible tragedies in his personnel life, as I was seeing the very beautiful Kamala Harris, the first women to get the role of Vice President, live on most TV news channels around the globe, including the UK. There were no huge crowds watching it because of the 6th of January debacle and only a few special guests near bye and nearly 25,000 troops on the streets of

Washington, to keep order in case Trumps useful idiots stormed the citadel again. To my knowledge no one has been charged directly for the five deaths that happened on the 6th apart from Trump being impeached for inciting the violence of it in the first place. However, what most people do not understand is that the basic underlying structures of society hardly move an inch on these occasions - albeit because of the huge chaos that Trump caused over four years in the White House is partly being rectified and overturned from day ONE. Trump snubbed the whole occasion and ran off on Air-Force ONE to his luxury resort at Mar-a-Lago in Florida, after a surreal send off from Andrews Air Force base, just outside Washington. Maybe because he would not admit he lost the election in November 2020 and hates to be called a loser? Like Boris Johnson in the UK Trump does not seem to have any 'remorse' whatsoever for the death of 500,000+ in the USA, and in the case of Johnson 150,000+ in the UK, from Covid-19, both two of the highest in the world….2022 over ONE million dead in the USA. Peter Oborne (see below as well) noted that 'when people started to die in large numbers, both the US president and the British prime minster responded with lies and fabrications' (19).

But like all presidents for decades, Trump pardoned dozens of his mates for misdemeanours. Steve Bannon, Elliott Broidy, Ken Kurson and 70 others mostly all committed financial crimes. Steve Bannon being the most surreal for stealing money from funds collected from Jo public's contribution to 'We Build the Wall' project - which Trump had bragged in 2016 would be paid for the Mexican government. Apparently even Nixon did not have the gall to pardon his cronies when he was forced to resign in 1974. Bannon was banned from Twitter for calling for the beheading of FBI director Christopher Wray and Dr Anthony Fauci.

In the UK Boris Johnson originally could not make up his mind about Trump, this was in 2015. But afterwards when he became president, he seemed to be deferential and sycophantic towards him, because Trump was also in favour of Brexit and wanted to give Britain a great trading deal when we left the EU. Johnson became more confused than ever because Biden's family originally came from Ireland, so not too happy about Brexit and seemed too see-through Boris Johnson from day one when he said Johnson 'is a physical and emotional clone' of Trump.... which is an axiom of this man, who lied about many aspects of the Brexit madness, which might well cost the British £80 billion a year? Also, most Americans are very confused why anyone would want to leave a huge trading block like the EU and be poorer for decades because of this action that David Cameron, Nigel Farage (King of Europe) Michael Gove and Boris Johnson are directly responsible for. Peter Oborne, a very well-known British journalist of the Right, noted (21st January 2021) on the Alex Salmond Show (RT UK) that Boris Johnson's Tory party was an alt-Right wing party, very much like the ruling party in Hungary, having got rid of all the sensible moderate Tories in this very old party, that may still be around at the end of this century? Peter Oborne's brilliant book about Boris Johnson and Trump et al called: *Assault on Truth* should be read by the whole world, because basically Boris Johnson like Trump trades as a charlatan and an extremely dangerous Nationalist. I would also suggest everyone in the world buy and watch Michael Moore's (DVD) called Fahrenheit 11/9 which again places Trump as another extremely dangerous nationalist/Right wing Populist, some might say returning to what happened in Germany in 1933 and Italy 10 years earlier, where to get elected you must have scapegoats to explain your rationale and internal logic.

Martin Jacques excellent book about China which I have used as a source in this book several times should be read by all Western leaders in the world, because he gives so many insights into this great civilisation, which he calls a 'civilization-state,' instead of a 'Nation state' which is how most textbooks on the subject predicate 'statehood' when explaining how societies work around the globe. The reason is that it is one of the oldest civilisations on earth, covering a huge land mass. The problem with countries like the USA and the UK is that most of the elites running society have just ONE agenda and that is to treat other nations as either friends or foes. At present China, Russia and Iran are the enemy states that must be controlled and kept down at all costs, very similar to how they treat their own citizens, or in the UK their subjects. At least Boris Johnson's father and half-brother seem more sympathetic to China, according to the Sunday Times (28th February 2021). Stanley, the father, first visited China when Chairman Mao was still in charge and Max, half-brother to Boris, is a businessman who lives in Hong Kong. Stanley at least seems to be aware that China must be involved in the whole climate warming debate or else it does not make sense. Will China turn out to be a much more caring actor on the world stage than most European countries over the last 500 years have been? This is open to conjecture, albeit this is what Martin Jacques is suggesting in *When China Rules the World.*

If I did not think that Donald J. Trump was/is such an existential threat to the whole of civilisation in the 21st Century I would not have written this book and spent over three years doing it. Ironically, according to the Guardian of 16th July 2021, which really upset the Kremlin (RT…UK), they claim to have got hold of documents that suggest that Vladimir Putin did try and get Trump elected in 2016. It said on the front page: 'Documents show Putin plan to back "unstable" Trump in 2016 US election'. They claimed the meeting to plan this took place on the 22[nd of] January 2016. This process 'would help secure Moscow's strategic objectives, among them social turmoil in the US and a weakening of the American president's negotiating position'. The report No32-04/vd is classified as secret. If true it is an explosive document because it says that Trump is an 'impulsive, mentally unstable and unbalanced individual who suffers from an inferiority complex'...which may or may not be true, perhaps because of his lack of a knowledge base? Also, it says that Putin has comprising material on Trump from previous visits, which others in this project have denied...albeit even Fiona Hill et al seems to think that Putin wants to weaken USA hegemony and was up to no good in 2016? The Kremlin and Trump rubbish this whole story but if we look back on the last 5 years, there does appear to be more than a grain of truth in what has happened, and like Caligula, Trump is perhaps unstable.

Two thousand years ago in Rome, people like Julius Caesar and Caligula (little soldier's boots) could not blow up the planet but did use their power to the full throughout the Roman empire and beyond, killing perceived enemies at will, often for mere amusement in the case of Caligula. Ironically, both men were killed in a similar fashion in Rome, being castigated as Tyrants. Caligula, (quoted from several sources) was probably insane, perhaps caused by some form of mental disorder, albeit for the first several months of his reign he seemed to go down well in Rome. He also became ill like Trump, perhaps by poison, built projects for society and luxurious homes for himself and spent large sums of money on sex and debauchery. He liked to sleep with other men's wives and bragged about it, so again very similar to traits in the 45th president of the USA. Tiberius understood that Caligula had a cruel and brutal nature and was a 'natural actor' while living with him for six years on the island of Capri. Trump seems to believe in the power of Christian thought over his actions: Pliny the Younger thought that Christian thought was a 'wretched cult'. Tiberius believed in his soothsayer called Thrasyllus of Mendes who noted that Caligula had 'no more chance of becoming emperor than riding a horse across the bay of Baiue'. A very big mistake because once he became a Roman Emperor, after the death of Tiberius, whom he may have killed, Caligula built a bridge across this bay and rode his favourite horse, Incitatus across it with the breast plate of Alexander the Great on his chest. He also made this horse a consul and a priest and built a huge racetrack for chariot racing, with a huge Obelisk, (brought from Egypt) at its entrance in Rome. This same Obelisk still stands in the Vatican square, over two thousand years later. The final straw leading to his assassination may have been not only upsetting the praetorian guard, but very similar to Trump he wanted to be worshipped as a God and thus acted in such a manner, with the intention of leaving Rome and setting up home in Alexandria as a living God.

Trump still asserts that he did not lose the November 2020 election to this day and sued Facebook, Twitter and Google for censoring conservative voices like him. He is now running for the presidency in 2024. He is also trying to turn the narrative on its head about the 6th of January debacle, asserting that it was all Nancy Pelosi fault. Albeit, the US House select committee investigating the 6th of January 2021, is televising all of it; which may change public opinion long term, has over time been collecting as much data as it can to form a solid case against a very dangerous man of the Right. Even Attorney general Bill Barr, who was trying to convince Trump he had lost the election, said at the time 'Trump was becoming detached from reality'. It also seems that Trump knew the crowd had guns when he urged the march on the Capital. Cassidy Hutchinson, a former Republican aide testifying at the US House select committee, said that Trump approved of his supporting that the crowd was chanting 'Hang Mike Pence'. He also wanted to go to the Capital to support his followers but his bodyguard would not allow it as there were guns at the siege. The seventh session of these public hearings chaired by Bennie Thompson noted that:

'Donald Trump summoned a mob to Washington DC and ultimately spurred that mob to wage a violent attack on our democracy'. (Quoted in the British Guardian 13th July 2022). As I note in my conclusion to this project, conspiracy theories are a good part of what Donald J. Trump has built his base on, and good old Nationalistic tosh (framed in working class patriotism) to hang his legitimacy on. According to Hugh Tomlinson in the UK Sunday Times 25th September 2022 Trump got so desperate in his latest rallies that QAnon concepts became more to the fore of his discourse, a Hitler type hand signal of ONE figure pointing forward being deployed at times. Ironically the FBI calls QAnon a 'terrorist threat'? Fuelled by right-wing media this movement seems to getting hold of the political agenda in the Republican movement around Trump, especially after the FBI raided Mar-a-Lago for top secret documents that were taken there after Trump was defeated in November 2020. Trump (a bit like Putin in the Ukraine debacle) is increasingly backed into a corner, signalling to the Justice department that if you prosecute me, I have powerful supports that will use violence against the State.

I would have thought that it is very unlikely that Putin would use nuclear weapons against the West and blow up the Planet? Albeit, if NATO had been dismantled after 1991 (probably others have said this as-well), we would not have been in the serious situation we have in Ukraine today which the West seems to be ramping up and pouring fuel on the fire, and perhaps maybe over 200, 000 people would not have lost their lives? However, Fiona Edwards in the Morning Star (9th February 2023) agrees with myself and the very few (so it seems) who believe 'the US is on a warpath against China'. This is mostly due to 'the extraordinary economic social and technological development of socialist China' and so it seems the USA 'has given up on peaceful economic competition and is engaged in a drive to world war'. For this to happen it is more than likely for this to happen will be by created a 'false flag' situation in the pacific by the

Western powers and this will be the end-of-life forms on Planet earth for millions of years, or perhaps for ever? A recent BBC documentary, fronted by Jane Corbin, called *Inside Taiwan* shown on the 23rd March 2023 which I replayed on the iPlayer system here in the UK (so saw twice) tries in a roundabout way to be objective, about the main problems myself and others have mentioned and reaching the same conclusions? In this book however, the underlying problem in the Taiwan straits stems from Chiang Kai-shek fleeing Taiwan in 1949, with perhaps another million people from mainland China and the 17th April 1895 cession by China of Taiwan to Japan. Albeit, the Portuguese in 1542 sighted an uncharted island and noted it as 'Ilha Formosa' meaning the beautiful island. Only in passing did Chiang Kai-shek get mentioned as a tyrant in this documentary; which apparently, he was until his death in 1975. Instead concentrating on President Tsai Ing-wen's election win in 2016 and 2020 elections and the so-called disinformation that the Chinese mainland is using against her and the citizens, of Taiwan. President Xi wants 'reunification', I presume going back to the 17th April 1895 forced agreement made with Japan: perhaps on the One State two systems (very similar to the Hong Kong) model made with the British in 1997. It seems that the citizens of Taiwan are very proud of their Chinese heritage, but the younger generation wants to have an independent country, sometime in the future. Also, the incredible modern technology of semi-conductor manufacturing may form a sort of 'shield' around Taiwan because the whole world needs this technology, including mainland China.

As I have noted in other projects of mine this is one of the most surreal epochs in world history and nothing emphasises this more than when the British State brought Volodymys Zelensky to the UK (8th February 2023), where he addressed the British Establishment, including labour MPs, in Westminster Hall, basically begging for armaments, including jets.

Ironically, at roughly the same time from Switzerland, the great Roger Waters (of Pink Floyd fame and often allowed on RT TV) was addressing the 15 members of the UN Security council. Condemning the 'illegal' invasion of Ukraine, while also saying the 'Russian invasion was not unprovoked, so I also condemn the provocateurs in the strongest possible terms'. This speech, now on You-Tube, was to me just as important as anything said by Fidel Castro and Gorbachev. Roger Water is a a very well-read intellectual who it seems to me has probably read Gore Vidal and many other important people of influence, like Noam Chomsky. Apparently, his late Mother had told him to 'read, read and read' which he has done, like Frederick Douglas, and myself and hopefully a few million others?

A footnote, to the very sad story of Afghanistan debacle should be added here, as Trump is now saying that Biden is responsible for the chaos that happened in that country, as of August 2021. In fact, it was Trump himself who signed a peace deal with the Taliban in February 2020 over the heads of the official Government in Afghanistan, albeit the original objective had been achieved when bin Laden was killed in 2011 in Pakistan, by American Seals.

The only conclusion I can make about this whole project is that Caligula had/has a lot in common with Donald J. Trump, albeit two thousand years apart! Caligula was murdered at the age of 29 for being a monster and a cruel tyrant, Trump is still with us in 2023. But sadly, as Cas Muddle (Guardian 17th May 2022) said, 'One and half years later, the Republican party has declared the storming of the Capital to be "legitimate political discourse" and is attacking both human rights and the democratic system across the country'...which helps to legitimise conspiracy theories like 'the great replacement theory', which originally goes back to the 19th century. With the last word going to amazing Dr Fiona Hill ...born working class in the UK but now an American citizen from 2002, who noted on Desert Island Discs (BBC - Radio4) that having read *Alice in Wonderland,* by Lewis Carroll was a good grounding for working for President Trump!

SOURCES

(1) William Blum - Rouge State - fp 2000 p, 308 - 309 my edition 2014 paperback.
(2) Joseph Choonara - unravelling capitalism - 2017 paperback p, 120 – 121.
(3) Ibid p, 121
(4) Joseph Stiglitz - Globalization and its discontents - p, 173.
(5) Ibid p, 173
(6) Ibid p, 176
(7) Noam Chomsky: The Umbrella of us Power – The Universal Declaration of Human Rights & the Contradictions of US Policy - 1994 p, p49
(8) The Guardian - 30 January 2019
(9) The Sunday Observer - 3rd February 2019
(10) Private Eye – No 1493
(11) Private Eye – No 1496 p, 37
(12) Will Hutton: The writing on the Wall – China and the West in the 21st Century -2007 my paperback edition p,155.
(13) The Guardian – 19th July 2019.
(14) The Sunday Times – 5th January 2020.
(15) The Sunday Times: 5th July 2020.
(16) The Morning Star – Left leaning daily newspaper sold in the UK.
(17) The Guardian – 15th September 2020.
(18) Noam Chomsky: Year 501 p, 26
(19) Peter Oborne: The Assault on Truth 2021.hardback edition p, 68.

Other Sources

I Independent newspaper: various editions
The Sunday Times 12th May 2019
Private Eye: Various editions
RT - TV station paid for by the Russian State and now outlawed in Britain and Western Europe because it is a threat to Liberal capitalist democracies?
The great Cicero, put to death in 43 BC.
Sunday Times: various editions
The Guardian: Various editions
BBC TV Panorama
Sunday Observer: various editions.
Donald J Trump: The Art of the Deal – 1987
Julius Caesar: The Conquest of Gaul…. written while in action, in Europe…we presume?
The Daily Telegraph.
The Daily Mirror
The Riot Club: a brilliant movie about the ruthless nature of the British Ruling Class, at Oxford University.
Fox News USA
Kitty Kelly: His Way 1986.
William Blum: Rogue State – 2014
Michael Woods: DVD on China
BBC 4 British TV channel
John Bolton: The Room Where It Happened.
Richard Tomlinson: The Big Breach.
Morning Star: various editions
BBC TV Andrew Marr Show
David Niven: Bring on the Empty Horses…2nd Autobiography.
The Holy Bible – the American version, I presume?
Alexis de Tocqueville: Democracy in America.
Kim Darroch: Collateral Damage – 2021

Washington Post
New York Times
More4: British TV Channel
Oliver James: Affluenza -2007
The Rich Get Richer and the Poor go to Prison. A VIP book I read in the West Midlands, about 1989, in a University Library.
Yesterday: digital TV Channel in the UK....re: the Himmler piece about the formation of the SS and its derivatives.
Channel4 News in the UK
BBC2: The Trump Show - TV channel in the UK.
James Comey: his autobiography.
Martin Jacques: When China Rules the World.
The Letters of the Younger Pliny - paperback edition - Penguin Classics
Peter Oborne: The Assault on Truth (2021) - Boris Johnson, Donald Trump and the Emergence of a new Moral Barbarism - hardback edition 2021 (read so far 3 times)
Mary Beard who is a professor of classics at the University of Cambridge who recently made a documentary shown on BBC Four TV about Julius Caesar and on now Amazon (2020) in it suggests that Caesar has been a good role model for all sorts of strong men especially in the 20/21st century, like Hitler and even Trump...which may or may not be true because in Trump's case he may not know who Caesar was? Albeit the strong man act is what he seems to like to be?
American Gangster a brilliant movie made by Ridley Scott and in theory based on fact?
Tom Bower: The Gambler about Boris Johnson - fb 2020
The Washington Post by the Fact Checker Staff ...Donald Trump and His Assault on Truth 2020
PBS America: Lies, Politics And Democracy...shown in the UK on the 1st July 2023.

The Snowden Files by Luke Harding…..who exposes the depth of spying on the whole world, especially by NSA & GCHQ which even includes hacking 'Chinese mobile phone companies to steal' their SMS data?

Printed in Great Britain
by Amazon